Bush

Twenty-Seventh Letter
The Official History

Jennifer Nine

First published in Great Britain in 1999 by Virgin Books
an imprint of Virgin Publishing Ltd
Thames Wharf Studios
Rainville Road
London W6 9HA

A catalogue record for this book is available from the British Library.

ISBN 0 7535 0189 9

Typeset by TW Typesetting, Plymouth, Devon

Printed by Creative Print and Design (Wales), Ebbw Vale

Years ago, my heart was set to live
And I've been trying hard against unbelievable odds
It gets so hard in times like now to hold on
But guns they wait to be stuck by, and at my side is God

And there ain't no one going to turn me 'round . . .

There's people around who tell you that they know
And places where they send you, and it's easy to go
They'll zip you up and dress you down and stand you in a row
But you know you don't have to, you can just say no

I've been built up and trusted, broke down and busted
But they'll get theirs and we'll get ours
If we can just hold on . . .

Big Star, 'The Ballad of El Goodo'

'I've always felt like an outsider . . .
but with plenty of kindred spirits.'

Gavin Rossdale

Acknowledgements

All the ladies and gentlemen
Who made this all so probable . . .

Without the co-operation of Nigel Pulsford, Dave Parsons, Robin Goodridge and Gavin Rossdale, this book would not exist. Without the help of the other four dozen people who agreed to talk to my rotating cast of cheap tape recorders, and the tireless work of transcribers Ngaire Orsborn, Lisa Hire, Colleen Browne, Jennifer Blair and Leila Boyd, it would have been an awful lot shorter. And without the selfless and unstinting collaboration of Heather Redmond, Ian Gittins, Glyn Brown and Kirstie Addis, the assistance of Giles Baxendale and David Dorrell, the wit of Mark Armstrong and Alex Tate, and the love and support of Angus Batey, Victoria Segal and Pete Paphides, I wouldn't have made it to this page.

Thank you, friends. Wouldn't be here if it weren't for you.

Foreword

A book title is almost as hard to write as everything that comes after it. Even if you cheat a little by recycling some of your subject's own lyrics.

Still. How could a handful of words on a book cover sum up what Bush think about Bush, let alone what anyone else has to say? It's probably no wonder then that, even with three albums' worth of hallucinatory, razor-sharp and fiendishly contradictory lyrics to choose from, I kept threatening to duck the issue of what to call this biography.

Which was probably why the man who writes the lyrics kept smiling every time I said I still didn't know. So Gavin Rossdale kept offering suggestions. Tactfully. Offhandedly. And possibly not always seriously.

'*Crown of Lead*, maybe?' Gavin would propose as we sat at his kitchen table and flicked through sheets of his lyrics, which he'd hold up and look at intently as though he was surprised and more than a little pleased to see what had ended up there. '*Poison Crazy Lush* – yeah, how about that?' he'd muse, one eyebrow lifted just in case. Or '*Coppertongue*. Now that's a good one . . .' Or 'Hey, *A Slice Of Help*?' Or '*Gasoline Choir* – that could work!' In fact, before I came across the words 'Twenty-Seventh Letter' in 'Bonedriven', a glancing reference to the imaginary extra letter in the English alphabet we all wish existed so that we could use it to describe our deepest desires, I even threatened to give up and just call this book *Four Men And A Dog*.

And not only because there are, of course, four men in Bush. And one omnipresent hound, Gavin Rossdale's faithful Puli Winston, who showed super-canine restraint in only biting me once. (Rather hard, though.) The other reason is a nod to that old, quintessentially black-hearted English joke about bands you come across, doggedly playing their sets in some toilet in a less salubrious part of town, when the world refuses to show up and the crowd is so very small that everyone announces later that the audience contained only four onlookers and a dog. I don't know how that expression came to be, but it's probably because it's rather cruelly effective in suggesting that the band in question is so deeply unloved, you'd have to press-gang the animal kingdom in order to have more ears in the crowd than onstage.

And, strange as it may seem for a band who could now probably circle the globe with the millions of records and tickets they've sold, the 'four men and a dog' joke has been told more than once of Bush. If I'd called the book *Four Men And A Dog*, as it's clear by now I haven't, it might have been a nudge to suggest that it's the Bush nay-sayers (hey, every band has them) who've been missing something. Then again, this book isn't for the nay-sayers, but for the people who said yes. And the band who gave it to them.

As it happens, Bush did play an early gig at the Camden Falcon in London in which the audience contained four people and ... well, two dogs, actually, if we're being fair, since Winston had company that night. I didn't see that gig, in fact; nor did I see Bush – who were Future Primitive at the time – make their debut in a car park in London's East End. But I know the people who did. And everything I know about Bush makes it easy to believe that from the very first day they took the stage, and back when they had a name only Brian Eno thought was cool and no record to put it on anyway, they always played with enough stubbornly unshakeable self-belief to satisfy about a half million pairs of ears. Even if only five turned up.

Sometimes, if you believe hard enough, long enough, big enough, the other 499,995 pairs of ears turn up too. And this book, in the words of the people who were there and the people who dreamed it so fiercely it couldn't be otherwise, and all jumbled up and full of memories and dates and road maps and contradictions and jokes and longing and truths and maybe even some lies, is how it all happened.

So I've left it to them. It's their name on the book. It's their story.

Jennifer Nine
London, May 1999

'Are you absolutely sure there's a book in all this?' Tanned, alert and smiling, Gavin Rossdale stretches his legs out in his seat in a pub full of summer sunshine and the passing noises of Primrose Hill. He wants to be very sure I think this book isn't a bad idea.

Of course, he knows what my answer will be. Great band, great records, great story full of multi-platinum albums and sellout tours and superlatives and mathematically astounding statistics. Great news that someone wants me to write this book, and even better news that someone has told me Gavin, Robin, Nigel and Dave have agreed to put up with me and my tape recorder for the duration. Nevertheless, I'm not sure what his question really means.

'I just don't think anyone needs a book about what they've done until they're, oh, sixty at least,' he laughs, when I ask him to elaborate. He mentions Pablo Picasso and Francis Bacon and Van Gogh: old people, dead people, people who made Proper Art, I suppose. By those standards, he and the rest of his band are barely halfway to the Age Of Reasonably Interesting.

I give him my answer again. Surely he doesn't need me to point out that bands far less important or successful than his own have books written about them. Maybe he doesn't see himself in that company: I've watched Bush triumphantly command the stage at the UK's Reading Festival and been struck by Gavin's surprise, astonishment and delight every time the crowd roars back. Every time it happens, it seems he can't quite get to taking it for granted.

We kick the idea around, we agree to disagree, and he agrees to help me with the book. 'Oh, don't worry, I can be a complete brat,' he insists. 'So if I didn't want to do this, believe me, I wouldn't.' He thinks for a minute, and begins to list the people I might like to talk to about him, jumping from name to name and noting, with a smile, that the things they have to say won't all be complimentary. And then he pauses, and says how much he wishes his Aunt Maggie, injured in a car accident some years back, could have been one of my interview subjects.

He shakes his head. And then brightens, and then says that whoever I talk to, he might learn something from it himself. It could be really good, he adds. And then suggests we go to his house over the road to talk some more.

I skulk in the hallway, more than a little embarrassed by the thought that he might think I'm prying, that I've got my journalist eyes swivelling in my journalist head. I try to slip up the stairs tactfully, if such a thing is possible. 'What do you think?' he asks. It's a lovely house. I say so. 'What do you think?' he asks again as we pass a framed photo of Francis Bacon, his head a fiery blur as he moves forward at the instant the shutter closes. (Gavin has seven Francis Bacon paintings and on other occasions he will show them to me with such love and delight and awe, I'm struck by the unfairness of paintings ever sitting somewhere where they are not gazed at and loved this constantly.) Next to the photo of Bacon, there's a long-preserved note to Gavin's old flatmate Pete Black – 'Pete. Save the teabags. Times are hard!' – propped up on a desk next to the fax-laden fax machine.

'It's nice,' I say. We keep walking up the stairs as Winston, his dreadlocked blur of a dog, bounds ahead. 'What do you think?' he asks again as we climb to the top of the last set of stairs to his bedroom, where a guitar sits in the corner with stacks and stacks of records, and huge windows face front and back, over London. 'No, what do you *really* think?' he asks again. My professional composure drops and I grin. 'Wow, your house is amazing!' Because, of course, it is. 'I want you to know about all this,' he says simply. 'I don't have anything to hide.'

'Nothing to hide,' Gavin repeats, smiling. 'Nothing.'

B

Barbara Stephan could charm the birds from the trees. Arms outstretched and a delighted smile on her classically beautiful face, and her effortless model's poise is still in evidence as she waves you to a place on the immaculate sofa. This is the mother Gavin Rossdale's childhood friends remember with awe and, amongst the boys, something rather like unrequited love, even now, years later.

Born in Aberdeen, Barbara's parents ran a country hotel: her maternal grandmother was a concert pianist, one uncle was a violinist and the other a magician, and her mother, widowed young, was a dancer. 'I think my mother had great ideas that my brother and I would take on the hotel,' Barbara recalls, 'so one summer before college I found myself working at the Central Hotel in Glasgow. One day all these models arrived from London for a show, and a wonderful man named Michael Whittaker came running to the desk and said, "You must help me out; one of my models has missed her plane from London." And I was so shy, I just went red like a beetroot. All afternoon they marched me up and down and that night I did a show and loved it. So I thought, "I'm not going back to college, thank you very much. This is *much* more fun!"'

So Barbara came down to London, and found herself staying in a very respectable young ladies' hostel just across the park from where Gavin now lives; in fact, his local pub was her local. But it was 'all very prim and proper,' she laughs. 'I didn't see much of the swinging 60s side of London.'

Young general practitioner Douglas Rossdale, himself the son of a doctor, was originally from Hemel Hempstead, but brought up in London. One night, he came into a restaurant to join some friends for dinner and Barbara was amongst the dinner guests. 'We didn't court long,' Barbara says. 'We met in January and got married in August; quite a big wedding at Caxton Hall. I continued modelling, and we both decided we wanted to work and keep our independence. I don't think I realised how independent I was,' she says. 'Though the longer I was married, the less independent I became, until our marriage unfortunately broke up and then I *had* to be independent. I'd no idea how to do it,' she admits.

But back to the Rossdale's early days. The couple set up house in Albion Street near Hyde Park, with Douglas' practice downstairs. Lorraine was the first of three children; Gavin was born two and a half years later, Soraya nearly a decade after that. When Gavin was three, the family moved to North London, on the border of the working-class Irish/black neighbourhood of Kilburn and the slightly more upscale West Hampstead, in a home where Douglas still lives.

Lorraine adored her brother, Barbara recalls. Blond, curly haired and rather reserved, 'Gavin was her baby; we practically had to ask permission to see him. She liked to be part of everything – feeding and all the fun things, like talcum powder going everywhere. They went everywhere together; we'd be tasting a new food in a foreign country and if Lorraine liked it, then Gavin would like it. He's a bit more careful,' laughs Barbara. 'Very shy, very reserved.' The family story that Gavin didn't speak until he was at least four has, she laughs, become a bit exaggerated in the telling.

'I don't know where that came from! He didn't say much because he was shy, and Lorraine would more or less speak for him, but I think older sisters do that. He didn't have a problem with speaking, he just didn't find the need to.'

Young Gavin had other enthusiasms. 'He was car mad,' says Barbara. 'Knew every single car on the market, and had a whole collection of Scalextric cars. He loved books too. They were all like that; preferring to read and play music in their own rooms, rather than watch TV.'

From an early age, Gavin's nickname was Jim. In fact, one of his nicknames is still Jim, and that's what he calls his father, too. Douglas explains that it all came from a cereal packet.

'We do call each other Jim, and I can show you why.' Dr

Rossdale pushes a framed snapshot of Gavin, aged about five, and with a smile so wide it's almost bigger than his face, across his office desk. 'It comes down to the advertising for Force cereal at the time. The slogan mentioned someone called Sunny Jim. I started to call Gavin Sunny Jim, and we just kept it up.' As prone to blushing as his mother, Gavin was certainly sunny much of the time. 'A lovely little boy, as everyone said wherever we went,' Barbara notes.

'I was sure he was going to be a vet,' she recalls on another occasion. 'He loved animals, and used to come home with stray dogs. There was always someone who was moving back to America, and could we please have the dog? We had a toy poodle, Brandy, who became Gavin's favourite: a best friend, everything. She was killed one Christmas Eve, which ruined everybody's holiday, and lamb was banned from the house because the knuckle of the lamb bone had been her favourite. We weren't allowed to have lamb for a *very* long time.'

'Of course he spoke to people as a child,' sister Lorraine insists apropos the family legend of Silent Young Gavin. 'But I definitely helped out. He'd say, "er", and I'd say, "He wants a biscuit." ' But if Lorraine was her younger brother's official spokeswoman in his pre-school years, Gavin served as her long-suffering straight man. 'I used to make him eat soap in the bath,' she laughs, only a little guiltily. 'I was probably about six and he was four, and I used to say, "Gavin, look, eat this soap, it tastes really good!" And he'd do it over and over again. I used to try to get him to blow bubbles with it but of course he couldn't, he'd just make gagging noises. Then at night I'd say, "Gavin, Gavin, come here!" And he'd come into my room and I'd shout, "Help! There's a burglar, get into bed!" This would go on night after night and he'd always believe me. I remember going in the car to visit patients with my dad, when I must have been about six or seven. I'd tell Gavin to get out of the car . . . then lock the door behind him. The last time I tried this, I said, "Let's take off all our clothes." So, when my father came back after seeing a patient, he came upon two naked children. It must have been a bit of a shock.' she adds, laughing.

In summer, the family would take holidays in Spain, where the children played outdoors from dawn to dusk. 'We hardly ever saw them except at mealtimes,' Barbara recalls. 'It would be good morning, goodnight and "Oh, are you having a nice lunch?" '

'Summer holidays in Spain were wonderful,' Lorraine remembers. 'I think the first boy I ever kissed was the brother of the first girl Gavin ever kissed. Our whole year was geared toward that three-week holiday. I remember one summer when I was about thirteen, we got into *Joseph and the Amazing Technicolor Dreamcoat* and annoyed our parents on the two days' drive down from London by singing the musical from beginning to end.' Gavin's introduction to the world of musicals would lead to his first recorded stage performance, as Lorraine confirms. 'Gavin was chosen to be Oliver in the school musical, and he was a star. He was brilliant, running around in brown satin pants, and I remember my mother sitting there sobbing her heart out listening to "Where Is Love?" He was chosen for the part by a teacher called Mr Shaw, and when I recently came back to England from living abroad, and went to see if Jade [Lorraine's daughter] could go to that school, Mr Shaw was retiring and he remembered Gavin. He said, "Oh, it's wonderful to talk to you. How is he? Obviously, I follow his career . . ." And I said, "Well, actually, you're the one who started him off." '

Asked if the young Gavin was any good in his first starring role, Douglas Rossdale replies mildly, 'You know that chap Mark Lester? Well, I have a tape somewhere of Gavin singing those songs, and frankly it would be difficult to tell the difference. He had a very good producer, so I think he did very well.'

'That was his first musical experience,' Lorraine recalls, and then grins. 'Whether or not it had anything to do with him becoming a rock star afterwards, I don't know.'

When Gavin was twelve, however, his life would change rapidly. First of all, his parents' marriage began to disintegrate. Although he kept up a close relationship with both his mother and father, it was a difficult time. Longtime friend Pete Black recalls, 'When Gavin's parents split up, it was a shock. Gavin and Lorraine were deeply upset, though I think Gavin was more angry. And I think I probably got angry as well, because Gavin was.'

His mother, Gavin suspects, still feels guilty for having left. 'She doesn't need to, though,' he insists. 'I do understand how it's not possible to be with someone if you don't want to be. The irony of it is that it was worse before they split, with all the tension and arguments that happen when people can't be together. I've always felt weird about the consequence of human dilemmas, and that when things aren't right you shut up or you leave. Back then, though, when you mentioned the split to someone else, it was a bit like a death: too heavy. At that age, you're aware of what's going on, yet you're not quite old enough to understand. It only destroys a part of you, though, and from disarray and chaos comes knowing and understanding. I was really close to my mum when I was growing up, and then we went through a weird time when she was obviously unhappy. Which is strange, because now she's the coolest person on the planet. She brought me into life, so it's hard to be critical, and I'll always feel very protective towards her, even though we've had some bizarre twists and turns. I just feel she's good now, and I respect her a lot. I think she went through this whole period of her life just looking for happiness. She's in a good space now; you have to make decisions and be accountable to yourself emotionally. And worse things happen to people. You deal with it.

'I'm not a great fan of blaming your life on other people,' he will say later. 'The adversity you have is the adversity you have, and it's not really engineered by the people around you. You can't expect people to be your totems and not be as fallible and frail as you know yourself to be. I'm talking about your parents, your support network, your siblings, your friends. Of course it's a shock when you see any of them fuck up. People aren't meant to fuck up, are they? When you're a kid, your parents are everything, they have godlike status. The realisation that they're human makes them twice as valuable, though.

'I find that people lay blame too much: that therapeutic American idea that if you've been abused in any way, you must tell everyone. People being interviewed do it a lot. You can give away stuff about your life, and your truth, and milk that, and come across as very intense and "Oh my God, what a life, what a struggle." But the people involved,' he emphasises, 'the protagonists, are usually all still alive and would be absolutely crucified. Don't do it,' Gavin says, as if to himself. 'Don't go anywhere near it. Because there are plenty of other things to go through, and certain things are sacred.'

Gavin can, he says, see echoes of both of his parents in himself. 'Definitely. It's evolution, isn't it? I can see parts of them in me – physically, of course, too. My dad's quite reserved, so I guess there's elements of that in me.'

'Oh, Gavin's very much like his dad,' ex-girlfriend Lindsey Thurlow will say with a smile. 'His dad's very quick witted, with that dry, dry sense of humour, just like his.'

'The best thing about my dad was that he didn't really give any standard-issue parental guidance or stuff like that,' Gavin adds. 'I never had a conversation with my dad about morals or personal politics, I was just left alone. I think I was pretty self-sufficient when I was about twelve. I just did whatever I wanted to do.'

Douglas observes, 'One thing I think I've managed to be to my children, as a father, is their friend. Everyone should be allowed to develop on one's own . . . and one of the most important things about children is that they be allowed to discover what they want to do in life.'

'It's funny,' Gavin adds, 'because I often have these conversations with Gwen [Stefani, his girlfriend] about her family, because she's so wholesome, such a good person, and you just think "Wow, it's so instilled in them to behave in a certain way." For me, it's been a voyage of understanding how you should be – sometimes getting it completely wrong. I think I just intuited, to a degree, how to treat people. How to be.

'You know,' he interjects, 'I went out for lunch with my mum on Sunday. There she was, chatting away to the head waiter, charming everyone. There were four generations there: my nan was down from Scotland, and my mum, and Lorraine and Jade. Then they came around to my house . . . and I couldn't get rid of them!' He laughs. 'There I was, trying to watch the football . . .'

'Actually, I don't really know my family,' Gavin will say at one point. 'I grew up with my aunt Maggie, but that's a chapter in itself. It's a weird one. A big subject, and a really sad one.' In fact, he says, what would happen to his aunt would be the most significant event in his young life.

'I lived with Maggie from the age of twelve to fourteen. She was really my second mum. When I was a kid, she came down to London from Scotland, and lived with us and ran a boutique in High Street Kensington. She was obviously trying to make a good impression on my dad, but she got arrested for taking acid and dancing on the roofs of parked cars in Berkeley Square – she was just crazy! I'd be getting up for school and she'd just be coming in. She was the only person I ever spoke to about sex. She was really cool.'

Later, Maggie ran a pub, The Pepperpot, in Dock Street in London's East End. 'For a time, I lived and worked in the pub,' says Gavin. 'Sometimes I'd come up and stay with my dad [in Kilburn], but generally I lived with Maggie. And she was the one who introduced me to all the music I loved, like *Ziggy Stardust*.

'But she got hit by a car,' Gavin says abruptly. 'Eighteen years ago. It was devastating. It's so sad. She absolutely loved her life, and she was the wild and crazy one, and now she lives in Edinburgh Infirmary. She's almost fifty. You can visit her, and they say she has the mind of a twelve year old, but it's not a twelve-year-old kid in there. She'll recognise me and be really pleased to see me, and then she'll forget. It's a National Health story,' he says, referring to the lack of facilities in underfunded public health institutions. 'They keep her on drugs, all locked doors, and she lives in a brain injury unit.' He pauses for a long time. 'She would have been the one who would've got the most out of my life now, you know. When I see her, I try to talk about it. And she would have been great to interview. It was so painful to lose someone like that. And because Maggie's still alive, I go to see her, and obviously I just want her back to how she was. It would be so much easier for her if she would have been allowed to die gracefully with a brilliant memory. Unfortunately, she's left in this terrifying limbo.'

When it's suggested that he's always been around strong women, Gavin immediately agrees. 'And Maggie was the strongest. She was amazing. So brilliant, so cool, so helpful and instructive.'

'Did Gavin tell you about his old woman?' Lorraine asks. 'He looked after her when he was about twelve. She had no money and he used to visit, take her tins of beef. It was a purely nice thing to do. That's what he's like: not trying to say he's a saint or anything, but he is genuinely a nice person.'

'Bella Mostyn?' Gavin recalls. 'She was an amazing woman.' Gavin met her one day crossing the road near his house, and a friendship between a twelve-year-old boy and an old woman began, probably to his father's bemusement. Douglas recalls drily, 'Oh, yes. He adopted her. They were told at school to do that sort of thing. But she obviously took a little bit of advantage of that fact.'

'It was so weird,' says Gavin. 'She was lost in time; a sweet mad old thing in a weird cape. Tiny, had no cash, and lived at the top of West End Lane. She was quite scary, but I wasn't scared of her, just a little unsure. You know how old ladies have lipstick all over their faces? *That* kind of scary. I remember going to her flat, and it was one of those mad old person's places; newspapers all over the room, really filthy and crazy and hot. I used to do my homework at her house. I don't quite know why, but I used to go around there and study. It wasn't at all like *Harold and Maude*,' he smiles, 'but she did look like Maude!

'She wanted me to be a musician, and go to Munich – this is before I was ever interested in music – because her husband, who died some years earlier, had played with Shostakovich. She was senile but she was wonderful and I used to go around and she'd make tea. I found a lot of solace there; it was peaceful. She was just happy to have me sit there, and I didn't ever want to leave. And she thought I was brilliant.'

And that, Gavin says baldly, was because 'I used to tell her I was. I didn't do well at school at all, but it made her happy to hear I did. "Oh, what a great student you are, Gavin!" she'd say. So I told her I was a straight A student, and she loved that, and of course it gave me self-esteem. When in fact I was an academic fuck-up. I screwed it up; I couldn't pay attention. Sometimes I wonder if I ever *have* listened to my powers of concentration,' he admits. 'It's like a crazy wild African dance going on in me all the time, and I have to really listen to things and concentrate, and I can't. But what can you do?' He shrugs. 'It probably helped me to think that I could have been a good student. I was really good verbally, and I could talk a good answer. I could talk good theory, but when it came to writing it out . . .' He shakes his head.

'Then one summer I went away on holiday and couldn't see her. I saw her down the road when I came back, and I felt really bad. But when I went back, there was no one at her flat. I phoned the council to see if she'd been taken into a home or something. I'd never met any of her family, so I couldn't ask them. And I never found out where she went . . .' His voice trails off.

Of his youthful weakness for lying, he admits, 'I just couldn't help myself. I suppose I was pathologically insecure. I so much wanted to be someone else.' Even if, according to other people, Gavin seemed the very image of the attractive, popular boy.

'Well, I wasn't that popular! I loved sport, but that was really the only help I had socially, being able to play football. That was the only time at my school that I'd speak to people. I was friendly with an older lot, but I don't know if that cartoon image of a popular, well-rounded, athletic young boy is right. It's just . . . flawed. But all those questions, all those unanswered things about what anyone was really like when they were young are hard to settle . . . You know, I probably had a different recollection of it three weeks ago, let alone ten or fifteen years ago.'

One thing he does remember is shoplifting. 'From the age of

about ten to fourteen,' he notes, and then shrugs. 'All boys do it. So do all girls. But I had this weird fetish, or weird twist to it; I always used to have to steal two of everything, even though it was only sweets and stationery and stuff. And then I realised it wasn't that cool. Still, there was one amazing Christmas Eve when I hid out in Fenwick [classy London department store] . . .

'But yes, the fact is that I couldn't stop lying at points. Objectively speaking, it's not really a healthy way for a child to behave. I don't think I ever represented myself to anybody as *me*.'

Was he ever caught out?

'Yeah,' he nods, 'because it was usually outlandish; I probably laid claim to loads of accolades for myself. Something I thought would give me bonus points in the social world. It's obviously an inadequacy, isn't it? You feel inadequate, so you need a shrink . . . or you shrink, and you lie. I think I just recreated myself in order to be somebody, be something.'

He can't recall any specific fibs. 'I think it just started with . . . *winner*. Common or garden winner. I used to have this obsession that my dad would be ashamed of me, though I don't know why. He certainly wasn't austere, but he was really busy, working hard from eight in the morning until eight at night. I just wanted to get his attention like any kid, and thought that by being good I'd get it. I used to have this scenario where I imagined him being ashamed of me, so I wanted to be whatever it was that he wouldn't be ashamed of. The opposite. Of course that's something that's filtered through with everyone else in my life. I don't do it anymore,' he smiles. 'I try not to.'

On the bright side, Gavin had Lorraine. As older sisters go, Lorraine Rossdale had it all and more, beginning with impressive skateboarding prowess, years before the sport caught on in the UK. 'My friend Alisha and I were queen bees, and we went into competitions and shows,' Lorraine says modestly, without mentioning all the competitions she went on to win. She had a gaggle of friends who were admittedly 'all in love with Gavin; in fact, I think half of them were around because of him.' She also had, Gavin says, great taste in music, and a cool line in punk attire.

'Well, I wasn't really allowed to be *too* punk,' says Lorraine. 'My mother used to make me walk behind her in the street! We were Hampstead punks, really, where it was definitely a fashion thing. I remember painting my mouth black and dad saying I looked like I was dead.'

'She *was* a punk,' insists Gavin. 'Lorraine was the coolest person. Everything I learned was from trying to hang out with her friends when I was twelve and the whole punk thing happened. At the top of my road was this record shop and I was always going in and getting one single at a time. That's why I've got X Ray Spex and The Buzzcocks, practically the first edition of everything. Her friends would come round and, as they were fifteen to seventeen, I thought they were wicked. And when they'd come round, *I'd* have the music. And they'd be in her room smoking bad dope and drinking bad cider and I'd try to lure them to my room: "Hey, look, my Buzzcocks single is on white vinyl!" '

Lorraine, now back in London after living in Spain for eighteen years, laughs at Gavin's story and suggests that his record collection may well have been appropriated from hers. 'He was very crafty.'

'Girls were right there from the beginning for Gavin,' she adds. 'He's always been sensitive enough to know what women like.'

She goes on, 'We hung around a lot. We were quite close. There was only a while when I was skateboarding that I wasn't very nice to him. I'd say, "You can come down and watch me skate as long as you don't talk to me." ' That was as far as sibling cruelty went. 'Well, that and hitting him on the head with a frying pan once,' she laughs. 'I don't think he ever pushed me again!'

'I was sure she really didn't like me and really hated me hanging with her friends,' Gavin insists. 'She'd be mad as anything, though. She'd be suspended for stupid stuff, just for being a real punk. It was right at the beginning: bleaching your hair, putting egg white in it, all of that. She used to be really feisty and I used to dote on her. Typical sibling dysfunctional thing,' he laughs. 'We'd go away to Spain with my dad on these mad driving holidays and I'll never forget it; it was just like a switch going on when she had peroxide hair, and that made her seem even more brilliant. I just thought she was *out* there.'

'We'd go out to the Camden Palace to see bands. Gavin didn't really come along to those things, because he was too young,' recalls Lorraine. 'Though I remember going on the number 31 bus somewhere and some skinheads got on and even then he said, "I'll protect you, it'll be all right." And when they closed World's End [a legendary Camden club] I took Gavin down, and lost him . . . I thought, My God, what am I going to do? I'm miles away from home, and I'm going to get the blame because I've lost him!'

The same neighbourhood boys in awe of Barbara had a crush a mile wide for Lorraine, of course. One such admirer was Pete Black, now a respected photographer whose varied credits include everything from record sleeves for Gavin's first band Midnight to a best-selling book of Bush live photos from the *Sixteen Stone* tour. Two years Gavin's senior, he and his brother John lived on an estate near the Rossdales' home.

How did Gavin and Pete become friends?

'Because I fancied his sister,' Pete says frankly. 'I worked at a newsagent's and Lorraine used to come in in her school uniform with her mum. I was a little kid and there were these two beautiful women – God, they were stunning! – and so I said hello a few times. Then one day Gavin came in, this little guy with blond curls and a big black skateboard. We just got chatting. He invited me round and it went from there. I didn't really have a great home life, so I'd go round and stay for tea. His mother was so nice to me that I ended up spending nearly every night there, though I didn't know his father that well. For the first five years or so, I rarely saw Douglas because he was at work in the surgery. It's funny now, looking back, that I was actually terrified of him, because he's the friendliest man you could meet. Of course, when you're a kid and he's somebody's father . . .

'It's really weird,' Pete admits. 'I wanted Gavin's life. And maybe Gavin looked up to me because I'd come up with stories from living in a council estate: people getting beaten up or things getting nicked. Gavin was quite impressed by that. I used to go to a rough school and I had a couple of tough nuts as friends who would come down and sort people out. Gavin's family weren't wealthy, they were just middle class, but they had a lovely house, and his mother had a TR7 sports car. I was like, "Wow!" I didn't know anyone who had a car.'

His crush on Lorraine never quite worked out, laughs Pete, now happily married to his longtime sweetheart Lisa. 'I swamped her with gifts, to no avail. The worst thing is that when you have a crush on someone you become a prat. I was probably embarrassing to Gavin; you know, "How could you have a crush on my *sister*?" I'd spend nights throwing pebbles up to her bedroom window, ending up with Douglas telling me to get lost or he'd call the police. Gavin and I spent a lot of time in his bedroom watching Elvis movies on a little film projector, against his bedroom door. I'd go round after school, I'd see him at weekends, we'd play football down the road, we'd play tennis. Looking back, we spent hours and hours together.

'Gavin was always good at everything,' Pete adds. 'He had the looks, he had the girls; even right from the beginning, he was always cute, and as he got older he was much better looking. I'm probably the friend he's had longest, and over the years we became stronger friends. Of course, we'd fall out and run away and cry, but then his mum would get us back together again.

'You must have noticed, because everyone does, and if they don't they are blind, that there is *something* about Gavin,' says Pete. 'There's always been something about him. When I first met him, he was a little boy and I was after his sister. But when I became friends with him, we just clicked. Whatever the reason, it's irrelevant, because it's so many years ago now that it doesn't matter. The friendship has built beyond that. I can have rows with him all the time now, whereas if you had rows with a new friend you'd worry – and believe me,' laughs Pete, 'we've had some big ones.' A veteran of several North American Bush tours, Pete adds, 'On tour, I can tell him to stop acting like a prat, with absolutely no fear. It's Gavin, for Christ's sake, not God! Of course some friends just worship him, and that's fine, but it annoys me. He always says, "Look, I know what they're doing, just chill, it's fine."

'But he's the same guy he was twenty years ago,' Pete insists. 'He's got a bit more money and a bit of success, but it's irrelevant. There's just something about him. When I worked in a stables as a teenager for five years, all the blokes liked him and all the girls loved him . . . and I didn't have a chance! Forget the fame factor, because he wasn't famous, but he would walk into a room and people would look at him. And it's nothing to do with the beauty aspect, either,' adds Pete, his photographer's appraising eye coming to the fore. 'Actually, I've never found Gavin beautiful. Probably because I've known him so many years, y'know, so you see all the imperfections . . . and there are lots!' He laughs as only, perhaps, your oldest friend would.

But we're getting ahead of ourselves by a few decades. Back when Gavin was twelve, more than his home life was changing. Crucially, he changed schools, and would go from a comfortably laid-back local school to the intensely competitive, academically rigorous and overwhelmingly well-to-do environment of a famous 'public' (i.e. fee-paying) school, Westminster. And it certainly wasn't his own idea. In the years since, in fact, he has paid his father back all the fees spent on his Westminster education.

His father Douglas, for his part, makes a strong case for having sent Gavin to a school with such high standards and, as he points out, a high-quality peer group. When Gavin balked at the move, and his father suspected he was attempting to get himself expelled, Dr Rossdale played a deft game of verbal chess with Gavin's housemaster to make sure it didn't happen.

'Gavin had lots of friends who weren't at that particular school who wanted to manipulate him into not wanting to be there,' Douglas recalls. 'Obviously, being particularly intelligent, he decided the best way to leave was to be rather difficult, and I knew this was what he was doing. Gavin nearly had his way and I was summoned to the school. Gavin had been there two terms, and they thought it was best for him to leave. As my brother says, I can be extremely brittle. So I simply said that if I allowed them to expel him, they would be allowing a twelve-year-old boy to manipulate two grown men in charge of five hundred boys. That they would be giving him what he wanted, and aiding and abetting him.'

Needless to say, he won his point. Douglas allows himself a brief smile when he is asked about the looks on the teachers' faces. 'Oh, yes. I know. Quite something.'

According to Gavin, however, there was much not to like at Westminster, not least the bullying that required deft avoidance. Lorraine says regretfully, 'I was away. I was too selfish, and too wrapped up in my own world. When he first started at Westminster he was bullied, I know. I knew someone who was there, and I found out that he'd been really horrible to Gavin, and I said, "Look, don't, please look after him." It was one of those things that happens, and to be honest I don't remember giving it that much thought. But they hit him and he stood up for himself one day and it stopped. He was a pretty little boy, and children are very cruel. I don't know if it was all about that, but it wasn't easy for him.'

In the meantime, Gavin sought solace back in the old neighbourhood. Where, in a mixed but largely working-class area, he was certainly the only Westminster day boy to be found playing football at the Abbey Road Youth Club.

Pete Black recalls, 'He hated Westminster. I think he just didn't like the pompous people at school. He used to come back up and we'd go to Emmanuel's, this Lebanese restaurant on the Finchley Road, and we'd hang out in the back and play pool. And he was very good. They had this Space Invaders machine, and of course he was very good at that as well. Straight from school we'd go there, and weekends: have a bowl of chips, and stay there for the whole day just playing pool and trying to be Jack the lad.'

According to John Black, Pete Black's brother and a builder and contractor who would later give Gavin work in the lean pre-Bush years, 'Gavin's dad said to me once that he couldn't understand why his son was hanging around with the likes of us. We were as rough as they come,' he grins. 'One thing I've always said about Gav is that, although he came from quite a good background – they had a few quid behind them – he was never stuck up. He always wanted to be one of the lads, and I think he enjoyed the fact that he had some mates who would swear a lot and run around causing trouble.

'After school, we'd meet up and play in his street and my brother would come round and a few of my friends would turn up, and we used to play football in Kilburn together.' Asked whether Gavin was, as he claims, a tasty footballer, John laughs long and hard. 'Well, I was the goalkeeper and he never scored past *me*!

'We all used to go round his house, where he had his own room and stuff that we weren't used to having. His old man used to leave us alone, so we'd just go up to his room and play records and smoke cigarettes. And I think every one of us had a crush on his mum. When I saw her at Pete's wedding [at which Gavin was best man] I hadn't seen her for, oh, it must have been fifteen years. And she came straight over and put her arms round me and said "John!" and reckoned the last time she'd seen me, I was having a piss in her lavatory!

'I think Gavin wanted to be more common that he was. But because he was so genuine, everyone took to him. And if we got into little scrapes, he'd hold his hands up with us and stand beside us. My old man always said, "You can tell who your mates are because, when you come across another group of lads and it looks like you're gonna get a hiding, your friends stand beside you and don't run away." And that meant a lot to me, as a kid. If we ever had any trouble, with just a phone call everyone used to come round and Gavin would be one of the first there. And things like that – loyalty – really matter.

'I think going away to Westminster got to him,' John suggests.

'Especially because he'd have to go in to school on Saturdays and for us, Saturday was *the* day. We were up early in the morning and we were out and that was it. He finished school at one or two o'clock on a Saturday and he'd spend the day trying to find us, 'cause in those days we didn't have mobile phones! Unless we were around the area he had no way of knowing where we were, and he'd be lucky if he'd get in touch with us by Saturday evening. I know there were a few Saturdays where he didn't go to school 'cause we were planning to do something and he'd rather hang round with us. I think that's one of the things his dad didn't like about us. But at the end of the day, it was his choice. We'd never say to him, "Oh, don't go to school." But I can understand his point. He wanted to be with his mates. I suppose it was a posh school and there'd be all these posh people saying "Daddy's this" and "Daddy's that". And he'd be saying, "Yeah, well we was running round Kilburn High Road kicking footballs about." Even if,' John laughs, 'he did talk a little posher than everybody else and tried to sound rougher than he was and learn a bit of slang. Though he was never that good at it, actually!'

As far as John remembers, though, Gavin was quite good at nicking birds. In fact, Gavin's first ever girlfriend, Jill Hurley, was spotted by John Black first.

'Oh, yeah, I was seeing Jill for a few weeks,' John Black nods, 'and then suddenly she didn't want to know. I found out Gavin had slipped in through the back door somehow. In fact, I can remember when I found out: later that day, we were playing football and I went in for a tackle, and it wasn't a very nice one.' He grins. 'And he said something, so I gave him a good slap, and that was about it.' He winks. 'So you can put that in the book, then . . . "I gave Gav a slap." '

Now a qualified aromatherapist and sales and marketing representative, Jill Hurley still lives in the old neighbourhood, and looks not much different from the thirteen year old who, Gavin says, was 'just unbelievably beautiful.'

'I met him through a neighbour, Robert,' Jill remembers. 'All of a sudden, this guy appeared on the scene, and everyone was tittering and twittering about Gavin. I don't remember exactly where I met him, he was just there. When you're that age, it's just sort of like, "Will you go out with me?" It wasn't my job to ask, he asked me,' she smiles, remembering the strict codes of decorum of youth.

'We used to go to the Youth Club on Abbey Road and play table tennis and table football. And Gavin was just not the same as the other boys, who were all into being skinheads and fighting and toughness. But he came in, played football, and got accepted and I think that surprised everybody, really. He was a good footballer, too, and he didn't ever seem puny the way boys often are when they're young. He was from a completely different background anyway. One thing me and my mum remember was Christmas that year. We were all sitting in the kitchen waiting, because this was mine and Gavin's first Christmas and he was coming round. And everyone was tittering, "Oh, what's he going to buy you?' Anyway, Gavin turns up, and he's got his hands behind his back, and he had this little Snoopy love heart for me. It was so cute! He was lovely, and he's still got that shyness about him. That little smile, sort of embarrassed.

'I remember us all going to his house – me, a couple of girlfriends and a few of the lads, and being so scared, thinking, "Oh, please don't break anything . . ." Gavin was dead cool about it, but I was really nervous. My house is very nice, but going to his . . . well, everything was just so. And that lovely picture of his mum on the wall; absolutely beautiful. I bet she's beautiful still.

'We used to hang out at the Youth Club, outside, kicking footballs and pinching each other – the way you do when you're young and you don't know what to do, so you just pinch each other. We'd listen to Cockney Rebel, the Sex Pistols and ska. Most of the boys were skinheads; not shaven, but just really short hair, with tight jeans, little turn-ups and monkey boots. Gavin had short hair and he wore jeans, more sort of American-style. You know,' she adds suddenly, 'we broke up because, and he won't forgive me for this actually, but I packed him in to go out with someone tougher.

'I told him first, of course. I think he was a bit shocked. My friends thought I was mad. He was gorgeous. He had a pretty look then and he's still pretty, 'cause he's got perfect-shaped eyes and lips. I remember my mum telling him "You've got make-up on!" He hadn't. It was because his eyelashes were so long.

'But he never would have grown up with us, he was just too different. Even from a young age, you could see he was going to go on and do something. I remember him singing, and saying "I'm gonna be – ", well, something. And I'd say, "No, Gavin, you won't," because he had a terrible voice! He'll probably hate me for saying that,' she adds mischievously.

'But he was a good kisser,' she adds, laughing. 'Very soft and tender compared to most lads, who were usually horrible and sloppy. I'd say he must have practised . . . the back of his hand, a teddy bear, or something! He had very well-conditioned lips,' she teases. 'He must've been using a good lip balm.

'He really wanted to be accepted by people, but he never went around pretending to be something he wasn't, like most people do. He never started spitting and swearing, it just wasn't him.'

A few days after we speak, Jill sends me some photos of Gavin from the time they were dating, and a letter in which she tells me of a youth club camping trip she, Gavin and the gang went on. 'I think I deliberately didn't tell you [in the interview] because I wasn't the nicest to Gavin, in my sister Lynn's words. In fact, she said I was really horrible to him. Still, I can remember us all getting drunk on a few cans of beer, and Gavin listening [on the radio] to John McEnroe in the tennis finals. He got really excited about it. Which was so strange, really, considering all the other boys we knew got excited about football and went to matches on the weekend, whereas Gavin would play tennis.

'I just had a look on the inside of my wardrobe door. Everyone who used to come into my room used to sign it, and sure enough, Gavin 4 Jill is written there a few times. It's been a little bit of a challenge over the years explaining Gavin to my boyfriends. I don't think any of them have ever really liked the idea that we are still friends – especially as, if he is on the telly or in a magazine, I get excited as I would about any friend.' Here's how Jill's letter ends. 'Before I close off, I would just like to say a few more words to sum up the Gavin I know. He has always been unique, with a deep soul and a deep passion. He never let go of that desire, and he's done everything it took to arrive. He still has that same air, that same warm aura, and still has an amazingly modest, shy way about him.I wonder sometimes, though, if Gavin would like to be just Gavin and not Gavin from Bush, because he's much more than just a singing voice and performer. You can feel it in his spirit. I'm proud that I have Gavin as a friend, although sometimes I forget . . . because he is a bit of a devil with phone calls!'

C

Coincidentally, or perhaps not, it was on that very same Abbey Road Youth Club camping trip when Jill Hurley was 'really horrible' to her then-boyfriend that Gavin realised it was time for a change. As he would tell the *Sunday Times Magazine*, 'That [trip] woke me up. I realised I didn't want to be a postman or an electrician. Overnight . . . I smoked red Marlboroughs and wore a dirty mac and carried a copy of Jean-Paul Sartre.'

And so a new world of possibilities beckoned, and with it the opportunity to meet new people and possibly even become a new person. Westminster schoolmate Mark Armstrong would be there to accompany Gavin on his forays into a London of clubs, parties, scenesters and artists, charlatans and creativity. A cultured, witty and strikingly handsome man of Milanese and English parentage who is frequently mistaken for soccer star David Beckham, Armstrong has spent more than a decade as one of London's most sought-after events organisers and club owners and promoters. Sitting in Soho's exclusive media-and-entertainment club The Groucho, he recounts the story of his friendship with Gavin Rossdale, all the while treating both the teenager Gavin was, and the successful artist he is now, with the sort of irreverent affection only the longest-standing friends would display.

'Oh, we've had some great times,' he drawls. 'And we'll carry on having some great times, of course.' Looking back, Armstrong insists that Gavin's dislike of the air of privilege at Westminster, where he would spend four years, was misplaced. 'It's one of the few public schools that are actually in the centre of London, so you're not only learning about trigonometry and physics, you're also having hands-on experience of life, because you're where the action is.

'On the very first day we were put in the same class, and that's where we met. We'd just turned thirteen and that's where it all started. Now,' he laughs, 'Gavin's going to say to you that Westminster was really poncey and really uncool, because it doesn't necessarily go with his image. But nevertheless he must admit it was a very good school, and we did learn to speak Spanish and French. And, even better, you go and have your lessons and then that's it; you're not controlled or anything. You finish about quarter to four and then you can do what you want . . . like a hotel. It's fantastic for a kid, really.

'London clubs were really starting to blossom at the time, with all that glamorous hanging out that doesn't really exist now; the New Romantic thing, very visual and very cool. Even then, Gavin was fascinated by it, because he always had this star quality about him, this aura, which you could see even when we were young. And he was totally fascinated by this nightclub world.' In fact, laughs the man whose name would become a guarantee of the most sought-after party invitations, 'Gavin was the one who introduced me to it. We used to sneak off to places where we were probably the youngest people by about five or six years, hanging out with all these people who later became celebrities. Everyone was congregating around the Camden Palace on Thursday night, which was the coolest night to be there, so we used to go and meet people. It was great fun. The music was really happening. Completely fascinating.

'Of course,' says Mark, 'being that young, it was very overwhelming, because you're meeting celebrities when you've never met anyone famous before. We'd go out with them, then watch them on *Top Of The Pops* the next day. And obviously, we liked our girls,' he adds lightly. 'It was pre-AIDS time, and we were doing our bit of pulling. It was great; we were real *smoochers*,' he smiles.

'Parties and clubs and girls. They were things that were always around us, whether we had no money or lots of money. Somehow, we managed to lead this semi-fantasy lifestyle, which was fantastic, because of course at the same time we were both still students, going back to our lessons. We used to sit in the back row with our notebooks, and I had Gavin's page and he had my page and we used to write each other messages – "Do you remember that girl last night?" – while some teacher would be droning on about the historic past tense. We'd take it in, but have a laugh as well.

'It was crazy to think we did as much as we did, but when you're a kid you want to do everything and it's all very new and very inspiring. You look forward to the night.

'Gavin always used to get caught [misbehaving], whereas I kind of got away with it. And when it came to exams we tried hard to be stupid, but we always did quite well. So even though we were naughty – especially him – we were liked. The teachers didn't punish us heavily 'cause we were quite humorous. I'd sit there and hear, "Rossdale! Get out!" and I'd see this little head sticking round the edge of the door. Once, I came in late to English class from the clarinet lessons I took. Our English lessons were taught by this really old ex-major who thought he was still in the army. Gavin had saved a seat for me, so I strolled in and Gavin said, "Hey, how you doing?" And it was "Armstrong! Get *out* if you're going to come in like that, get out!"

'And that,' he says, 'is pretty much the way it went. The irony is that, of the two of us, I used to be in the orchestra. I did grades for the clarinet and play a bit of piano, so I have quite a good classical background, whereas at the time Gavin wasn't that much interested in music. And every morning we had to go to this morning service at Westminster Abbey; only about 15 minutes, but every morning a song, a lesson and a little talk. If you missed it, they kept you back and made you run around the green a few times, which was pathetic really. So for five years we spent time in one of the most important abbeys of the world walking all over these famous graves and everything and he just wasn't interested in the music. Well, certainly not *that* kind of music.

'But Gavin was interested in everything that went with pop music. I don't think he necessarily wanted to be famous, although there are a lot of advantages,' Mark smiles, 'if you are. I think he wanted to be successful more than he wanted to be famous. And he was fascinated with a lifestyle that included so many girls, and the fact that you could get a message across to a large number of people just by having a lot of power. He wasn't necessarily out to be a star, even though he had all the qualities. And it almost didn't matter what the music was like, because he's great looking and a good talker, and he'll always make you feel good.'

Needless to say, says Mark, Gavin 'had no interest to study any further after we took our A levels. He wanted to get out there and start living.'

Just after Mark and Gavin met, Mark's father died and, when the boys finished at Westminster, Mark returned to Italy where it was expected that he would stay and take his place in the family's business concerns, rather than going on to the London School of Economics, as he intended. 'I remember having a few chats with Gavin, and basically the most important decision I made was to stay here and not go over there like my little brother. You're in the best city in the world; you're having a great time; all your friends are here. You're English, so what the hell are you going to do back in Italy?' Mark did go to Milan for a long holiday – but he returned. Not only to the LSE, but also to the music and club scene.

'And I came back and saw Gavin,' Mark recounts, 'and he'd totally changed physically. He had longer hair, for a start; obviously, we weren't allowed to before that. And he pulled out this tape and said, "I've got this band, The Heroes, together. Do you want to hear it? Do you want to get involved?" He played me the tracks and they were great. And completely different, I mean totally different, to what he does now,' he adds with a wink.

Somehow, quite without anyone seeing it coming, Gavin Rossdale had decided on music as his life, and found some musical partners to do it with. It's perhaps not an unusual move for a seventeen year old who'd already been a fan of music for some time. Lorraine recalls, 'I remember him saying he wanted to do it. You know, we're not a musical family; no sing-songs at Christmas or anything like that. I was away [in Spain] at the time and I remember him telling me on the phone, "I know what I want to do now. I want to be a singer.' And I was like, "Oh, really?" But that's what he wanted, and he knew it. And anyone else would have given up two years down the line, but of course he didn't.'

Alex Tate, now a film director and producer who was, at this time, beginning to hang out with Gavin and Mark, comments. 'It was an incredible scene we found ourselves in. These pop stars were just two feet away from us at clubs, so you did start to have that feeling of, well, you know, "I can do that. Look, he's only standing right there . . . we'll just pick up on the moves and do it too." Total disrespect for any craft or work involved, of course.' Alex laughs at their youthful optimism. 'It was all about *front*. You just had to gird your loins and say, even though you were only eighteen, "Yeah, I'm a producer; yeah, I can do that film for you in a week."'

'Yes, of course that scene can be shallow and hedonistic,' Mark allows, in response to comments Gavin would later make about the glittering world he observed as a wide-eyed teenager. 'You take it for what it is, but at the same time, it's a very important part of the creative world. It was like being at school or something; it was where all our friends went. It was where you spent time on a social level, especially in those days when you weren't working and you were out clubbing. It was where we met a lot of people. It's completely different now, but then, if he hadn't been at Madonna's party, say, he wouldn't have met a particular producer. It's how things happen. The same way people go to a pub or a bar, we had this large circle of creative people and I'm sure that gave him a lot of inspiration to go out there and do his stuff musically, because a lot of these people were going out there and doing it, too.

'And where else,' he adds emphatically, 'are you going to get that sort of crowd? Hanging out with fashion designers, artists, the most beautiful girls. It inspires you to be successful. If you're going to stay at home and watch TV and have a quiet life, you may not have opportunities to bump into people and create opportunities.'

By now, the almost-inseparable twosome even had their own bachelor pads. 'We always used to hang out together and there were more and more girls, and there was more and more fun to be had. We'd go to all the great parties, the openings, and the nightclubs. I got my first car, and Gavin had just moved into this basement flat in Montagu Square [where Gavin's aunt Maggie had once lived] and he was so sad to leave this little room at his dad's house. And I'd been living on my own; I had my own flat too. I always used to go pick him up to go out clubbing, and he'd spend hours getting dressed,' says the immaculately-attired Mark. 'Worse than any girl I've ever seen; the look had to be *perfect*. Of course, he could have worn a T-shirt and a pair of jeans and it would have been fine. But no, about 17 different pairs of trousers went on . . . And this was all while I was waiting, saying, "Come on, let's go." And he'd say, "Well, I'm not sure about this hat. I don't know whether it goes with this green top." Not only did I pick him up,' Mark laughs, 'but then I'd have to wait for him to get changed, listen to his demos in the car and then talk on and on about his music in the club. It was frustrating, but funny at the same time.'

As Mark recalls, there was no shortage of friends and friends-of-friends around to believe that Gavin's talent, looks and genuine charm would result in something special happening, almost immediately, for The Heroes (or Midnight, as they would later become). In the heady 80s climate of sudden fame and conspicuous consumption, a nice fat record deal was expected any minute almost as a matter of course. 'But for some reason the deal wasn't happening, and it was nearly as if people were too scared to approach Gavin,' Mark frowns. 'You know, everyone thought that he was all sorted out. That he was doing well, that he didn't need that deal. But the reality was that the deal wasn't there . . . and it was time to go out and get it.'

With Sacha Puttnam as his first musical partner, that was exactly what Gavin Rossdale did.

D

'Do I think we could have made it? I remember having a very weird feeling with Midnight, which was that I couldn't quite push out of the boundaries that we had. I remember looking at a song, really trying to work out how we could make it better, and absolutely not being able to at all, which was a really, really frustrating feeling. Nowadays if I looked back at it, I would completely turn everything inside out. I knew that we had to go an extra ten per cent, and I just couldn't do it. It's funny, looking backwards now. We were so tame. We thought we were actually pushing it out there a little bit; two-string chords instead of single-finger plucked lines. But now, when you hear American music, or when you hear Bush's music, it's total mayhem in comparison. But great mayhem. Controlled mayhem.' – Sacha Puttnam

Sacha Puttnam recalls that his eighteen-year-old self fell in love all the time. When his attention fell on 'an absolutely beautiful girl' named Ana, it was natural that he'd want to know who she was rumoured to be seeing, if only to know what his own chances were. The object of Ana's affections, and therefore the object blocking his path, was Gavin Rossdale.

As it happened, meeting Gavin was the start of a relationship for Sacha: a musical one. 'I'd been shut away in a public school and I knew exactly what I wanted to do. I'd met all these people, musicians and different bands, at school. But when I bumped into Gavin, I just knew he had everything I needed. The thing I noticed instantly was an incredible sexual energy. If we walked into a room, people used to notice us; we'd walk down the street, and people would look. I was eighteen, but a very young eighteen. I'd just got out of school and had my first cigarette, so I was a little bit behind everyone. But Gavin was much more mature than I was, so he kind of became my protector.' Even today, Sacha – who would go on to study as a conductor and composer in Russia and at Berkeley in Boston, and who now works as a teacher and film score composer – says that being in Gavin's company 'is like coming away from one mother and going to another mum. He's my mum, or my big brother, and he's brilliant to me. I can be really callous,' he adds impishly, 'and know that nobody's going to hit me, because of Gavin.'

Back when they were still teenagers, Sacha recalls, 'There were a couple of guys from Gavin's school who I knew, and who'd say to me, "Listen, you don't want to get on the wrong side of Gavin." For two reasons. First, on the popularity level, because if you weren't with him then you were with the wallies, because he was always top dog, absolutely always. And secondly, because you didn't want to have a fight with him. I've seen him deck people before, in fact. Not because anyone was having a go at him, but because someone was having a go at someone else. For example, there was a guy called Richard, a really sweet little gay dude, who was walking out of the gardens one night, and some big idiot was heckling him: "You fucking poof!"

'I was watching Gavin and could see the hairs going up on the back of his neck. He hates anyone being picked on. And he just turned and smashed this guy so hard he hit the wall and slowly dropped to the ground.' What you could see, Sacha suggests, was two parts of a personality mixing – the Kilburn rough boy and a gentler soul. 'He could have been a really bad sort if he'd wanted to be. And he didn't really hang out with the artistes, though he has got that side to him. He's an enigma. A real enigma. I don't understand him, but I love him. And I think if all people were like him, we'd be just about all right.

'When I first met him, I knew he had something really special. He already had some really good demos, but they were very light. So we just spent every hour of every day together, talking about how things should be. We talked about music, music, music all the time. We listened to a lot of Prince, and The Family, all of that Minneapolis sound, and whatever was a very big album at the time, usually by male artists. And, of course, we'd talk about what we would do with our band. What we'd do when we went on tour, how it was going to be.'

'I remember when we first got the band,' Gavin recalls. 'Dave [Norland, another ex-Westminster boy] and Sacha were the first two people I had met who were musicians. I would write lyrics, sing them into a tape recorder at my dad's house, and give them a tape and ask them to put music on it. Sacha's stuff was really beautiful: in fact, if it had continued like that, it probably would have turned out to be something like The Verve – obviously a young, bad version – in the sense of being very English and very rolling, because Sacha has such a beautiful feel. As a guitar player, Dave was really good too, but Sacha was just so supremely talented. Sacha's the only person I've ever been in a band with that I was best friends with.'

Mark Armstrong recalls the initial Midnight results with some enthusiasm. 'It was the early 80s and it was perfect for the times,' he says. 'The package was all there: a love song, a song that was gloomy and depressing, and a couple of fast ones that were essentially really poppy.'

As luck, or coincidence, or merit – or all three – would have it, it wasn't long before the band found themselves in the ideal situation to get a record deal. 'We were sitting in our friend Jordan's house, and Jordan's sister was going out with Lee Barrett,' Sacha explains. Lee, a band manager, was particularly hot at the time, managing the quintessentially 80s, smooth soul outfit, Sade.

'We'd just signed a publishing deal with Warner Music with a guy called Johnny Stern . . . who rang me up not so long ago to try to release the old Midnight tapes,' Sacha adds. 'Silly man. And so Lee was there, and asked us a few questions about our band and said, "Oh, that sounds really interesting, send us a tape." We had one song called "Tell Me Girl" that he thought was a really big hit. I think we signed with him almost straight away. For us, he was a really big cheese, although it was actually one of the worst things we ever did. I think he'd just been lucky with Sade, because the first single went for them and it was all plain sailing, and I don't think Lee really knew how any of it happened. But we weren't to know that at the time and, to be honest, we probably got our deal with [record label] CBS because we happened to be hanging out with Sade.

'But we never really saw anyone [at CBS] ourselves,' Sacha explains. Despite all their daydream planning, 'we never really called the record company to say, "Right, this is the way it should be." Lee had a policy that we didn't speak to anyone, and we were very overshadowed by CBS's ideas. It was difficult to be yourself when they'd come up with a formula.'

At the time, Gavin admits, his teenage view of what it would be like to be in a band was simple, and not particularly unusual. 'What appealed to me about being a rock star? Freedom and money. Freedom to do what I wanted, and loads of money. That's what I thought it was.'

'The truth is,' Sacha smiles, 'he really wanted to be a star. When we had our boys' conversations together, he really used to worry about looks. He used to say that I had the most perfect forehead. He has quite a big head, and was worried about it. I'd point out that it's great for the camera and he'd be really pleased, and say, "Oh, so in films . . . that would be really good, would it?" It always showed me that if a film came up, he'd be the first one to jump in. It's that thing of recognition; he loved it. But ultimately, once he latched onto music, *boom*, music was definitely the way.'

As Sacha recalls, even in the earliest days of the band, 'Gavin's lyrics were really quite awesome. Really quite awful in a way, too. There was a lot of pain there. I used to say, "Can we have something to go with a nice melody?" What he was singing about didn't go down well with those melodies at all. And it was probably terrible of me, but I was always trying to Hollywoodise him, I guess. "Look, can you write about something good?" And he'd look at me like I was bonkers. I think it's just what came naturally to him.'

As for Midnight's career, Sacha won't venture to say they dwelled on their prospects for success, or how, exactly, it might come about. 'To tell the truth, a bit like the sound of the band, I didn't really think about it. It was almost like it was totally in the hands of the gods. And again, maybe one of the reasons we weren't successful was that we just allowed things to happen. Of course, we all believed we were going to be the biggest band in the world,' he adds wryly. 'Some guy told us, "You guys have a long way to go." But although we knew that, at the time we also thought we were really good.'

Mark Armstrong, ever the behind-the-scenes overseer, had high hopes. From the band's earliest days, 'I was always the organiser, the impresario, and Gavin was always the creative mind. It was a bit like *Midnight Cowboy*: I was Dustin Hoffman, and he was the cool boy, and we did these fantastic shows. Loads of them, all over the place, in the trendiest clubs. We always used to pack them in. Each time, we'd meet more and more people, and *everyone* liked Gavin. But for some reason, the deal wasn't happening. It was frustrating that the success wasn't there. The record company didn't do their stuff; it wasn't promoted enough. Otherwise, of course, everything was there: a good-looking band and easy-going pop songs. But it wasn't being played on the radio, and that's what you need.'

Between 1985 and 1987, the teenaged and early-twentysomething Midnight would have the opportunity to release two twelve-inch singles. ('They never trusted us with a full album,' Gavin recalls wryly.) Debut single 'Run With You' introduced the first lyrical collage from a songwriter who still builds his songs as a series of serendipitous images and juxtapositions. In this case, the words were taken from random bits of graffiti scribbled on Jim Morrison's grave in Père Lachaise cemetery in Paris. ('Did Mark Armstrong remember that?' Gavin says, surprised. 'Even I'd forgotten that. But yes, that's exactly true.') 'King of the Mountain', the second single, presented a particularly bleak bit of Gavin's writing that completely undercut the triumphalism of the title. Gavin laughingly says Sacha 'forced me to use it'.

The results, in terms of chart success, were less than anyone involved had hoped. The gigs, on the other hand, had their exciting moments, starting off with crowds both on and off the stage. 'Our first show, I think there were fifteen people onstage,' Sacha recalls with amusement. 'The classic case of hiding behind a whole lot of people. Or we wouldn't play unless we'd bought a new pair of shoes. The percussionist then hit me with a bill for £1,500 – for the shoes! Sheer madness. We were hiding, basically. Although as soon as we started stripping away because we could only afford to have the four of us, suddenly it started coming together.'

'We found a place in clubland,' Sacha continues. 'We were liked, but it was a club audience who would never have bought any records anyway. In London, the people who saw us were probably just hoping there were free drinks. All the bands we were around, like Curiosity Killed The Cat, were much more successful than we were. So we used to sit and watch all of them doing really well. Then again, if you can keep it alight during those times, you're so much stronger.'

Midnight would also bring Gavin Rossdale his first encounters with the press, and his first indication that, in contrast to the famous diktat, it wasn't where you were at, it was where you were from that gained or lost you credibility in the eyes of the music and style press. Although the band attracted only a few magazine articles in its short life, Sacha believes most interviewers were less interested in the music than in being sceptical of a band of well-spoken, attractive young men, including a bass player whose father was famed film producer David (later Lord) Puttnam.

'I never did an interview, though,' adds Puttnam's son, Sacha. 'Gavin used to go in there and rub them up the wrong way, I think, because he was probably being honest, and the difficult thing with the English press is that they really do want you to come from nowhere. Which is why it's so schizophrenic; after all, Shane McGowan [of The Pogues] went to Westminster as well, but, because of his bad teeth and the way he looks, people don't take that on board. As long as you're filthy and look like you're struggling a little, then that's acceptable. But then you'd have Gavin coming in, looking good and being polite, and it was all over.

'It did bother me a little that people always talked about my dad, because neither he nor his friends ever helped me do this. So I got frustrated and decided, right, I'm going to use what I've got. I went to see my godfather Charles Saatchi [the advertising magnate] and said, "What can I do to really advertise this group?" And his response was sort of, "Well, hmm, I dunno." ' Sacha rolls his eyes. 'I couldn't win either way. It wasn't like I was getting help from the powerful guys, yet I was being linked to them, so I couldn't possibly be assumed to have come from the street.'

Guardian music critic Caroline Sullivan, then writing for *Melody Maker*, remembers her surprise that the Gavin Rossdale she interviewed in 1987 was nothing like the man the band's press – or even her experiences with other bands at the time – had led her to expect. 'I think I assumed he'd be rather thick, because not only was he quite exceptionally pretty, but I'd seen him tipped in *Elle* magazine's style roundup as a face to watch that year. In fact, he was quite nice, and not at all stupid . . . much brighter and nicer than most musicians, actually. If one thing stands out, it was that he seemed anxious to distinguish the band from the impression given by that *Elle* piece. And to stress that the band weren't just young clubgoing male bimbos, but a bona fide rock group who had paid their dues.' She also notes that the band didn't seem to be

CBS's number one priority: 'I was used to doing interviews with Next Big Things in posh hotel suites but, when I went to meet him, we were shoved away in an office the size of a cupboard. You could tell how much faith the record company had in them ... just enough to get someone to step out of their office for half an hour!'

'Maybe if the press had gone, "Oh my God, maybe there's something interesting going on here" when I was doing Midnight, I would have gone off into some sort of self-built greenhouse for destruction,' says Gavin in retrospect. 'And instead, up until this day, that negative kind of reaction has just always pissed me off and been more of a challenge. I remember one of the first reviews we got. The writer said, "First off, you can't call yourself Gavin and be in a rock band." '

The man fatally named Gavin laughs, incredulous. 'Where does that come from? I'm nineteen years old and thinking, Fuck, great, even my name's wrong. I should have been J-O-N.' He shrugs. 'Of course I come from a middle-class background. We had three bedrooms and I had my own small room. Well, John Lennon grew up in a seven-bedroom house by the seaside, and Joe Strummer's dad was an ambassador. I don't know how many true working-class bands there are, or if it matters. Maybe it's supposed to be about how good you bluff it. I guess I've always been guilty of having a shit press angle ...'

Nevertheless, the band continued to tour, supporting Big Country, then Cyndi Lauper, and making it as far as Ireland. 'It wasn't a great tour,' Sacha remembers. 'The fun bit was just being with your friends. The hotels weren't anything to write home about, certainly! But there were a couple of moments, like being in a hotel in Ireland and watching Live Aid on television all together, which bind you closer as a band.' Outside of London, he adds, 'audiences were much more receptive. Our very first gig in Ireland was amazing. It was the first time there were people who were really enthusiastic that we were playing.'

And the songs? 'It's like Sacha said, I've always written the same kind of lyrics,' Gavin theorises. 'Always, always, always. I know I used to work really hard at them. And they wouldn't ... well, they wouldn't be totally embarrassing,' he smiles. 'They'd just be like a younger, different version of myself. Ever since I began, you know, that's what I always cared about. Just trying to get better at music, at words. I've always loved words, and I always felt I should sing them, which is a weird confidence to have. In retrospect I could say, well, maybe what I did in Midnight wasn't great – but at the same time, I can't even remember it that well. I suppose I've got the records, but my record player only plays albums, not singles, so I haven't got the chance,' he insists. 'Still, it certainly wasn't just pop. I'd like to listen to them someday. Quietly, on my own. Alone.'

Perhaps Gavin Rossdale needn't sound so tentative. For a young musician barely out of his teens who had yet to write music for himself, who had yet to discover many of the bands that would later inspire him, and who was trying to make sense of the Bowie and Pistols touchstones in his head while the glossy sounds of 80s clubland – and the commercial inclinations of his record label – swirled around him, Gavin Rossdale's work with Midnight is hardly an embarrassment. It's indubitably of its time; a time when even the best works have not aged well. But in amongst what hindsight would call the over-polished pop and pallid drumming of tracks like 'Burning Up' or 'Tell Me Girl', you can hear an individual voice struggling to get out. In a live recording of a show in Belfast, you can even hear a vocalist fighting against a hardened punk audience's suspicion of London bands, as Gavin encourages the audience to enjoy themselves and even asks for volunteers to be his best friend, while the band go on acquitting themselves creditably with a cover of Bowie's 'Rebel Rebel'.

And in the demo tapes of unreleased Midnight songs Sacha digs out of a jumbled box in his West London flat, you can hear hints of what Midnight could have become. A few untitled numbers are Sacha's instrumentals, movingly elegiac and haunting; elsewhere, you can hear a younger but identifiably hoarse-voiced Gavin scratching, laughing, stumbling and ultimately roaring into a bluesy, twangingly acoustic kitchen-sink narrative called 'In America Tonight', which sounds as if it was recorded straight to four-track and, aesthetically, wouldn't sound out of place today.

'It's a little bit bruised, and it's full of love, and it's full of yearning, and it's full of isolationism and all that stuff,' Gavin says of the music he makes today. In fact, it was true even then.

E

Even if Midnight wasn't quite setting the world on fire, there was plenty of excitement to go around. With Mark Armstrong as a friend, Gavin was never short of a social event or two.

'I remember when [archetypal 80s London scenesters] Steve Strange and Rusty Egan and I organised a trip to Ibiza, long before it became the commercial clubby town that it is today,' Mark remembers. 'Midnight were playing at the Ku Club and we took along the wildest bunch of hardcore London party animals. The gig was fantastic, and afterwards the dance floor opened up to reveal a pool full of foam and everyone was falling in it. And then we got invited to [film director] Roman Polanski's house up in the hills. For some reason, Gavin decided to drive up on a scooter. So I was in this taxi with Steve Strange, and all of a sudden I saw Gavin fly off the road and into the bushes. We got really worried: it was midnight, we were going to a posh dinner, and now there was blood everywhere. He'd cut his neck and all down his arm, but kept insisting, "I'm fine. I'm perfectly all right. Just a little accident." So he got back on his scooter, and when we got to this house, we rang the doorbell and a really weird little girl answered the door in a Pink Panther outfit. And in fact, all the girls were dressed in these outfits. We sat down and Steve Strange just passed out, and we were left with all these people we didn't know. So we got really drunk, and then I was made to put on a red Cleopatra wig which Gavin refused to wear, and then all the Pink Panther girls started jumping into the pool . . .

'It was like a party clip in a Peter Sellers movie,' laughs Mark. 'Gavin had cut a bit of his shirt sleeve off to make a sling for his arm, and by now I had this huge bruise on my head from jumping into the pool and hitting a giant wooden crocodile that I'd mistakenly thought was inflatable. Anyway, we went back to the hotel and it was daylight, and really hot and, just like every other day, there'd be someone sleeping in our beds, because someone had had a row. I remember I had to sleep on a table because it was the only space in my room. I could hear people talking absolute gibberish outside my room, so I thought fuck it, I'm just going to go sleep on a beach. So I went into his room and said, "This is not happening for me, Gavin. I tried to sleep for an hour on this table . . ." and he said, "Well, look where I slept!" He'd had to put an inflatable mattress on about fifty bottles of beer because the room was so full of glass and dirt he couldn't even put it on the floor. So we ended up sleeping on the beach, finally getting some rest – until all of a sudden the guys from Frankie Goes To Hollywood turned up, and Paul Rutherford took this huge pile of seaweed and threw it all over us.

'You know I call him Rock,' Mark says of Gavin, 'and he likes it. It just came out: rock and roll. He went to Amsterdam to do some writing once, and I went out to join him. I had organised, through Warner Brothers, this fantastic suite with champagne and everything at the American Hotel. I had no idea it was the best hotel in Amsterdam. I called Gavin and said, "Look, I've got a hotel just in case yours isn't very nice." So he came to pick me up from the airport, and I thought he'd have a nice car or something, but he caught the tram. Then we went to his hotel, which was horrible.' Mark grimaces. 'It was like a youth hostel. And he'd checked in with my name, met some girl and brought her back there . . .' Mark shakes his head. 'I said, "Let's go and see my hotel because we might like it more." So he got his bag and we walked out, and the owner of the hotel was shouting at Gavin, "Mr Armstrong! You don't pay your bill!" I was turning around going, "What?" And Gavin's muttering under his breath, "Just keep walking." We got to my hotel and it was *much* better. And we spent the whole weekend in bars and coffee shops. We were in and out *very* quickly from the museums.

'We did acid for the first time together, too. We went to Roger Taylor's fortieth birthday party at his house out in the country, and we took this tab of acid called Batman. To our disappointment, absolutely nothing was happening. Nothing. For about two hours. Then I lost Gavin, and I was with Steve Strange going through a long hallway which had all these Queen gold records on the walls . . . and then I started tripping. Steve Strange became this horrible little gnome and I was thinking, I've got to find Gavin because he must be feeling the same. So I looked around and I saw Gavin standing right in the middle of the party, motionless. So I ran up to him and said, "I'm really out of it!" and he said, "Oh, no, so am I." I thought, Everyone must know we're on acid, so let's go and hide and join the party later. We went away, but bumped into Roger Taylor's new wife, who was a model – the Flake [chocolate bar] girl. She's like, "Hey guys, are you having a good time?" and we're like, "Oh God. Erm, yeah, we're having a good time." And it's a fancy dress party, and everyone's in school outfits. She's in a schoolgirl's outfit, and we're in shorts. "Roger's happy," she says, "and we're going to bring out the cake now." And then Gavin goes, "Erm, so, how are you?" And she says, "I'm fine, Gavin, how are you?" And he says, "Oh, I'm fine. Uhhh . . . how are you?" We weren't making any sense whatsoever. And Pink Floyd were there, and when we saw them, we *really* didn't know if we were tripping.

'Eventually, somebody gave us a lift back to London. Unfortunately, we'd totally forgotten about Steve Strange, whom we'd gone with. We went back to my house and crashed out. Then Steve turned up with a man in a suit and he said, "You have no idea what trouble you've caused me – but I've hitched all the way back from London, in this nice man's car!" Of course, we were still all in fancy dress as we stood there arguing: Steve wearing a headmaster's outfit, and we're in purple shorts, having this really serious conversation . . .

'We were also friends with this aristocrat, Lord Bristol, who was a society guy but a rock'n'roll guy, too. He had a fantastic house in the country and he'd throw huge, decadent parties, and he liked to invite Gavin and I, because we were young and funny. And he was, of course, completely mad. I remember one night we were asleep and he burst into our room – woke us up at four o'clock in the morning, and gave us these really Sloaney outfits, Barbours and so on, to put on. We walked outside with him, and he got a gun out, shot a rabbit and said, "OK, Armstrong and Rossdale, back to bed." The next morning we still had no idea what it had all been about.'

Meanwhile, Alex Tate was spending more and more time with

Gavin and the gang. 'I was hanging out, at first, with Mark Armstrong, and Gavin was sort of somebody I knew, but he was still practising "Moody Rock Star" on me. Yeah, the moody look – you know the one? So cool they can't even *speak*.'

And all the while wearing the coolest clothes. 'The first time I really noticed him, he was wearing this incredible hat, a bolero-type thing on top of long hair.' Remember, this was the 80s, and no one else was dressing that way. 'And I just thought, "Wow, how do you get away with that one?" And he wouldn't even give the hint of a smile to anyone, otherwise there was the risk that everyone would crack up, probably.

'Places like Taboo were our first introduction to proper freaks: weird and wonderful and rebellious and crazy. And "sartorial" was the most important language; it was one of the languages that you had to learn quickly and had to understand. Those people were just fantastic, real lotus eaters. They had the best clothes, they had ridiculous hair. Fashion is always changing if you hang around very fashionable places, and how you presented yourself was very important. I was going through a similar buzz to Gavin: he wanted to do music and I wanted to do film, but we were always chasing the same goal. And eventually, through parties and connections, we'd see each other and have a laugh and so we became a small gang.' Staring at the bigger gangs, in fact. 'Oh, yeah, glammed-up supermodel types. I mean, our eyes were on stalks. We couldn't even talk to them. I remember there was this one woman who came to Taboo with Mick Jagger and I couldn't even buy a ticket, mate, let alone talk to her. We probably thought we were nerds; in suburbia we would have been really happening, but here, we were just trying to get on the guest list. When you're the bottom of the pile and all the cool people are much cooler than you, well, you're always looking up. Trying to social climb your way up to the really cool people. We quickly discovered that it was a competitive sport: who could pull the most beautiful girl – that was one for the boys – or who could wear the most incredible outfit, or who had the weirdest drugs on them. You know, there were all kinds of different ways we were trying to be somebody. Even if it was also quite nurturing, and we also wanted to be nice to each other.'

According to Sacha Puttnam, Gavin 'was always ahead of fashion. Every time someone looked at him they would be thinking, "Fuck, you look really great. Where did you get that outfit?" He always looked like that, and he actually looks great in anything anyway. But in the 80s we were running around in whatever we could find. I remember once he had this great Jean-Paul Gaultier coat, and he used to wear it all the time. But he was never really feminine; there was always this macho side, there was always the side that showed you that he could have turned around and thumped someone, decked them completely.'

Still, as Sacha, Mark and Alex all point out, there was an unpleasant undercurrent to the omnipresent club scene.

According to Mark, 'It was all very camp. There was a big gay subculture, which carried over into making the whole thing very bitchy. You could get caught up in this bitchiness and end up being a bit bitchy, too. The whole attitude then was more aggressive, and maybe that's why Gavin used to be a lot nastier than he is now. Now he's more laid back, and of course he's a gentleman; everyone goes on about how polite he is. But there is still that side, and it was more obvious in those days, because of who we were hanging around. Even now, he's very good in an argument, and I hardly ever argue with him, but when he has disagreements with people he can be absolutely ruthless.'

'And that was a great training,' Sacha adds. 'Because so many of the people we were around had such wicked tongues, you had to fight for yourself mentally, very quickly. There was nothing physical, they were just unbelievably cutting all the time, whether it was about what you said or whatever you were wearing, trying to make you feel small. And Gavin learned a lot from that, I think, and has really torn some people to shreds with his tongue when he needed to. I suppose it definitely helped him later on in dealings with the record business.

'But those people could be very unfair with us, too,' he says. 'They pushed their cruelty to extremes. Still, in terms of that training, if you can learn how to stand up to those people, it makes you really strong.'

During what might have been called Midnight's heyday, if there'd been any real heyday to speak of, Gavin would meet his first long-term girlfriend, Lindsey Thurlow. Now living in London after several years in Los Angeles, she works in the film business – but, back in the mid-80s when she met Gavin, Lindsey was a supermodel before that term had been coined. Sacha Puttnam and Gavin met her in a club and, just as Sacha was hoping to arrange a date with her, 'Gavin found out about it and rang me up.' She laughs. 'And he came over and that was that. We started dating and we were together for five years.'

'I could tell he was in love,' Mark Armstrong says, 'and that he really did care a hell of a lot about her, and probably still does. She was a stunning girl, but very jealous, though she was always surrounded by good-looking guys, the same as Gavin was surrounded by good-looking girls. And she was a mad girl, really, a lunatic. I think she's calmed down a bit now,' Mark adds fondly. 'They used to have tremendous rows, really passionate Italian-style rows with things being thrown around. And in a funny way, I think he liked the fact that for the first time he'd met a girl that he couldn't control, couldn't manipulate. I think he's always been attracted to relationships that aren't easy to deal with. I think Gavin is one of those people who likes to suffer in an arty way. And I think he always wants a girlfriend. It's a psychological thing. He doesn't like being single and, even in between relationships, there isn't a long gap until the next girl comes along. In the twenty years I've known him, it was only at the beginning that we were both single. Since then he's always had a girlfriend.'

And this one was special. Just before Gavin moved out of his father's home in Kilburn, Lindsey would stay with him in his bedroom for six months – 'I spent the night there and I never left' – hiding from the imagined disapproval of his father, although Douglas Rossdale says mildly that he believes he always knew she was there. Later, when Gavin took over the tiny basement flat in Montagu Square that his Aunt Maggie had lived in, Lindsey would live with him. 'I was away in Paris and then I came back and it was lovely; he'd painted some furniture and fixed up the whole flat.

'My God, we were in love!' says Lindsey of their time together. 'He was so sweet. He wrote me little books; it was a very kind of surreal love, and it was all like a fairytale. It was very romantic. I was always on the move, because I was modelling, and I was doing very well, so my whole life was planes and then coming home for the weekend. And then I moved to New York, and so I would fly home weekends and Gavin would fly and see me in New York. Or we'd meet in Paris, and he was gigging at the time, trying to get Midnight off the ground. And so it was really weird, because my life was what *his* life is today.

'Midnight were cool. They had a rival band at the same time called Curiosity Killed The Cat, and they were all really gorgeous guys. There was Gavin's band, and then there was Curiosity, and they were very competitive, but we were all friends as well. We went to the same parties and they often gigged pretty much at the same places.'

Even before he was a star, Lindsey says, 'Gavin was a star in his own right. And even though he was struggling on the dole and trying to get this band together, he lived and acted like a star. Not in an ostentatious, arrogant way; but, even though he had no money, he was famous. I don't want to sound sycophantic about it, but I think he always knew he would do something. When you spoke to Gavin he'd never sit there and talk about when he was going to make it; he'd never say, "Well, when I get big and become a pop star . . ." He always knew, but he was very quiet about it. He had this demeanour of somebody who was so focused, and really had immense presence even then.

'Gavin was gorgeous, number one, and yeah, I was into sort of the visual aspect of the opposite sex at that point,' she says. 'The good thing about Gavin is that he is very intelligent, he's got a really amazing, sensitive side to him. His female side is very developed and he was always reading books and taking me off to see amazing lectures and Russian films, so it was a bit of an education for me. He loves the arts, not just music, and he was a great fan; he was always interested in poetry and literature, he was – dare I say it without being pompous – hungry for knowledge. He has the ability to be very sharp witted, very funny, always on the ball, and he can hold himself and be very cutting when he needs to be. But at the same time he's quite soppy as well. He always had friends that were not doing so well, and he tended to take them under his wing. It used to annoy me a little, this trail of sad faces that he wanted to nurture, but I think that probably comes from the break-up of his parents' marriage; he was quite young when that happened, and it affected him very deeply. And a lot of people were envious of Gavin: all the girls loved him, but all the boys kind of resented him. He was so popular, so confident, and not in a show-offy kind of way, so I think guys thought he was big-headed. But you know, it was water off a duck's back to him; I think he found it very humorous.

'He was in the gym every day, running every day, played football and worked out. He got himself physically fit, and mentally he was ingesting all this material for the songs, from poetry to literature. So he was feeding himself. He used to drive me nuts. I bought him his first [acoustic] guitar for his birthday, and he decided he was going to teach himself to play. That was a nightmare to begin with. Gavin used to strum on the guitar, and it got to the point where he could only play two hours a day in another room at the end of the house, or when I was out, because he used to drive me mad. So it took him quite a while to learn to play, because I wasn't very supportive. But he worked like I've never seen anyone work. One great lesson I've learned from Gavin is that, if you have faith in yourself and if you put the work in, then it is possible. He really does deserve every success, because he worked religiously. His whole life was his music.

'But it was hard being with him, because keeping up a long-distance relationship was pretty tough. That, eventually, was the downfall of our relationship. I tried to go home every weekend and it was costing me a bomb, and I was going in one direction and he was still struggling with his music. And so that was the end of it, really. But it was fun while it lasted. We had a very volatile, passionate time, and it was one of the great romances for me, even if I don't know how he feels about it.

'Gavin was a very private person, even with me and our intimate relationship,' says Lindsey. 'He was very much a loner, very closed, and it wasn't often that I got to see those weaknesses or that frailty, that vulnerability. He didn't reveal it too much, he kept himself to himself. Everyone has demons and, when he was facing his, he was such an enigma. It's not good for a girlfriend, because the girlfriend then goes smashing up picture frames, and demands, "You tell me what's going on, I want a reaction." I was very much like that, and he'd retreat. He was very private, inaccessible. He still gets like that.'

'It's hard to say where his mum's leaving came into all that,' Sacha theorises. 'I think it's probably not ever getting close to someone too much because someone's already been close and left. And it's much more subtle than just being cruel, and he's not cruel. What he can do, though, and what was always difficult for me, is he can just follow his own agenda. I remember when he was with Lindsey, and he'd just be sitting playing the guitar, and I'd hear Lindsey saying, "Gav, do you want a bite to eat?" Some question like that. No answer. Long, long pause; no answer. He was too absorbed by his own thing. I know that if *I* was with someone like that, at that point I would belt them!' He laughs. 'I would just be like, "Oy! I'm talking to you." When I did do that, he'd snap out of it and say, "Oh, sorry, what did you say?" '

Jealousy, Lindsey admits, was a factor in their relationship. 'And for good bloody reason. Gavin liked women, and he still does. He's got a lovely girlfriend now; I've met her, she's wonderful. But I guess every good-looking young guy who's struggling and wants to be a pop star likes women, so I had to battle with a lot of other beautiful women while I was with him. Gavin liked his women too much. I think he's very different now, and he's grown up, but at the time I think it was a man thing entirely. And he had women throwing themselves at him. It was a nightmare. I remember when I flew out to Paris to see him play a gig [with Midnight], and he was singing and smiling at some girl in the audience a bit too much, and I went mad. I was dragged backstage by his manager, Lee, and told to calm down, because I was going to kill Gavin and this girl. I was livid.

'No, I didn't take any of his shit,' Lindsey continues. 'That's the kind of person I am, pretty aggressive and strong, perhaps to my detriment. But at the time, I didn't have to take that kind of thing, and I'm a pretty outspoken person, and I think Gavin liked it that I wasn't passive. I didn't just let it ride and I was very confrontational when I needed to be. And he still has a go at me, you know, sometimes when I have a go at him. He says, "Do you realise you're the only person whom I let speak to me like that?" ' She laughs. 'And I say, "I don't give a shit!" I've always been like that with him.

'Gavin and I have remained very good friends. You know, he still calls my mother up for chats, which I find a bit bizarre. He is so lovely like that, and he has always been really good to me. His whole family really took me under their wing. I lived in this house with his father, who is adorable and wonderful, when we first started going out. I'm godmother to Lorraine's daughter Jade, and Lorraine is my closest friend. She and I hated each other at first, because I was the girlfriend, and she was the sister. Gavin used to say, "Why don't you two get together, you'd really get on." And eventually, in fact, we became very, very close. And Gavin's still such a sweetheart, because when I came back from LA things went horribly wrong for me, and he was there for me without question. He's always said, "I'll always take care of you if anything happens." '

After Lindsey left Gavin, it would not be long before another important partner would leave him as well. 'I guess there's a part of him that still will never trust me,' Sacha Puttnam says of his decision to move on. 'I'd say maximum ten per cent. But I think he'll never quite get over my leaving, the same way as if someone has an affair with someone else while you're with them. You might forgive them, but it never quite repairs. Maybe after fifty years, but that's only because you've got so many other memories covering it up.'

Prior to Sacha's departure, Midnight had more or less fizzled out and Gavin, Sacha and a guitarist named Emil Lobo were working on a new band called the Little Dukes.

'I thought they were kind of all right,' Sacha says. 'I remember doing a showcase for EMI and that was the first time we played where I knew we'd all played well. The sound, which our friend Nigel Luby did, was really amazing. We had a guy we brought in called Andy Gungadin, and he and Emil, who were both Indian, were fantastic. I remember Clive Black from EMI was there and the word we heard back was that they never realised we were such good musicians. But then we never heard back from them.'

Of the events that brought about his departure, Sacha says: 'I'd done a terrible thing. We had a new drummer, Ali Cash, who was really good. But Gavin was away and the three of us were rehearsing every day, and I just got more and more annoyed that Ali wasn't drumming a half beat. I made his position untenable. And Gavin came back and acted like a mother hen and suddenly threw me out as well. Then I realised I'd ruined the band and ruined that friendship. It's not about ability, in the end, it's about much stronger things like love and longevity, and I had gotten rid of a great drummer.

'But in a way, Gavin made my decision to leave a lot easier. I can see both sides of it and, in the years since, a lot of people have come up to me and said, "Well, you made a bit of a mistake, didn't you?" Which is very English: in America, if you grow a beautiful tree in your garden, someone next door will try and grow a better one. But in England, someone will want to come round and cut it down instead.'

Sacha left for Russia to study composition and conducting, and would not see Gavin again until the next year when, he says, he returned to hear Gavin playing loud, angry American underground music. 'When I came back on holidays, he was listening to really serious grunge, some really mad music, a Steve Albini record, I think. It was really uncompromising; it was just sounds and rhythms and I didn't really like it. It was all about anger, I'm sure. He would turn it up to eleven and all the neighbours would complain like crazy. I think after I left, something happened. He became very uncompromising. Perhaps he realised that you can't wait for someone to give you something, you've actually got to force it to happen. Get a little elbowing going on.

'I think I was just being really selfish,' Sacha says of his departure. 'I thought I was going to be the greatest conductor to ever happen in the world. So I was just thinking about that and, to be totally honest, I forgot about what we had been doing straight away, because I just went boom, headlong straight into it. It was only later that it hit me, suddenly finding myself sitting in Russia on my own going, "Hang on, where are my mates?" '

Years later, Sacha says, he was watching television in a hotel room in Cannes, where he had gone to score a film, when he saw a hit video by a new English band called Bush. 'Everything Zen' was in heavy rotation on MTV, and Sacha was astonished and delighted to see that his former bandmate had done what he always wanted to do, on his own terms, and 'brilliantly, with a lot of anger, really good anger'.

'I got really self-conscious listening to it. And if I was being egotistical,' he says, 'I might think that line about "my asshole brother" was about me. And it may well have been; I never actually found out. Gavin smiled once when I asked him, but he didn't really reply.'

But that was still some years in the future. Back in London, with Lindsey and Sacha gone, gloom descended more and more frequently on Gavin's world. No matter how hard he and Alex, who was by now sharing Gavin's Montagu Square basement, tried to cheer each other up.

'Gavin and I were invited to a party,' Alex remembers. 'There was a guy called Nick Trew who used to organise this event called "Dinner With The Good Guys". It would be in a restaurant and there would be fifty guys who all knew each other. I think Gavin and I were both recovering from our disastrous inability to have anything but predictably bad relationships with women, and wondering what we had to do to find something better, and then this party came along and we thought, "Great! An opportunity to meet some women – not our normal crazy ones, either. This is gonna be great!" We were so intent on trying to gear each other up, going, "Come on, boy, you're going to win tonight!" You know, checking out what each other was wearing – "You wearing those trousers? Oh I see, right, okay, well in that case I'm going to wear . . ." Getting all excited and fighting over the eye drops and getting each other into that spirit of "We're men! We're single! YES!" '

He laughs. 'And, of course, we were completely heartbroken, and a mess, and we thought we were pulling it off. Looking at each other, laughing, chatting away to everyone . . . And then suddenly the guy whose party it was comes around and takes Polaroid snaps of everybody. We're smiling and laughing and looking at the camera, but suddenly the truth was there on film. We looked so sad! Through our smiles, you could see the saddest eyes ever. "Oh, no, man – we're *frauds*!"

'When we were eighteen, it was fine. And we were competitive about everything: your shoes, your hair, your car, your girlfriend – your girlfriend's car! But later on, it just wasn't the same, and I started to get quite judgmental of that scene. And think, What the hell are we doing here? Why are we sitting alone in the park with your dog, and close to tears? Somehow, this is *not* how it was meant to be.'

Should I fly to Los Angeles
Find my asshole brother?

And so, the Little Dukes trundled along after Sacha's departure for Russia, doing the usual things: making demos, playing the odd gig, trying to get someone interested. But it wasn't the happiest of times for Gavin, as Mark Armstrong recalls.

'After Lindsey, Gavin went out with a girl called Amy Fleetwood. She left him and we went out for a pizza and I remember him saying how terrible everything was: "My music's not getting anywhere, *and* my girlfriend's left me." It was the time of the Gulf War, a real gloomy year, and he was really down in the dumps. Then a week later my girlfriend dumped *me*! You can imagine what a pair we were: two suicidal cynics, desperately playing the most outrageous games to try and get these girls back. We wrote letters for each other. Called each other in the middle of the night: "Right, I've left four messages on her answerphone. What do you think?" "Well, I'm asleep at the moment, but sure, I'd say that should work."

'We were so scared of being alone. I'd go round to his flat and say, "I can't stop thinking about Caroline. I don't know where she is. What do you think?" We really loved these girls and we certainly didn't like being shoved out of the way. So we went through this really depressing stage, and it lasted a good six months. And Gavin's band . . .' Mark shakes his head. 'I suppose he didn't know what to do, because he'd been round to every label. Music had moved on and he wasn't sure if he wanted to be in a U2-style band or to create something entirely new. At the same time that he was having problems with his music, I was having problems, too. It was a recession and people weren't going out so much. The money goes, the girlfriend goes, and you're left with your friends. But sometimes when you go through these real lows, you come up with your best writing.'

But not right away, perhaps. Alex Tate recalls that at the time, 'I just didn't think Gavin's songs [with Little Dukes] were good enough. I said to him, "You know, there's a real problem here, Gav. You're writing *these* songs, but you're listening to *these* albums, and never the twain shall meet. I don't know what Emil's doing to you, mate, but he's not got it down." I was a real avant-garde wally, I guess, and maybe I wanted to be his Yoko Ono. I was anti-retro to begin with, and Gavin seemed to be coming back from Emil with all these retro tracks. I thought Jimi Hendrix had pretty much cornered that market. I said, "What are you doing?" I don't think he knew. And then . . . he went to LA.'

'I just felt everything had got too comfortable,' Gavin recalls. His musical career might not have been going swimmingly, but nevertheless, 'I was pretty plugged in here in London. You know, I could go out and have a good time. I could get by. And maybe I'd learned to survive too well: I was in a situation where at least I could get studio time from people; where I could gig, do this and that. But I knew in my heart that it was bullshit. I realised it wasn't the way I wanted to be, having been around for a while, always being that semi-familiar face.

'I guess my superficial assumption was that if I went to America, somehow someone would save me. A manager or someone who would say, "Wow. You're really great. Everyone's told me about you!" But the truth of it was, all I was doing was trying to get away from myself. Because I saw that my music wasn't working. My world wasn't the world that I wanted. I didn't want to die this way. If I got shot now,' he says, years after the fact, 'I'd at least feel like I have a legacy of time with my friends, of making records, of having done something. Whereas at that point I felt I didn't have anything. I wasn't with anyone, my band was crap . . . well, it wasn't crap, it was crap*py*.' He laughs again. 'It just wasn't good.'

Alex theorises, 'Gavin had to go on a journey of discovery, and he did. You know: ditch everything, pare yourself down. There were supposed to be a couple of people out there in LA who were going to give him a bit of a break. Strangely for me, he was staying with Claudia [Alex's ex-wife] some of the time, which probably saved his arse.

'I figure he went because you have to create some kind of new situation or you go into a real depression. But what's interesting about Gavin's character is that he's quite Calvinistic. "I must work! I must create! Do something!" And I think he just *created* the idea that he was going to get signed in America. So he collected some photos, got some demo tapes together, bought this beautiful art binder and did all the layout. He was trying to put together a package, just like a producer would do for a movie, trying to be a bit creative and get some bloody attention. He'd just been around the block so many times in London. You know, "Gavin who?" "Oh, we haven't cast him yet. *Nobody's* cast him." Someone had decided that he was old hat; yesterday's bread. Maybe he didn't have a strategy, or maybe the strategy was just stubbornness. An attitude that said, "Look, I'm eighteen. And it hasn't worked. Okay, I'll piss off for a while." Eighteen and a half: another demo. Twenty and three quarters: another demo. Twenty-one: another demo. He kept knocking on the door with his work unfinished, or maybe with his songwriting skills not up to scratch. He was in denial, I think. And many other people, me probably included, might have looked at that deck and gone, "Ooh *dear*. Maybe it's time to become a writer." '

Instead, Gavin got on a plane.

'I went to live out in LA,' he says simply. 'I had a certain amount of money, I'd worked and saved up. At first I stayed on a sofa at a friend's house in Venice. Then, a few weeks in, I got a call that her mum was coming home and I had to leave. So I lived in her car for two weeks.' He smiles. 'Even in California, it's really surprisingly cold.

'I had a few appointments to see some managers. I must have seen all the managers out there, but it takes months to see them because they're so busy and you're just another Joe. And it made me realise how, when you move away from London, you can finally see how small it is, and everywhere else is . . . so much bigger. In fact, everything just seemed to confirm how irrelevant I was. Going to LA, seeing the size of it, seeing the difference between it and London, trying to see people, trying to get myself together. After the two weeks I stayed in the car, then I'd stay at different people's houses for no more than two or three nights at a time. Never wanting to outstay my welcome, because I thought if I fucked up and stayed, like, ten days or two weeks, then no one wants you back if you really need to go there again. And I'd just get exhausted, because when you stay at people's houses, you often end up doing whatever they're doing. And you're in this weird limbo where you have no time to just be by yourself.

'I had my one little black canvas bag; I was like a nomad. It was brilliant because it was really confrontational. I didn't even listen to music. I borrowed someone's guitar and played a bit, but really it was nothing to do with music. It was just about surviving and trying to figure out what's going on. It's very romantic in retrospect,' he admits, 'but, at the time, it was just difficult. It's weird how, in those situations, vulnerability makes you twisted and less fun. It certainly didn't make me – well, it didn't help my openness.

'Then I stayed with Lindsey [Thurlow], who I'd split up with a few years before. I stayed with her and her boyfriend at the time, Jake Scott [son of film director Ridley]. I'd lived with her for five years, my first major girlfriend, the first time I knew what it was to really love someone. They were very kind to let me stay, but it was just really weird, and all I could think of, looking around their wonderful place, was, "What have I done?" It would be the three of us all sitting there, someone I'd lived with for five years, and then it would be, "'Night then" and I'd go into the little spare room and sit there. Thinking, What have I become? I felt like such a loser. I'm sure when I got signed with Midnight, I thought I was pretty shit hot. But since then, what had I done?

'One night after I'd gone with a friend to Joshua Tree for the day, I came back to Lindsey and Jake's, and they'd left me the key to the front door, but not to the main gate to the flats. So here I was, climbing over the gates with a guitar, and someone saw me and called the police. I ended up lying there in the road, spread-eagled, with two guns trained on me, and they're searching through my stuff. There was a tiny little joint in the front of my bag which they didn't see, and which really could have changed my whole destiny, because if you're found in possession, you know, you're done for. I had no money, I would have been deported and everything. When I get inside, after the cops came, everyone in the building went mad and I had to leave there, because I was causing trouble for Lindsey.'

When he could, Gavin got casual work as an assistant on video shoots. Lindsey recalls him 'standing there on a beach with a big reflector, reflecting a light at the set about fifty feet away, holding this thing all day long and all night, getting paid about fifty dollars. And I remember him saying he thought, I'm supposed to be doing music, I've got no money, and I'm standing here on the end of Malibu Beach.'

'I had a couple of saviours there in LA,' Gavin admits. 'There were a couple of girls who were really brilliant, Tamara and Linda. They were real socialites, and they'd just go out, meet people and chat to them and remember to ask them all about their apartments, and so I'd get to go stay for bits. Really weird. I think I lived in about twelve different places when I was there.

'At the end of the time I was in LA, I went to where my friend Claudia was staying.' Claudia Brightman, sister of singer Sarah Brightman, was not only a friend from London days, but practically family: she'd been married to Alex Tate. 'Claudia's sister Sarah had this . . . palace, really, in Coldwater Canyon, which was quite a change, because I'd just come from a place in Westwood that was really grotty and really scary, though it was very kind that I was allowed to stay there. And then I went around to Claudia's, just as my money was almost gone and it was clear that nothing was happening in music. I stayed at Claudia's for a bit, then had to move on, but she rang and said, "I found you a place to stay" and it was this palace. And I was like, "Wow," because by then I was nearly at the end of it all.'

Aside from bringing relief from the constant search for accommodation, something else of great future value happened to Gavin thanks to Claudia. One weekend, she held a party for friends and friends-of-expat friends. One of those friends-of-friends was David Dorrell – a band manager, a club DJ, a hit songwriter and the man behind M/A/R/R/S' UK number one dance hit 'Pump Up The Volume'. Dave – not surprisingly, given his huge sphere of music business contacts – had some memory of Gavin from his club days in London.

Meeting up again at Claudia's, not only did they get on well but Dorrell, on his way back to England via New York, promised to take Gavin's Little Dukes portfolio to someone attending the New Music Seminar in the Big Apple. Unfortunately, as he never tires of joking to this day, the man who went on to become Bush's manager handily managed to hasten the demise of the band that preceded Bush by losing that portfolio. He still grimaces when he tells the tale, but there's a twinkle in his eye. And just before he abandoned Gavin's precious package to whatever taxi or airplane or airport lounge it ended up in, he also met Gavin's friend Claudia – who is, today, Claudia Dorrell. Evidently, he was better at keeping telephone numbers than he was at handling promo kits.

But we're getting ahead of the story again.

'Out of the blue,' Gavin recalls, 'I get a call from this band manager from New York. He says, "I heard the tapes and they're brilliant. Do you want to go to New York?" You know, this is after six months of being in Los Angeles. And now something at last had happened. So I went to New York to meet him. I was going to drive across the country with this guy, in five days, but Figs [an old friend from London] bought me a red-eye ticket instead for ninety-nine bucks, which would have been a fortune to me. So I went to New York, thinking, Well maybe this is it. I arrive in NY, and Figs tells me he's trying to sell a brownstone, because he's got no money – he's been rich, then lost it all six times, something crazy like that. His boyfriend met me at the train station, Grand Central, and gave me the keys to the apartment. It was deserted, but there was one flat that had nothing but a sofa bed in it and no one had occupied it for months. It was really creepy, because the lights were on twenty-four hours a day, and I was on the fourth or fifth floor and all the other apartments were just open doors – no one in the building.

'And it was all because I had to see this guy. The day of our appointment, it was raining, and I had to walk all the way downtown to meet him in St Mark's. And the moment I laid eyes on him, I could see that he was some idiot twat who just looked like . . . well, fuck, he had loser written right on his forehead. I'd been a loser long enough to know another loser when I saw one.' Gavin laughs softly. 'And I just thought, Whatever happens, man, let's not be losers together.

'If I were to do it again, if I ever had to, I'd be more clever about it,' says Gavin. 'But to have left Los Angeles to go to this empty building on a whim of a phone call just seemed so crazy as I sat there. I had a meeting with him for twenty minutes, sat in a bar, and he looked at me to pay the seventy-five cents for the cup of coffee. Not that I wouldn't have offered. All I wanted to say to him was, "I don't think this is going to work." I just kept trying to talk about what I wanted to do, what music I wanted to make, and what I wanted *him* to do. But that didn't really seem to wash, and it fell through. But on the other hand, there I was in New York City. I decided I didn't want to come back to London until I had my head straight.

'It wasn't all horrible. This girl Suze, who eventually introduced me to Nigel – I'd been kind of seeing her on and off, but she'd been away in Australia. Then she came to see me one weekend in New York in this empty building. It's so romantic in retrospect – I'm sure I shouldn't keep using that word – but there I was, with four inches of dust all over everything in the apartment, madly cleaning everything before she arrived, and happy. A lot of times I'd go to The Strand, a bookstore off Central Park, where they sell cut-price books. I'd been in the void of LA for seven months, so I just read and read for two months. Walked around. Went to museums. Did things that didn't cost money. I lived on a few dollars a day, and I just walked everywhere, the whole of New York. I never took a cab once, and I lived there for two months. I don't think I ever really knew anyone there. Of course I was lonely,' he admits. 'I mean, often I literally didn't speak to people for seven, even ten days at a time.' It was, he says, an existence straight out of Paul Auster's novel *Moon Palace*.

'When I think of that time, it just makes me feel . . . heavy. I feel about two stone heavier when I think of it. But it was brilliant as well, invigorating. Just wild. I was so desperate to experience it all, because I had grown up reading Allen Ginsberg's *Howl* and *Kaddish*, and I wanted to be Jack Kerouac and Jim Morrison and the Sex Pistols too, and just live this crazy life. And that's exactly why I felt I was too plugged in to London, I was too settled. Anyone would be who's been around for a little while and knows how to survive. You get that thing where you're coasting. You're not improving and you're not changing, you're just digging your path like all those people whose lives are predestined when they're eighteen or nineteen.

'I'd say it was a deliberate disassembly. I had to deconstruct myself. I had to accept that, in everything I'd been doing, I'd merely been just good enough. It's too strong to say I'd been lying to myself, but I'd been in a complete state of denial. My work wasn't good enough, and yet I had always thought it was, and everyone else was wrong. I had to do something that would just disrupt everything. And the funniest thing about it all is that I didn't really pay any attention to music when I was there. It was obviously after Pixies and stuff like that had been and gone and anyway, at the time in LA, it was still all Poison, Mötley Crüe, Guns N' Roses and Bon Jovi. There didn't seem to be anything there worth looking up to.'

And what about newer bands? Gavin sighs, and says evenly, 'You know, when Bush started out, so many people asked me to justify the fact that we supposedly sounded American, and the fact that I loved bands like Mudhoney and Jesus Lizard and Pixies and Nirvana. So I once lied to an interviewer and said that when I was living in LA, I'd seen a show with Nirvana.'

He pauses. 'I didn't. In fact, the sad thing is that I even had tickets to the gig; a friend got me some. But I didn't go. Not because I didn't want to, but because I'd forgotten my address book at someone's house and I had nowhere to go. Basically, I had to call people up, friends of friends, and meet people and chat and then, really carefully, slip in the idea that I needed a place to stay, and hope for the best. And without that address book, I was out on the street. I would have loved to have seen Nirvana live . . .

'By the time I came back to London, I didn't think I had any future in music. I came back, my band had split up, and I had no future and no money. And you know, I actually thought, This is *good*. That's when I thought I should see if I wanted to work with anyone else and do new things, other things. That's when I started writing songs entirely on my own. And that's how it all began . . .'

And here's where the story starts. But first, we have to meet a guitarist.

G

'It was when I first heard the Bush demos that I knew: Nigel had really found a style of his own. I think he dabbled around for quite a bit in London trying to find his direction, and it's the hardest thing in the world to find people of like mind to play with. It's so frustrating waiting to find that magical combination of people, and some never do. People always end up playing in bands that they wish they weren't in.' – Jan Pulsford

Madeline and Kenneth Pulsford both came from Newport in South Wales, but didn't meet until their twenties, in 1948, when Kenneth came out of the army. He'd joined up underage, and during his time saw overseas service in the engineering corps. A civil engineer after he left the army, Kenneth would, in the course of work for the Central Electricity Generating Board, move his family from Newport, where his three children were born, to Bournemouth on the south coast, and thence to Leicester, Sutton Coldfield, and finally Lancaster.

'I met him at a dinner, we fell in love and we married in 1950,' says Madeline. An accomplished pianist and singer, Madeline might, speculates her daughter Jan, 'have gone into the music business if it had been different in her day and she hadn't stayed at home to look after the children – which she did brilliantly. When we get together, she's always the one on the piano'. Madeline confirms, 'My father had a very good singing voice. My brother was a brilliant violinist. It's all through the family.'

Jennifer Nine

Kenneth was a quiet, hardworking man, perhaps even quieter as a result of his wartime experiences, as Nigel, who has his father's piercing blue eyes and prominent nose, speculates. 'Kenneth wasn't at all musical,' Madeline says. 'But he was a jazz fanatic. There was nothing for him but jazz. We saw them all: Woody Herman, Buddy Rich, Duke Ellington, jazz quartets. I can't tell you all the bands we saw.'

Perhaps it's no surprise that all three Pulsford children ended up musicians. Nigel's two older sisters Janet and Angela played violin as children, with Angela going on to win a scholarship to the Royal Academy of Music and then play in a number of national orchestras; she still plays and teaches, along with raising a family in Hertfordshire. Jan, a folk singer in her teens and early twenties, became a much-sought-after backing musician, touring the world with the likes of the Thompson Twins and Cyndi Lauper, and moved to America a little over a decade ago. She lives just outside Nashville, where she owns and runs a studio, produces, and writes as an 'electronic musician – I do everything on computer, and I design my own programmes'.

'As the youngest of three, Nigel was rather spoiled,' says Madeline. 'He was quite nice as a baby, very sweet, and a very kind boy. If he had just five pounds and someone was in trouble, he'd give them the money. He was a nice little boy, but I think he liked to have his own way. And when he was at school, I think he thought everything was going to come to him on a plate. It was only when he got older, in the comprehensive school, that he suddenly pulled up his socks, and worked like a Trojan and got four A levels, and we realised what a clever boy he was. He excelled at English Literature. But he was very slow in getting in there.'

Naturally, in a musical household – 'we always had lots of young people playing guitars and singing; I was used to the noise all day and all night, and you know what violins sound like!' – it was rather expected that he would, like his sisters, learn the violin. Nigel had other ideas.

'He would *not* carry the violin around with him,' says his mother. 'Boys are very conscious of what they do when they are little. He certainly wasn't very keen on the violin or the piano.' ('I went to violin lessons for six months and hated it,' Nigel confirms. 'I hated walking to school with it; I felt an idiot, and I didn't really like the instrument either. I used to skip lessons and eventually mum found out I wasn't going, but at least I've had some classical training and I bless 'em for it.') Instead, starting when he was about nine years old, Jan taught Nigel (who she says 'stopped being a naughty little boy when he got into his twenties or thirties') 'a few licks' on guitar. 'He was always interested in pop music and pop culture – in fact, I remember he ended up on one of the pop quizzes on television later.'

'I just decided classical music wasn't really for me,' says Nigel. 'I don't quite know how I decided to play the guitar, but I just said I wanted to, and Mum and Dad bought me one for my birthday.' From where the young Nigel Pulsford stood, 'making music looked like a pretty cool life – work for three weeks a year and chill out'. He laughs. 'Well, it used to be true, but it's not any more.'

Eventually, both Angela and Janet moved to London, Angela playing in a symphony and Janet writing television jingles. Nigel tried his hand at attending university, in Bradford, but quit in short order. 'Bradford was a horrible place at the time,' he says briskly. 'And I hated students. When I was at school, it was the prefects who got to college or university. I was prefect for a day and then I quit – it didn't feel right, but it was probably because I wasn't put on with the girl I wanted to be put on with. But when I got to university, it was like, Oh, we're so cool, and I just thought, What a bunch of wankers, because I knew what they were really like. I just thought they were phonies. If I'd gone somewhere nice, I might have stayed. When I left and came back home, of course, my parents didn't think much of it at all. My dad was slipping me the odd twenty quid, but eventually my mum said I had to go and get a proper job.' And so, for one 'seemingly endless' year, Nigel Pulsford was a reluctant employee of a building society in Morecambe. 'I just didn't get on with the manager; he was a dick. I had a day off a week to do a course, and managed to get the lowest exam mark possible. But then someone who had done the course gave me all the answers so I could go off and rehearse.' Eventually, of course, his dedicated lack of dedication brought about the desired result: 'I got the sack.'

At about that time, Nigel recalls, 'I rented a room from a friend, Jenny, who ran the market record stall where I spent a lot of time. She lived with a guy called Mark, who was a fantastic jazz guitarist. They had the most amazing record collection; I had a real education in the year I lived there.'

By now, Nigel was playing in bands. 'That's what I'd really wanted to do for quite a while. I had been in school bands, and then in Lancaster I played in pubs: a power pop band for a while, and an R&B band, and with my friend Neil, doing covers and original songs. And jazz. Well, when I say jazz, I mean that I *wanted* to play jazz, I'd've loved to play jazz, but in fact,' he laughs, 'I play *fake* jazz.'

Neil Crossley, the friend in question, is now a journalist living in Devon. 'I don't actually remember how I first met Nigel,' he muses. 'But I guess it must have been in the early 80s. A few of us had just started playing Thursday nights at a pub called The Brown Cow, doing R&B with a few of our own songs thrown in. And one day Nigel just turned up. He'd been at university and he'd dropped out, so I had a bit of sympathy for him because that's exactly what happened to me. So he arrived, and everyone thought he was a shit hot guitarist. I must admit he never really impressed me that much, because I was just into songs. It struck me as a bit of a paradox that this eighteen year old, one side of him was into jazz, and his big hero was Larry Carlton who used to be the guitarist for Steely Dan, and at the same time he was into The Clash and The Ruts. In retrospect, all it really meant was that he had eclectic musical taste but, at that age, it struck me as a bit weird. He was into The Clash, but dressed in dark suits and Doc Martens.'

Crossley, Pulsford and the others would play around town together for a few years. 'I wouldn't say it was punk *per se*; we had this blues thing going, too. And then we started writing our own songs and bringing them in. He was always the lead guitarist, and I remember he said to me one night, "Why don't you do a solo?" I was never into solos, but I said all right, and I did one and he followed on. And I don't know what happened – in fact, I think it was an accident – but I trod on a fuzz pedal and it made a *great* sound, a real whining noise, and afterward he wouldn't stop laughing about it. "God, you bastard, you blew me offstage!" He was definitely the lead guitarist through and through . . .'

By then, both Angela and Jan were in London, and Jan recalls Nigel coming down to visit. It wasn't long – 'though it seemed like an eternity, because I didn't have the wherewithal to do it' – before Nigel would follow suit. 'I think Janet encouraged him,' Madeline recalls. 'It was awful when he left home, and I missed him terribly. But at the same time I wouldn't have discouraged him, because it's only right to encourage your children to do what they want to do.'

'By the time I left Lancaster I knew everyone in that whole little scene, and everything was the same: get drunk or sit around and take drugs, don't go out,' Nigel recalls. 'For me the anonymity of a big city appealed; you can be anyone. In the country, there's not much to do. London is just a feeling, it's really exciting when you're young. So I thought I'd go to London.

'Initially I stayed with an old friend called Alan Greenwood who had moved down from Lancaster. I shared a bedsit with him in Blackstock Road in Finsbury Park – with mould on the walls. It was all right for a couple of months, and I just hung out with Alan. Played in a band for a bit; went to some auditions: R&B, middle-thirties-aged bands. And then I met some guys who – well, none of them could play, they just made a racket for a while. I think we lasted a few weeks. They were all living in Finsbury Park. I wasn't officially living there, so I'd have my dole cheque sent to the dole office and I used to have to pick it up. And there was this huge, endless, depressing queue to pick up your cheque; you just sat there forever, crushed into a stinking queue. It made me go and get a job.'

That job led to another, and another, and somehow all connected back with music – via cutting up colour slides and sticking them into bits of plastic. 'Angela's next door neighbour ran an audio-visual company, and I started making slides for them: unrolling a film and cutting it up. I had a laugh, met loads of friends from doing it, and got some money so I was able to buy some equipment, get a studio together. Eventually, when they found out I did music, I got to do that – arranging, writing – and so really I could be doing music all the time, even at work.

'I started to meet more people, and joined a band called Taming The Outback, with a girl singer, doing James White and The Blacks-style funk. It wasn't very good, but I stayed with them for about a year and a half, because I ended up going out with their manager.'

Next, Nigel and Alan Greenwood would find themselves playing with an old Lancaster friend, Chris Haywood, who had a publishing deal with Zomba, went by the florid name of Oscar Van Gelden and led an idiosyncratic band called F1 Electric. And quite a band it was. Chris, who tragically would die suddenly in the late 80s while still in his late twenties, was an intelligent and gregarious young man full of charm and with striking good looks. (In fact, Nigel remarks, 'When I started working with Gavin, I couldn't believe how similar their personalities were.') He was, by his own admission, not much of a vocalist: Nigel recalls laughing hysterically in a studio as Oscar insisted on singing Bowie's 'Heroes' lyrics over his own song, but altering them to 'I . . . I wish I could sing . . .'

Nevertheless, the shows F1 Electric would put on were, in their modest left-field way, show-stopping. Long before modern editing technology would have made it a breeze to engineer, their stage setup included multi-media screens running in tandem, all featuring dislocated bits of Oscar's body moving in time to the music. 'In fact,' Nigel laughs, 'the screens were actually just cheap Radio Rental TVs onstage with videos running through them that took ages to synchronise, and we played with backing tapes, me and the bass player and Oscar. We had a great time; went to Amsterdam, and played The Fridge in Brixton a lot.'

Nigel would also start his career in film soundtrack music rather earlier than most recording artists, who generally save it as a semi-retirement hobby. 'I did music and some slide programming for a couple of David Larcher films in the late 80s,' he recalls, adding with some pride that London weekly *Time Out* described Larcher as 'the founding father of the English avant-garde'. 'He was a mad, intense sort of genius, really talented; they used to show his films late at night on Channel Four. We used to go to the Film Co-Op in Gloucester Avenue in Camden, watch the films on the big screen and get drunk. And he was an amazing person. He used to do his stuff with Anthony Phillips from the original Genesis lineup. Working with David was really good. I did a few soundtracks for some other odd arty movies, which I'd like to do more of in future, in fact.'

Eventually, however, Nigel took a year off from music. 'I thought fuck it, I'm fed up with being in crap bands. All I was doing was some experimental, ambient and noisy stuff, like Can really. I was also trying to be a writer. In fact, I wrote a novel. It was horrible! It was all about three imaginary soldiers who go around killing people from my past. They wipe out the whole of Morecambe, for example.' Nigel claims not to have a copy of the book himself. 'But a friend of mine has one, which I haven't yet had the chance to destroy.

'I came to the conclusion that I didn't have anything to say,' he observes when detailing the end of the Pulsford fiction-writing years. 'I think brilliant writers are ones who can get out of themselves. It would be nice to write again. Maybe when we all retire from Bush.'

* * *

A few years after Nigel had moved to London, Neil Crossley, who had been off to America with a short-lived band of his own, remembers hooking up with him again in the inappropriately named Paradise Road in London's deep South. 'It was probably around 1984, and by then he'd hooked up with a really interesting crowd. He was living in a block of flats in Stockwell, in a council flat on the ground floor. A real siege mentality place; he'd been broken into three times. I think that whole period was Nigel's gothy period,' he laughs. 'He was heavily into The Cure at the time, that was his thing. And he was living with a Bavarian girl, Petra, and a dog called Stupid.' (When Nigel mentions this fact, he laughs and warns, 'Don't get that confused, now, because on *Blue Peter*, Petra was the dog.')

Crossley continues, 'Petra was really nice, but the atmosphere at their place was bizarre. They just used to hurl insults at each other all the time. I mean, Nigel is quite cynical. Quite cutting, which can be the source of much amusement. It's weird, because he's also quite charming: he can be confrontational, but it's never particularly aggressive, he just likes a really good debate. But with Petra, it wasn't like being trapped with a couple who suddenly get very nasty in front of you. I don't know how to explain it, really. They did care for each other but it just got to the point where they didn't care what they said, and it was incredibly entertaining. Nigel would be struggling around trying to find a CD to play, and Stupid would be barking, and Petra would be saying, "Oh God, Nigel, you're a wanker, you're shit!" and he'd hurl insults back at her. He can hurl insults with a smile on his face. It's quite tongue-in-cheek. We'd spend a lot of nights drinking bottles of Jameson and waking up with Stupid hanging over us.'

Nigel recalls those argumentative times as something that 'almost became a display for the benefit of others. That said, it wasn't a very happy time. I do remember one night we'd just finished painting the flat white, and I had a full cup of tea in my hand, and as soon as Petra said, "Don't throw it" – well . . .' He shakes his head. 'All those beautifully white walls, ruined.'

'I think this was the time I really got to know him,' Neil Crossley continues. 'Back in Lancaster, the only real connection we had was music. He always had a great selection of CDs, and he always had great books: you could pull out any book he had and want to read it, it was just a little treasure trove round there, really.

'By 1987 I'd gone back to college in London and Nigel asked me out for a drink at the Windmill in Clapham. He said he wanted to get a band together; he wanted me to do the singing and he was going to write the songs. I thought that was quite intriguing, 'cause I'd always written songs. Certainly, it wouldn't involve a lot of work on my part, I'd just stand there and sing. So we got together with Hugh Garrety and an Australian guy, Kevin.' The band was called The Charms; the atmosphere, however, was not always quite as endearing as the name. Neil continues, 'At rehearsals, Hugh would be spitting beer over Nigel, and things got really vitriolic. But maybe it was almost pretence, like the arguing with Petra. Anyway, we did all this incredible rehearsing, and played one gig – out in High Wycombe supporting Thee Hypnotics – and split up! I went off to New York for a couple of months to stay with friends. When I got back, it had all folded.'

But all was not lost. For one thing, as Nigel recalls, 'It was fun, even if it was a lot of hard work organising everyone, doing the songs, motivating people.' For another, one of the audience at that 1987 gig in High Wycombe was charismatic archetypal northerner Ian Lowery, singer in the then-defunct John Peel favourites The Folk Devils, a supremely aptly named band whom onlookers recall as a frankly terrifying blur of drunken, amphetaminised aggression with swampy black-tar blues-punk undertow. With the demise of The Folk Devils, Lowery had already recorded a track which would later become a single, 'Mouthoff', with Screaming Blue Messiahs serving as his backing band.

The first time Nigel met Lowery, he was interviewing The Folk Devils for a fanzine called *Overground*, for whom Nigel's writing career was short-lived, but of course in the best of underground taste. 'He knew what we did, he didn't ask stupid questions and he gave us an absurdly good writeup,' Lowery says with some satisfaction. 'He'd always said that our guitarist, Kris, was his favourite guitar player. I remember meeting him again at a Tav Falco gig at the Mean Fiddler, and after the show he said, "You know, I've got a studio in Battersea, why don't we do something?" So I said OK.

'Nigel was brilliant to work with. I could say, "Well, I want to do this; can you get this drum track up?" And he'd do it in seconds. "Nigel, I fancy a Cajun feel to this", and he'll be, "What, like this?" The first time we worked together, we recorded three tracks in an evening. There was one called "Bagman" which was just basically one riff for ten minutes, and I remember Nigel playing the

guitar and reading a newspaper at the same time. He even managed
to turn the page while he was playing, which I thought was rather
impressive. The demos were just me, Nigel and a drum machine,
but Beggar's Banquet [Lowery's label] could see what Nigel and I
were doing; I'd found someone I could work with who could help
me realise my vision.' In fact, Nigel would work on two tracks,
'Bagman' and 'Drunk on Tears' that would end up as B-sides to the
'Mouthoff' single: the first record ever released with Nigel
Pulsford's name on it.

With an almost ready-made lineup that included Hugh Garrety,
Kevin Rooney and Kris Jozajtis, the Folk Devils guitarist Nigel had
so admired (and who would later introduce Nigel to his wife
Judith), King Blank was ready to roll. If, as Nigel says, he was
'completely in awe of both Kris and Ian', it didn't stand in the way
of working together. An album called *The Real Dirt*, released in
1988 on Situation Two, a Beggar's Banquet subsidiary, would be
the result.

'It just slotted together really well,' recalls Lowery. 'Beggar's
were really pleased with the results. I thought it might be difficult,
because with Kris and Nigel, well, there was loads of rivalry going
on. Perhaps rivalry isn't the right word, since Kris was, after all,
Nigel's favourite guitarist. Kris is a wonderful, intuitive musician,
while Nigel was technically better, but they both came up with
great ideas. The only problem with Kris was that he wanted a bit
more control than I was prepared to give, and sometimes I wasn't
prepared to listen when I should have done. Kris's approach was
upfront and in your face; Nigel, on the other hand, could insinuate,
and things would happen that way. He was better at dealing with
people, especially with egomaniacs like me. So Kris had to go,
which was stupid, but shit happens.

'Then we made a second album in 1989, *King Blank To The Ian
Lowery Group*, just as a four-piece, and Nigel's input was
consequently greater because he was doing all the guitar parts –
well, I played some, but my guitar playing is, shall we say,
idiosyncratic – and he helped arrange the album and played
keyboards, too. I'd say, "Nigel, I want a Hammond on there" and
he'd do it. He just knows what the song requires immediately. Then
again, we were always on the same wavelength. We read the same
books, liked the same films, and it's great when you've got that
much in common, especially since the films and books we liked
were fairly obscure. It made a change from talking about your

favourites and then having to stop to explain who they were. It's the same with music: Nigel knows his shit, so I could get a potted history of anything any time I wanted. "Nigel, John Coltrane?" And he'd tell me all about him. I mean, you're talking about somebody who loves music, unreservedly. Regardless of whether it's jazz, blues, rock . . . I'd never met anybody like that before. Oh, and he's one of the most irritatingly level-headed people I've ever met, too.

'Nigel is also a great collaborator, and makes the difference between sloppy work and crafted work. If I had a good song, I could never distance myself enough to sit back and arrange it properly. But Nigel likes arranging things; he's got a very musical frame of mind and can see the potential in anything. I mean, he's such a consummate player – not in a session man kind of way, he's just a damned good musician. To work with somebody who actually had a broader scope of reference than I had was utterly liberating. And I don't think I'm blowing my own trumpet here,' says Lowery, laughing, 'but he did like my songs and could always see how they could be developed and realised to their fullest potential.

'Anyway, we decided to produce ourselves on that second album, which in retrospect was a mistake. I think Nigel tried to talk me out of it, but I didn't listen. Patience at Beggar's Banquet ran out in the end, and consequently we were dropped.'

'After we did the first album,' Nigel suggests, 'great things were expected of us. But I think we only ever did about five gigs. We did the Astoria and it went really well, and then we didn't play for three months. Did a few more gigs, and Kris left. You know, it's not glamorous or fun unless you get the work done, and we just sat on our laurels. To be honest, I was going to leave,' he says frankly. 'But then we got a new drummer, Alan; we did the second LP as a four-piece and Joe Hammond came in on one track. But typically, Ian did the vocals in a day and a half, because his girlfriend was coming to visit. And we were producing it ourselves, and it was a very disjointed thing. It all got a bit silly, and the second album doesn't sound that great. We had a little tour to Holland; got there, played to about four people – when we were in Amsterdam there were massive storms and everyone was advised to stay in – and got five hundred quid. But just as I was about to leave, Ian was offered a promotional trip to America in February 1990, because the album was coming out there. So I thought I'd stick around.' Lowery and

Pulsford would go to New York, San Francisco, and Los Angeles and, Nigel recalls, 'We were just badly behaved boys in America being stupid. We played the RCA boardroom, played the Canteen at CBGB's. I didn't like LA, though I loved Frisco. And New York was really exciting. We stayed at the Chelsea Hotel, where I sat in my room with a door that wouldn't shut while Ian was down the street in some bar or other.

'When we got back home, that was pretty much that. It was really a shame it didn't work out, but it was inevitable. I think if we'd toured, we'd have done all right, but there was a very self-destructive streak in the band. Too much drink. Too many drugs lying around. It was good music – in fact, it was all the kind of music I wanted to do. But we never did the work, and all the boring stuff that has to be done. It was fun, but unfortunately the band preferred to misbehave.'

Back in the real world, however, after King Blank drifted apart over a period of months in 1990 and 1991, work was exactly what Nigel was back to doing. By now, he was writing, arranging and playing music for multimedia presentations created at the audio-visual company he'd been working for. Often putting in eighteen- or twenty-hour days, he found himself faintly amazed to be 'getting about seventy pounds an hour even if I wasn't entirely certain I knew what I was doing'. With the memory of an enjoyable first visit to his sister Jan in her new home in Tennessee still fresh, Nigel was bent on paying off all his debts and going away once again.

But in the closing weeks of 1991, Nigel would meet a new musical partner and, eventually, a project that would take him back to America and away from the audio-visual company for good. The twenty-hour days, on the other hand, would be sticking around for quite some time.

H

'Gavin and I already knew each other, in fact,' Nigel Pulsford recalls. 'I'd met him years and years ago, through an Australian girl called Suze DeMarchi, who sang in the band Baby Animals. I knew he was in a band but I wasn't bothered about seeing people playing in pubs particularly. I used to be friends with Suze when she lived in London, and we'd write songs together. But I kind of lost touch with her when she went back to Australia.' But one night, in November 1991, they'd meet again. 'Baby Animals were playing at Wembley supporting Bryan Adams, and I went along and Gavin was there. He'd just come back from America, and Suze said, "Why don't you two get together and see if it works out?"

'So we went back to his place in Montagu Square after the gig, and we got drunk and sang some Neil Young and Bob Dylan songs, basically. And then around Christmas and New Year, he came round to see if I wanted to work together. I didn't know what to think, because whatever was left of the band with Ian was a bit flaky. But I knew I didn't want to waste another few years with something that wasn't going to be carried through.'

The important thing, Nigel adds, is that he and Gavin liked each other. 'There was a little bit of hype surrounding him anyway, because he's quite a gregarious soul. But being in a band with someone is like being married. When people say things you disagree with, you just ignore them, 'cause that's the avenue they're going in. Gavin and I get on; we've never had a proper fistfight, though

65

we've had some screaming rows. But over the years we've got on quite well: mutual respect and all that.

'I was really pleased,' he says. 'Gavin and I liked the same sort of music, the same sort of bands. The Fall, all that British scummy underbelly, and Nick Cave, and John Peel bands – that was my thing at the time. But after The Smiths finished, British music seemed to go shit, and what was happening in America was much more interesting. At the same time, wherever it's from, it all comes from the same place. For me, the Pixies crystallised the two things, the Pixies got it spot on. And so did Big Black, Steve Albini's first band.

'We talked about music a lot. I started to lend Gavin lots of records, like The Gun Club, who he'd never heard of. And a 1969 Velvet Underground record which he still hasn't given back – he probably reckons it's his! I was more embedded in the whole indie scene, more so than he was, and I had more knowledge of all those bands. But then you forget, no one's heard of this crap – who the heck were The Gun Club? You think they're big fish, but in reality it's a very small pond.'

Somehow, Nigel adds, 'I knew it wouldn't be a waste of time with Gavin. Sure, we became friends, but I didn't even know what sort of bands he'd been in when we first got together. I guess I thought it might be heavy rock or something. I was quite surprised when I saw what his interests were.'

Of course, hooking up with another musician is always a blind date of sorts, regardless of shared interests. 'Yeah, but it's worth trying just in case,' Nigel says. 'It's always hard to work with someone, so you do spend a lot of time trying to find people with whom you get on well enough to work. And it started quite quickly: the first demos we worked included both "Comedown" and "Little Things". They were the only two that lasted – plenty of others didn't – though "Alien" is probably in there too. That started as a little riff and we developed it and jammed it.'

In other words, Future Primitive, the band that would later become Bush, had been born.

'Fairly early on, we worked quite naturally. I could do the things he wanted, or vice versa. We obviously had lots of hits and misses, but it crystallised quite quickly. He was into working hard, like I was. One thing I had learned is that if you make an album and sit on your laurels, nothing happens. Gavin, I think, realised that the only way to do it was to be obsessive about it. We worked really hard doing those demos, almost every day for a year.'

'Nigel is a great collaborator,' repeats Ian Lowery. 'I think he met Gavin and saw somebody who wasn't gonna sit around and scratch his head and wonder where to go next, but knew exactly what he wanted to do and how he was going to go about it. This may sound a bit simplistic, but I think Gavin had a bunch of songs and maybe Nigel was the missing piece he needed for it all to work. They used to play me the early demos, and I must admit I couldn't really see the potential in them then, because it was just Gavin and Nigel and a drum machine. They'd try again and again to get one song right, which is not a way I was used to working.'

Musical sympathies, too, were important. When asked if he had many friends who shared his taste in music, Gavin replies immediately, 'No. No one. I mean, I would end up forcing my girlfriends to share my taste. They'd listen to it because they didn't have much choice! The first time I played anyone a Jesus Lizard record would always be a bit of a leap.' He grins. 'Basically, it was always my problem that I couldn't find people to play with who were into the same music.

'I met Nigel after, oh, eight years of looking. He was the first person I met who liked The Fall. The thing is, I'd always believed in the people I worked with, believed that maybe we could work out our differences and that it was easier to try and steer them into the things I liked than to abandon the idea. Whereas with Nigel, it was right from the start. He knows so much; he's knowledgeable to the point of ridiculousness. Maybe if I'd met Nigel years earlier, my musical career would have been a different story. The whole thing about finding a musical soulmate is that people can go through their whole lives and not find one, so I'd rather have found one when I did than not at all.

'And,' adds the man who says his approach to life has always been 'I want it, and I want it now, and this afternoon would be good, but yesterday would be better', his bandmate Nigel is the kind of person 'who never says, Can you just give me a few minutes to get it together?'

Soon, other players were brought in to accompany the duo. Nigel recalls, 'The first few guys were Sasha Gervasi, a drummer, and Malcolm Pardon, a Swedish bass player who joined Kinky Machine and later disappeared into the wild blue yonder. He played on a couple of demos we did at my house in 1992, but he didn't actually go into the studio and make proper demos, 'cause it didn't really work out with the first two. He was too volatile, stubborn, quite bloody-minded. And Sasha was a nice guy, but I think he was going through some difficult personal problems at the time. We got an Iranian drummer, Amir, who later went off to be in an acid jazz band, and then my friend Kevin who'd been in King Blank for a while. And then finally we got Spencer Cobrin, who'd played with Morrissey, who was all right but didn't really fit, and he was doing us a favour, by filling in.'

Well, not quite finally. There was one more drummer yet to come, and he would start with the band just two weeks before Future Primitive signed a record deal with a new American label most people had never heard of. 'So, yeah, he got the easy bit,' says Nigel, laughing.

But we're getting ahead of ourselves. The bass player's spot, on the heels of Malcolm's departure, was sorted out a good deal sooner. 'He was very much a silent partner at first,' says his guitarist. His name, of course, was Dave Parsons.

I

'I think he always wanted to twang, you know. David never wanted to do anything else.' So says Annie Gration, mother of Bush's tall, rangy bassist Dave Parsons. Also known, somewhat inaccurately, as 'the quiet one'.

Third of five children and, 'everybody's favourite', Dave found his slot in the Parsons family sandwiched between Ralph and Trudi and then Fleur and Rosie. He was, according to his first-ever fan, 'a totally gorgeous, curly-haired thing who was always messy, and always got food in his hair and squashed fruit down the hole in the washing machine. One day he had bacon all along the windowsill and was busy putting marmalade on top of that and cornflakes on top of that. I suppose every mother says this,' Annie laughs, 'but when he was a fat little thing about ten months old, he was sitting in his high chair against the wall and I remember when his dad came home from work, I said, "this one's going to be musical." No matter what music I played, his fat little messy hands would go bam, bam, bam in time on his little tray.' Not that anyone else in the family was particularly musical, mind you. Annie laughs and confesses, 'I twanged the guitar a little bit, but only in the 60s when everybody twanged the guitar. I think I dabbled. I'm like an old rosebush – I'm never really good at anything special, but all the children have grown up to be lovely fat roses, and good at whatever I've dabbled in.'

Born in Uxbridge, Dave grew up in south Oxfordshire, his family eventually moving to Cholsey, near Wallingford, when his mother remarried. He liked football, books, astronomy, spelling games, geography. 'He liked knowledge, finding things out,' Annie says. Oh, and he liked first aid supplies: although he had no major illnesses as a child ('which is just as well, because he hates hurting himself'), the four-year-old Dave, when asked what he wanted for Christmas, 'said he wanted a box of plasters. He loved them. If one of the family hurt themselves, he always had plasters for them.

'When he got a bit older, he was a very quiet, cool little boy,' Annie adds. 'You didn't have to worry that if you went to the supermarket, he'd run off. If he left you, he'd just go and lean against the door with his little legs crossed, and wait. He loved school, and all the teachers liked him. He was the sort of boy who, when we went on holiday, all the waiters patted on the head.'

Growing up in a big, friendly household run more on love than money, Dave discovered that all of his friends eventually ended up at his place. 'It was a bit of a hangout, really,' recalls Pete Hislop, who would meet Dave at fourteen on his first day at his new school. 'His mum was the coolest mum around. Very liberal, very happy, very open, and there was always a good atmosphere in the house. We'd all go over, sit in his bedroom, listen to records, hang out.'

'I was counting on my fingers the other day how many of them there'd be about the house, and I got to about fifteen!' says Annie. 'They'd all be squashed in, and sometimes in the winter when it was cold we'd have quilts all over the place and all these little heads poking out watching television. They never used to knock, they'd just walk in the front door, and we'd say, "Hi, Josh" or "Hi, someone else." We had to have a rota for the washing-up because there were so many of them.' As a teenage punk wave spread out to the suburbs and beyond, Annie found herself elected den mother to amateur Sex Pistols who had missed their buses back home to neighbouring towns. 'So there'd be a knock on the door about half past eleven, and a little voice would say, "Annie, do you think Patrick can stay the night?" And I'd say, "Yes, of course, you can stay on the settee. But you haven't got a knife down your sock, have you?" I was happy to have them over. They were David's friends, and all of them were lovely, absolutely totally gorgeous. Though mind you, saying that,' Annie laughs, 'it does make me sound like someone on an American talk show: "Why Does My Mother Keep Winking At My Boyfriend?" '

Wallingford Comprehensive School was where Pete Hislop first met Dave. 'It was weird when he first came in, because not only did he come from somewhere else, but he dressed differently to us all,' Pete recalls. 'We weren't sure about him at first, and he was kind of known as the school punk almost immediately. He wasn't bolshy, but he was quite confident in a way when he arrived, because his older sister and brother were very confident, and they'd been up to London and worked at a clothing shop in the King's Road called Johnson's. We were all still in flares and jeans, and Dave came in with brilliant clothes; no one knew where he'd got them. In a way, he created the scene in our school. In fact, not long after that everyone started wearing black drainpipes and stuff. Obviously, everyone was kind of checking him out and wondering, is this guy dodgy or is he OK? But he got popular pretty quickly.'

'Oh, I'll tell you why he had the coolest clothes at school,' says Annie, filling in the missing part of the Dave Parsons Style Revolution story. 'It's his mother's fault. When we moved and he had to change schools, I went for an interview at the school with him and tried to listen carefully to everything the headmaster said. And so we bought David his uniform – black trousers, black jumper – for when he started school. Except it was supposed to have been grey and navy blue! So there he was, the only boy in the school with black trousers, which Ralph or Trudi gave him from Johnson's. It was a really cool shop, so David was exceptionally pleased with these trousers. I said to the headmaster, "I'm really sorry, I did think it was black that you wanted, and I honestly can't afford to start all over again." Eventually they said, alright, he can wear black, and gradually . . . Of course,' she insists, 'Dave was always really cool anyway, but the trousers were entirely my mistake!'

As it happens, Ralph and Trudi were responsible for more than Dave's fashion statements. Both music fans, they supplied Dave with his first records, from Clash albums to Bowie's *Ziggy Stardust*. 'I thought, This is great music,' Dave recalls. 'I don't know how old I was, but I know it was sinking in. This is it! *This* is what I want to do! I tried to learn drums, and then someone bought me a guitar. And punk was the proper thing to play, so it only takes three fingers – all you need is two fingers and a bar chord in fact – because they were very, very simple songs. And that was it. I was off, that's what I wanted to do. There was a guy up the road who taught me the guitar – I was a bit of a misfit at school because I didn't have so much money, and the way he taught me to play guitar, I could *really* stick out like a sore thumb, along with those weird drainpipe outfits I had. It's funny; in a way I quite liked it.

'Then I met even more musicians, older ones. Well, they were probably about seventeen, but they seemed incredibly old at the time. And I'd always say, "I can play bass for you," but they'd be like, "No, we've got so-and-so down the road." And you keep nagging them, like you do when you're young and arrogant.'

Eventually, of course, persistence paid off. 'I remember being stuck in a village hall in a place near Reading with a bass guitar around my neck and not being quite sure what to do.' The band was Dig Dig Dig; the singer was Julian Gammon, one of what Pete Hislop calls 'the cool guys from a couple of years above who lived in the village up the road', and the sound was poppy proto-New Wave punk. 'I remember one gig we did at a disco, and the DJ was at one end and we were at the other, and they didn't really like us, so they'd turn the music on and we'd have to turn our music up, and so it went on the whole night. We made a single; a thousand of them, in fact, because that's how many you have to make. I did have a copy, but I lost mine to someone else. I remember meeting someone recently, someone's girlfriend's friend's boyfriend's somebody-or-other, and he said, '"I used to love that band, and I've still got a copy." Which is a bit sad.' Dave shrugs and grins.

According to Pete Hislop, Dig Dig Dig's best song was '625 Line', though history does not record whether that was, indeed, the single. 'I remember going to Reading to see them play. And of course when you're fourteen, fifteen, there's this rivalry between groups, and so there was a band from another school, who were older – probably sixteen – and we were all sure that Dig Dig Dig were going to blow them offstage. Which, of course to us they *did*.

'I never remember Dave saying, "I'm going to be in the best band ever," or I'm going to do this or that. He just did it, you know, he did what he had to do. He's not someone who goes out to be upfront. And when you know him, he's certainly not the quiet one. Maybe he's a bit more of a thinker than some. Maybe he doesn't voice his opinions immediately, but he does like arguing. Arguing constructively – he doesn't shout – and he never gives in.

'We did the usual sort of teenage things: went to the town square, went to a couple of pubs where we thought they might let us in, tried to grow moustaches. But basically we just used to hang out at Dave's. He had this mad bedroom, really small, and you just

couldn't move in it. It was piled high with records; everywhere
you'd look, there would be records under the bed, piled in corners,
and a little record player. And we just waited until we could get
cars and start driving. Which meant,' says Pete, laughing, 'that you
could go to the next village, or down to Reading! And of course,
on Thursdays, we went to see Dave's band rehearse.' Pete
remembers two arrests in connection with Mr Parsons: one, in
which he went out with a couple of friends, and somehow a fence
was kicked in. 'It was probably on the front page of the local
paper,' Pete adds drily. Annie contributes her part in the drama.

'They'd all been out to a party. One of the boys jumped up
sideways and kicked someone's fence and the fence came falling
down. This bloke came charging out and everyone ran away, and
of course David, typically, and one other boy were trailing along
behind, and they were the ones who got caught. So they got taken
off to a police cell all night, freezing cold because it was a summer
night so they'd only got T-shirts on. I phoned the station about four
in the morning and said, "Right, I'm coming over to see my son.
And if he's covered in bruises and if he's got a burst spleen and
black eyes, I shall know you did it because he was all right when
he left home!" ' She laughs. 'So they said, "All right, you can come
and get him now." '

The only other trouble Dave appears to have given the
constabulary was in the company of Pete Hislop. 'I'd just learned
to drive, so I'd borrowed my dad's car to go to Devon, and we just
chucked a tent in the back of the car and set off. And one night we
were in Bude, a really nice little town in Cornwall, and went to the
pub and had a bit too much, and ended up walking out still
carrying our pint glasses. A police car pulls up and chucks us in the
back, and there we are, seventeen years old, oh *no*! And they're
ringing our home town to find out if we have police records . . . and
eventually drove us back to the pub, and made us walk through the
entire pub with them at our sides, put our pint glasses back on the
bar and then apologise to the landlord. It was fantastically
embarrassing!'

A year or so later, Pete moved up to London to go to college,
followed by a gaggle of other local friends who all availed
themselves of his hospitality, all ending up around Notting Hill in
West London, where both Pete and Dave still live. 'Initially, of
course, we all liked that area because [our friend] Kevin had his
own flat! But somehow it just had a real atmosphere – the pubs we

drank in, the clubs we could go to for two pounds, the cosmopolitan feel of it, the market keeping it down to earth – and we had the safety net of our friends, too.' When Dave made his move, Annie recalls, 'He was eighteen. Ralph and then Trudi had gone up, and then there was a little gap and David went. I said to him that he wasn't going to go until he had a job: no one is going to come and knock on the door and say, "David, I've got a really good job for you up in London." You've got to go up on your two little flat feet like everyone else and get yourself a job, and then when you've got a job you can go up to London and sleep on somebody's sofa. Then someone moves out and you get the bedroom floor. Then you get your own bedroom, but it's only as big as a matchbox. And finally you get your own flat and you have someone sleeping on *your* settee. So he got a job in a shoe shop, and he'd come back with the most hilarious pairs of shoes. But I used to say to him, it doesn't matter what you're doing, there's only one way in this world you're going to get some money, and that's to earn it. When you get paid at the end of the week, it's yours and you can be proud of it.'

In fairly short order, Dave (and later his friend Pete) ended up working at Johnson's. 'I worked there for about three or four years, I think. It was really good; all the bands used to come in and we'd get invited to gigs. I got really cheap, trendy clothes, too, so it was perfect for a skint teenager. Once, when I'd just started there and was still the young, fresh-faced bass player, Phil Lynott [of Thin Lizzy] came in. He was a friend of the manager of the shop, and I ended up talking to him because I needed to get my guitar set up, you know, the neck bends and stuff, and I didn't know much about it; I'd only played in the band I'd been in at school. And he said, oh yeah, he knew someone who could do that. And when he took it away, he looked me in the face – and when he came back, he gave me one of those famous basses of his with a mirror on it. It was brilliant.

'It was also quite funny going to rehearsal after that,' he adds. Having landed himself in a Welsh punk band, The Partisans, his musical peers were less than impressed with Dave's alarming non-punk tendencies. 'They didn't think I was punk enough, basically, because it was a trendy shop. And I used to wear baggy trousers sometimes, and that was a bit out. And, yeah, the Phil Lynott bass.'

He doesn't mention the rockabilly quiff that Pete Hislop confirms was *de rigueur* for Johnson's employees. 'In fact, Dave's was the most massive. We used to compete!'

It was Pete that Dave had to thank for his stint in The Partisans. 'I was studying Geology at Kingston Polytechnic, and there was a really nice guy in my class named Sharky – well, Mark Harris was his name – and he was a Welsh guy who had been in a band before he came to college, at about fifteen or sixteen, all anarchy and anger. Anyway, he became a really good friend of mine, and his band carried on when they moved up to London. They were looking for a bass player and I said, look, you should meet my friend Dave. It worked; he joined the band and they started gigging. They had an album out already and were writing a new one. I think Dave was really interested in participating in it, because I remember that when we went on holiday to Devon, he had a tape of three songs. I don't know if you know how long it takes to drive to Devon – it's about four hours – and he played the tape the whole way down, over and over. "This is brilliant! This is really brilliant!" "Blind Ambition", one of them was called. And he'd say, "What do you reckon to the bass line?" "What do you think of this?" '

Hislop laughs. 'Anyway, I remember a disastrous gig of theirs at the 100 Club in London. It was quite busy, there were loads of people, but suddenly it all just went horribly wrong. The microphone fell over, the electrics all got cut, and you could see them up there panicking. I felt really bad for them, because I think that was David's first gig with them. I saw them play in Brixton, too, on a bill of all the punk bands at the time, and they played really well, stole the show I thought . . . though they came back totally covered in gob. Dave was just dripping with phlegm. They did an interview for *Smash Hits*, I think, in which Sharky kept talking about anarchy and living in a field in a tent and stuff. Which kind of presaged the fact that they were about to sack Dave.'

For fashion crimes? 'Yeah, of course. They were going to sack him for wearing baggy trousers. Looking back, it's the funniest thing ever. They thought he was too trendy to be in a punk band. As much as Dave was pissed off, we did laugh about it. And what's more, I think that he was getting into a different style of playing, and I wondered if that conflicted with punk as well. So it was baggy trousers – and slacky bass.

'Around about this time, Dave had moved into a flat in Gravesend Road with his cousins, and he wasn't madly happy there. Too far away from Notting Hill, I think. And I had moved into a flat in Hammersmith with four girls that I knew from school. It was the messiest flat I'd ever lived in; I slept on a sofa in the tiny front room. But Dave used to come round every night and we'd just go to the local pub, or down the King's Road. So we stayed there for a while, and then decided we'd try and find a flat – this was in about 1986 – and we saw a notice in the window of a shop. It was the worst day, pissing down with rain, and we turned up absolutely drenched. We walked in and it was a dump, but we loved it. Two bedrooms, a perfect place in Notting Hill, right by the tube, and it was forty pounds a week each. We lived there for ten years, and the rent didn't go up the whole time we were there. We put Clash posters on the wall and played American football inside and had a wonderful time. We didn't care that it was a dump, we just wanted somewhere to live. We spent most of our time playing bar football – you know, tabletop football – down the pub.

'We got quite good at it, actually,' Pete adds. 'We used to go down to The Lonsdale pub in Portobello, and The Duke Of Norfolk in Westbourne Grove, every night.' It wasn't just with the aim of relieving other patrons of their money in bar football games, Pete insists. 'But that too, hopefully. But it was winner stays on, so if you won you'd stay on and compete against everyone else. And one night we were there and this guy called Nick [Sayer] started playing, and he was really brilliant at it, and we started to realise there was another level to this game. We started getting madly competitive. And one night, Nick's friend turned up, a girl we thought was quite a character. I just remember the first time I saw her, she had this mad blonde hair, with dreads sewn in, and she was wearing a mac with a French book hanging out of the pocket. And we used to take the mickey out of her a little bit, you know, and she was great, she loved it, and gave as good as she got. And it turned out that she was Wendy James, and Nick and her were forming this band called Transvision Vamp. And I remember this really vividly, Dave said to me, "I really don't know what to do, whether to join this band or stay at Johnson's." It was the one time I felt he wasn't sure. And I said, "Dave, you know, just do it!" I don't want to sound like I'm the person who made the difference, but . . .' Pete laughs.

'But I just said, "You've got to try, I mean, what can you lose?" And he said, "Right, I'll give it a go." And of course then they got a deal and things started to happen . . .'

And how. Transvision Vamp, fronted by the tiny, blonde and sharp-tongued Wendy, would fuse trashy glam, pop and punky attitude and notch up ten sugar-and-spite top 50 singles in the UK between 1988 and 1991. With an enthusiastic fan following and, initially, an irresistible press angle in Wendy's gleefully idiosyncratic fashion sense and willingness to shoot from the lip, for a few years it seemed as though Notting Hill's pub football champions might take on the world and win.

'It was only about two and a half years; it all went really fast, and it was brilliant,' Dave recalls. 'Nick and Wendy didn't jealously guard their control of the band, but they'd done a lot of the album anyway when I turned up, and it was very much their thing. We toured all over. And you know, when I look back on it, it was quite punk, having songs like "Baby I Don't Care".'

'They were a great live band,' Pete Hislop recalls. 'They started to perform really well, and Dave actually started to move onstage. It was quite shocking for us, really, because we'd never seen him move before. He was never renowned for his dancing – he was a classic bass player, just very motionless, very still.'

But even in a band driven by extroverts, Dave attracted his share of attention. Annie laughs, 'Wendy told me the girls all used to be hanging round after David; they all wanted to meet Dave. He went out the back door of some big venue in Italy and a horde of girls made a great big lunge for him, and he had to dash back in as quick as he could!' What's more, his semi-official role as 'the calm one' probably helped keep a band full of hot tempers a little cooler: 'Wendy said to me that sometimes Tex would be shouting at Nick, and Nick would be shouting at Wendy, and Wendy would be shouting at Tex, and she said Dave would be leaning against the wall with a can of lager, just watching them quietly and not saying anything. And after a little bit, he'd say, "Calm down." And eventually, Wendy said, he'd calm them all down and they'd sort out their problems because he never shouted, he just let them get on with it.'

As time moved on into the late 80s, you'd expect there to have been less spitting, at the very least, at a Transvision Vamp show than at a Partisans gig. It was, after all, a decade since the Sex Pistols had split up. But, according to Pete Hislop, 'A lot of people spat at Wendy, and I think it was more directed at her than anyone else, and the sentiment of it was obviously to bring her back down to their level.' And, although the band had hits and plenty of fans, they had their share of detractors – including, eventually, the press. 'Wendy had a very strong attitude, she knew what she wanted, and she wasn't afraid to say it,' Pete says. 'Obviously, it did put a lot of people's backs up. There was definitely a time when it was decided, let's go for them, and they really started to slate her and the band. A lot of it was brought on by the fact that Wendy probably said a few things that she might have regretted. And I'm sure that as things came to an end – the last album wasn't released, and there were wrangles with the record company – that probably did affect them. In the end, it may have helped break them up.'

'I learned a lot,' says Dave of his Transvision Vamp days, which finished round about the time that Nigel and Gavin were meeting each other. 'Touring-wise, and the experience, and money-wise. You know, when I stopped doing that, I managed to live for two years on the money I had left.' A somewhat improbable feat. 'Maybe it's just my nature.'

'I never thought Dave would quit music after Transvision Vamp broke up.' Pete shakes his head. 'I think Dave will play music forever. After they split up, he was very brave; he didn't sign on all that time, just lived on what he had made. I don't want to sound dull, but he's not the sort of person who'd go out and spend a chunk of money on a Ferrari. He doesn't like talking about money, that's for sure. But I think he thought to himself, right, he'd worked out what a survival wage would be, and paid himself that, regularly, out of his money. We were very lucky having our flat, still costing us only £40 a week plus the phone bill. And he went through some very hard times, but he'd play the bass every day; practise all the time. He'd go out and buy books, and learn more about bass playing. He didn't want to sign on, but he didn't want to work, because he wanted to find another group.

'And then,' Pete recalls, 'I remember him having met two guys with a band, and they were making minor waves, *very* minor waves. But I got the feeling that he really liked the way they were going, he liked the music they played; it was *his* sort of music . . .'

And before you know it, we're back to our story again.

'Robin was *always* really cheeky, really upfront. Garrulous, gregarious, all those g-words. Very kind of "what you see is what you get", and as tenacious as a dog with a bone. Vociferous, and always very good at getting his point over. You know, Robin would be exactly the same if he was in a room full of music business types, or speaking to your mum and dad down the pub; he never changes. I think fame definitely suits him: in fact, he acted famous when we were teenagers in Horsham, really. He's still the same: playing the drums, larging it up, and talking very loudly through all of it.'

The day Rob Leggatt, who is now an assistant film producer, met Robin Goodridge, who is now a drummer with a fairly successful band, Rob was six years old and had just started a new junior school. 'I walked up the drive and one of the first kids I spotted was Robin, running through the playground and showing the other kids ... well, he was actually re-enacting a scene from *Starsky and Hutch*. He was about seven, and he was shouting, "This is how Starsky runs! Like this!" He was a year older than me, and he was quite an intimidating character ...'

The second of three children born to Sheila and Sidney Goodridge, a clerk and a manager for British Rail respectively, Robin spent most of his life around Horsham in Sussex, though he came into the world in a hospital in nearby Crawley. (Robin enjoys noting that Crawley is also the home of Robert Smith of The

Cure, whose only visible similarity to Goodridge is a large quantity of unruly hair.) Robin's first memories of music came courtesy of his dad, a quiet, thickset, level-headed man who played the trumpet and whose sense of humour and musical talents, his widow recalls, both Goodridge boys inherited.

'My mum wasn't interested in music much,' Robin recalls, 'but I certainly remember the music my dad played when I was a kid: something by Herb Alpert and the Tijuana Brass was one he used to play all the time. I must have been really little, but I remember it was always there on Sunday mornings. You know, working all week and Sunday was for playing music and reading the papers. I can remember the tunes now, it's quite funny, and for years I never even knew what instruments made those sounds.

It was a normal childhood, Robin insists, though one that changed radically when he was four and a half. 'My dad died suddenly. In fact, he dropped dead at 38. He played badminton, and had a heart attack at the gates of the school backing onto our house. Here's a weird one, actually; it was the same school I went to from age seven to eleven, so I used to walk past those gates every day. I didn't really think about it at the time, but later it seemed strange.'

With Robin, his brother Steven and sister Samantha to support, 'my mum was a full-time single parent for twenty years', says Robin, who describes Sheila as 'tough, resilient, cool, and understanding – she let me get on with things. She never remarried for twenty-five years, not until two years ago when she met a man from Brighton and sold the house in Horsham and moved to Bexhill on the south coast. She used to work in Tesco, or secretarial stuff, things she could do when we were at school. It was hard for her.'

Sheila recalls that 'both boys coped very well when their dad died. I don't think Robin would remember very much of his father. After he died, I went out to work, but I always made sure I was there when they came home from school. I'm afraid I was one of those mums who said, "Sorry, I've got to be there when they get home." So that when they rushed in to tell you what they had been doing, you'd be there.'

Robin's childhood was full of 'the normal things, really: cycling, fishing, football. I played for the town, but I was asthmatic, and back then they never really had the hang of the right drugs to give you, so I couldn't run around as much as I would have liked to, and I used to start wheezing. So I ended up being goalie. I was actually quite good at it, sadly,' he laughs. 'Yeah, being a goalie *is* like being the drummer of football. The man at the back. I can't believe I play drums and am a goalkeeper as well. It's classic. That's why as soon as the drugs got better, I got out.'

'He was very hyperactive when he was little, up until he was about five, he was always on the go. But he did have several bouts in hospital when he was very small,' Sheila recalls. 'At about eighteen months he was in the hospital in a steam tent, and he had to have an inhaler. Despite that, when he was at school he was always very active. He loved skateboarding and I remember him going off for hours, days almost, and coming back bruised and battered.'

'I wasn't really fond of school,' Robin confesses. 'I liked the social aspects of it, but didn't enjoy the education, although I liked certain teachers and therefore liked certain subjects, English mainly. By the time it came to the crunch of exams, I'd already left school mentally – at about the age of fifteen. I was meaning to go to college, but my mum said, "Well, your brother's left home, and you're sixteen, seventeen and you need to eat." She couldn't really afford for me to go to college.

'So I got a sponsorship and a job, working as an electronics engineer for the railway company, where I went to a college in Crawley and worked at the same time. I hated it, but I got the qualifications that I apparently needed to prove that I wasn't an idiot. I'd made the mistake at school of not taking the chance to prove I wasn't an idiot, and it made me grow up pretty quick. I hated all that "prove you're not a moron" attitude. And the work; dreadfully boring. The first year, I was really bullied at work, though it didn't piss me off, I'd just go home. I'd be home by eleven in the morning, and no one would tell on me, because they'd caused it. It was just the sort of standard male thing: you know, I was sixteen or seventeen, and I was around blokes in their mid-twenties. The older ones ignored it, or thought it was funny. And so then you try to win them over; I mean, I was mouthy enough to win over the smarter ones while taking the piss out of the ones that were bullying me. Eventually I was actually doing the job I was training for, after about the first year, doing sick cover. It would be me and another guy working together, and the guys who were smart used to say, "Well, I'd rather work with him than with someone else I think is a complete wanker." So in the end, quite a few of them liked me.

'And then I took the exams, and passed them. And the day after I finished my exams, I walked in and handed my notice in. They said, "Great, we've paid for your education for three years, and now you're going to leave." And I said, "Yep, that's the breaks." They were like, "We can't believe you're going, you think you're going to be in a band? Well, we'll see *you* in a couple of years' time. You'll be back here." And I was like, "Oh, I don't think so." '

Because, by this point, twenty-year-old Robin Goodridge had spent almost half his life certain that being in bands was what he wanted to do. And he certainly knew what instrument he wanted to play, after getting a brief flirtation with the trumpet out of the way.

'My dad's trumpet was sitting about the house, and in one of the schools I went to at the time, one of the teachers had a brass band and wanted to form one at the school, so I joined and we used to go on tour around other schools and all that rubbish. We just played television theme tunes. I loved playing in the school band, but when they tried to get me in the district band, I just hated it. You know, the idea of going from my school to another school to get shouted at by some guy I didn't know was really nasty. And I was like, "Hang on, isn't this voluntary?"

'My older brother played the drums, in a local punk band called The Gonads. When he was 18 and I was 13, he left home and I inherited a drumkit.' Not a great drumkit, but perhaps a sonic improvement on the saucepans his mother recalls him playing as a toddler. 'I had that kit up in my room, you know, in a semi-detached house, and I can't believe my neighbours never complained! I remember when I was about 16, my mum was chatting to the next door neighbour, who said, "Oh, Robin's got a lot better on the drums, hasn't he?" This had gone on for years and years, and I guess I'd actually got to the stage where I was pretty good, and the neighbour said, "He's actually sort of tapping in time now, you know." I had one drumming lesson at school. It was boring, and I thought, What's the point? It suddenly had become a discipline, and it was much more fun when I just kicked the shit out of my own kit. I taught myself, but I also watched my brother. I guess I had a musical ear.

'I owe a lot to my brother. He had a brilliant record collection and, before he left home, we used to share a bedroom. He had two yards of vinyl going across the floor, and I used to dive in there and pull out everything. When you're twelve and you can only afford an album, what, only every three weeks or so with your paper round money, that's great. My brother, being older, had a serious collection. Everything from The Beatles, Rolling Stones, 60s music, right through to the first punk stuff. I was really lucky. And there we were, the pair of us, sitting opposite each other in the bedroom listening to the first Clash album and drumming into the air.

'Rob Leggatt, when I first met him, he was a year younger than us, so that wasn't quite cool enough for us at that age – we got to know him later on. But Rob Wells I met when I was eleven, and we've been mates ever since. Me and Wells, we were into punk music when we were kids, then got into The Jam, and Wellsy got me into Stevie Wonder; he played Stevie Wonder records when we were still listening to punk. In fact, I was in a band with Rob, the first band we were ever in, and we were called Boxing Clever. Dreadful name. For sixteen year olds, I suppose, we weren't bad. We were a three-piece, and I was drumming.' Of course.

The rest of the time, Rob, Rob and Robin did what teenagers do. According to Robin, 'My mum was good, let me go out at weekends: Friday, Saturday night, come home Sunday. I learned to smoke dope, though I hated it, still do. Doesn't seem to have improved since I first smoked it. Made me nauseous. As I got older, going drinking seemed much more fun. Trying to consume ten pints a night, chatting up girls . . .' Mostly, says Rob Leggatt, 'Horsham was always really the sort of place where you'd sit around and talk about what you were going to do when you got out of Horsham. I think we were all fairly gobby, quite cheeky. We'd get into the usual scrapes.'

Sheila remembers Robin's flirtation with punk quite well, as it happens. 'At certain stages in his teenage years he wanted to be a punk. I thought that if I couldn't beat him, then I'd have to join him. I even sewed chains on his jeans and made rips in them for him,' she adds, deftly blowing Robin's credibility retroactively. 'Mind you, I drew the line at earrings and coloured hair. Of course, he didn't really look that terrifying. He wasn't a bad boy at all. He's always been articulate and clever; he was talking from a young age and even though he was shy with people when he was younger, he was always very sociable. He didn't do terribly well at school, of course. I mean, he didn't do too badly, but he could have done much better. But by then, he was already saying that he wanted to be a drummer.'

And become a drummer he did. From his early teenage years, Robin Goodridge was already playing in bands.

'A local guy called Jim Dougan, who was brilliant, a real hippy geezer, used to put gigs on in Horsham when we were seventeen, eighteen. He'd rent the back room of a pub, charge us a quid, and put local bands on. And without that, we would never have played gigs for years. You know, normally you had to sing "Tie A Yellow Ribbon", that was the sort of thing the landlords of the time thought live music was all about. I played a lot of shows in the back of the pub. Jim's still around, but he eventually gave up the idea of fighting the establishment; Horsham's quite conservative.'

Still, it was enough to give Robin Goodridge, Drummer and Future Superstar, his first platform. 'It wasn't so much that Robin was the top dog,' Rob Leggatt recalls, 'but when you're in a town that has about three bands in it, and they're all shit, but yours is the *least* shit, *and* you've been up to London to buy your clothes – well, you know, you can rise to the top of a small barrell!'

In the meantime, there were also proper bands to see. 'The first band I ever saw was the UK Subs, in Guildford at Surrey University,' Robin recalls. 'That, or the Civic Hall, were the nearest venues. We got the tail end of punk, around 1979, and of course Guildford's quite close to Woking, where The Jam were from. And I saw The Clash at the Crawley Leisure Centre, and that was probably the turning point of my musical education, because it was the 16 Tons tour, for the *London Calling* album, and it was the first time I'd seen what you'd consider to be a superband, rather than a punk gig with spitting. They had a serious presence, looked amazing, with a light show and all the stuff I'd never seen before. So we just stood at the front gaping and leaping up and down. It was one of those sort of revelatory moments. It didn't look like a bad job from where I was standing. And they had a great drummer!'

In the meantime, there was real life to attend to. After leaving British Rail, Robin found what some might consider to be a plum situation for a young musician, in a rather more genteel environment. 'When I first left home, I lived in Chichester, and I got a job as an accompanist at a dance school. Actually,' he grins, 'it's one of the better jobs I've had: girls dancing, me playing percussion as an accompanist. Being a teenager, staring at all these girls the same age as me leaping around in leotards – and I got paid for it! For a while, I thought I'd died and gone to heaven.' Perhaps even heaven couldn't compete with Horsham, because shortly thereafter, Robin returned, and his drumming career became more serious.

'Don't eighty per cent of kids want to be in a band? Well, I was. I was really lucky.' In fact, Robin was in demand by more than one band. 'I started playing in a blues band, playing all the blues shacks down in Brighton and the south coast. The singer, Bob Brooks, had a building company and he gave me a job. I was around nineteen, getting up in the morning with my drum kit in the back of the car; drive to seventeen different places, work on a building site all day, come home, play the drums, used to kill me. Other than touring with Bush, that's the most tired I've ever been. I was absolutely knackered: four gigs a week at night. I remember that Saturday mornings were just a joy. I used to literally hum in bed, knowing I didn't have to get up, from pure joy. I enjoyed it all, though. Even when it was a shitty old pub, it was better than not playing. They were all older guys, in their thirties, and very good musicians, the best around. I was lucky. I got chosen. In fact, I actually got a call a couple of years ago to see if I was available to do a gig! I'd have loved to have done it, it would have been a riot. Unfortunately, I wasn't around at the time, but even though they knew I was in Bush, they rang up Glynis [Robin's partner] out of the blue and said, "Robin's not around by any chance is he? Got this gig going on somewhere" . . .'

Like all small town youth, inevitably, even Robin made a move to London. 'In 1986 I went up to live in Hounslow. Tried Lewisham, too – yeah, I know how to pick the places,' he grins. 'It was financially driven, because Hounslow and Lewisham are pretty cheap places to live. I was only up there for about two months; I moved up because of a band I was in, and moved in with a member of the band, but it wasn't going very well. I didn't enjoy it; thought it was a shitty place to live. London's no fun if you haven't got any money. I don't care what anyone says; walking around Leicester Square with no money in your pocket, what's the joy in that? I'd rather be in Horsham where someone might buy me a beer. Everything I could get in the world was here, musically or otherwise. I could still play in pubs, do the blues bands. There was always revenue. As soon as I went to London, the whole thing would cut off. You find yourself sitting in your car, driving back to work here. Sure, the music industry was in London, but I mean, I was only ever treading water. Playing down here was quite a good way to learn. Instead of being in bands with people who wanted to be pop stars, I was in bands with people who were musicians. So, in that respect, it was a better education than being with a bunch of pretentious wankers who thought they were the next superstars. Because you don't learn anything that way,' he adds, 'except how to spot wankers quicker!'

Of course, by this point, Horsham had one more thing going for it besides the quality of the air, the relative lack of wankers and the possibility of someone to buy you a beer. In 1986, Robin met Glynis Evans, a Horsham-area resident who had just begun working for her family's ice cream-importing company. Thirteen years later, they're still together, with a much doted-on daughter, Ruby Rose, born in 1996.

'I met Robin because my brother used to play percussion in a band that Robin used to occasionally drum for, so I'd see Robin either watching them or playing, and I thought I quite liked the look of him. It was one of those funny things,' she adds. 'I spent quite a few months going to places where he was, and knowing that something was going to happen, but having to wait. Eventually, my brother introduced him to me. Some friends of ours were running a club near where Robin and I were both living, and we both used to go there a lot. He didn't ask me to come up and see his stamp collection,' she laughs, 'but he did ask me if he could come over so he could play me a cassette of his music. He brought his tape over, and I played him my tape of *Les Miserables*!'

'She was going out with a friend of mine, sort of,' Robin elaborates, 'and I just waded in. Or maybe she waded in on me, is the truth of the matter. We moved in pretty soon after we met. It was one of those things; I never moved in officially for about six months, but I started moving my clothes – about three days' worth, and then I'd go back to my mum's place.'

'At the time,' Glynis adds, 'I had my own house, which I shared with my brother, but he wasn't there much of the time because he worked in France. And then there was a point where we really had to think about setting up home together. He was very funny about it, because he never actually moved in at any specific point. He was just staying – but he never went. Finally I managed to persuade him to use a wardrobe and a cupboard! Anyway, although there's an awful lot of things we don't have in common, there are many more things we do, and we're both outgoing. We clubbed a lot, we partied a lot.'

'She worked for her dad's company; Glynis was fully functioning in the work department, and really I was doing fuck all!' Robin laughs. 'Well, I was working, but I was mainly trying to be A Man.

Kind of "girlfriend supports boyfriend while he tries to be a musician" scenario. Which is quite common. But I think she was like me and didn't think about it that much. When you think about it, you worry. I was twenty-eight before I started making any money. Well, I'd made some money, but never enough to buy a house. That's the first goal for musicians, to end up with enough money to buy a house. If you have a really good year, you can make ten years' salary in one year. I just figured that I wanted to make enough money in a couple of years to buy a house, and then if I had to get a proper job, I could earn enough to keep it. If it all went right, I'd be thirty years old and own my own house. Most people are thirty years old and they haven't even started paying for it yet, and they've been working and presumably having a lot less fun.'

Soon Robin, Glynis and their friends were regularly coming to London to clubs like Shoom! and Boys' Own nights. 'There was a clique of people from Sussex who were quite in there at the start of all that,' Rob Leggatt recalls. 'And Robin was one of the first of us to go; he pretty much embraced it.' So much so, Rob laughs, 'that he used to wear a leather fez at one point. Dark green, I think; yeah, a lot of fashion crimes slipped through! But seriously, the great thing was that he didn't stop playing live music. It was a few years before bands started to incorporate any dance elements into their music, and so for the first few years we went, it was all just house music. But Robin managed to be into it and still do two things at one time.'

When the two sorts of music mixed, it came as cause for hope: prior to that, Robin hadn't heard much to inspire him in rock and pop music, particularly as a drummer. The era of the omnipresent 80s drum machine wasn't as funky as it liked to think it was. 'That's why it sounded so boring. A lot of a band's energy comes out of the drumming, and if you don't have it there, you're losing something,' he contends. Which is why, he says, he ended up getting into dance music 'in a big way. The reason I got into raves is that it was a dreadful time for any other kind of music. 1987, 1988 – can you name an album that was worth listening to? Thankfully, in the 1990s, you were allowed to play guitar again; in most of the 80s, you couldn't. It was lovely to get rock music and a bit of punk music somewhere together. I mean, they called it grunge, but it was just a fusion of rock and punk. You were allowed to look cool; you were allowed to be exciting again, to really let go.'

That fusion of styles to which Robin refers would pop up in his own work sooner rather than later. The Beautiful People, the band for which he was best known prior to meeting Gavin, Nigel and Dave, began as an attempt to mix the ultimate rock guitar sounds – Jimi Hendrix and his band – with modern beats and grooves.

'Basically, two friends of mine, Duncan Kane and Luke Baldry, were in a pub one night, and they told me they had this idea of sampling Jimi Hendrix stuff. And it's 1992, and nobody had done it. We wanted to get guitars on dance records. And we did!

'We started with three songs. And Eric Clapton lived nearby, so we took it round his house. We didn't know him, but we didn't know what else to do. He thought it was brilliant. And he said, I can get you in touch with the bloke you need to talk to, Alan Douglas, because you'll never get away with it unless you get permission. So we did, and Douglas offered us £50,000 to go away and do it. And he sent us all the DAT tapes of Jimi's stuff, including studio out-takes, which were amazing. We sampled a lot of it.

'It was quite a big underground record,' Robin says of The Beautiful People's album, *If 60s Were 90s*. 'And it sold about seventy or eighty thousand copies, but the thing was, unfortunately, that U2's *Achtung Baby* came out at about the same time. Not that we were trying to compete, or anything, but it was the same type of thing. And they had Flood as a producer and a million quid to work with, and we had a bedroom sampler and loads of spare time! Still, I was proud of that record, and in fact that was the record I gave Gavin when I met him. Actually, I remember on our first [Bush] tour, being in Seattle and hearing *If 60s Were 90s* on the radio. So of course I'd say, "That's another of *my* bands, actually. Hey, you lot, any of the rest of your bands on the radio in Seattle?" '

But that's getting ahead of the story.

If you're a good drummer, it's not uncommon to be in more than one band. At around the same time Robin was working with The Beautiful People – which obviously had its limitations as a live act, given Jimi Hendrix's lack of availability – his path was also crossing with that of another band. Soul Family Sensation, a wonderful and underrated London-based outfit who blended melancholy indie songwriting with Jhelisa Anderson's gorgeous soul vocals, had already made some inroads with an album *New Wave* in 1992. Robin had met songwriter Johnny Mayall, now the chief songwriter of Republica, 'just by socialising in London, going out every weekend, going to clubs, meeting people. I loved his work, like "I Don't Even Know If I Should Call You Baby".' By the time Robin met Johnny, Soul Family Sensation had shortened its name to Sensation. 'I loved working with Johnny, because he's a songwriter, same as Gavin. If you're a drummer, what you really want is to find someone who writes good songs. It's complete and utter talent, but also, it's not some magical and unquantifiable thing, it's work. I got on with Johnny the minute I met him, and we sat there out of our heads as usual and just rapped about music, and a few months later, he called me and said, "Do you want to play drums?" I thought, *Finally*! One of those evenings in London worked, after all this time! After talking so much shit for so long, someone heard me.'

And so Robin joined Sensation in late 1992, playing a few showcase dates and working on a second album, *Burger Habit*, with producer Mike Hedges in France. In the hope, as always, that the band's career was on the up. Robin was getting paid a wage, albeit a small one, and playing with like minds. But then, as luck would have it in the never-rains-but-it-pours department, Gavin Rossdale's flatmate Alex Tate got talking to a friend and occasional club promoter, Lee Collier, about his friend's search for a full-time drummer. As it happens, Lee Collier had just been down to Horsham for the weekend with friends and had stayed at Robin Goodridge's house.

'Gavin didn't really know I was a drummer. Or didn't know I did it seriously. But, within a few days, Gavin phoned me and said, "Will you come and see us sometime?" And I said, sure. And then he rang me Saturday night to reconfirm that I would be there for the Sunday night gig. And then rang on Sunday again to ask if I was coming.' He laughs. 'You know, I spend one weekend with a guy who stays at my house, and then the next weekend a friend of a friend of his ... well, I really genuinely wasn't going to go, because it was a long way up to London and I wasn't quite sure I could be arsed.

'Gavin was keen, I guess. Same as me. But I phoned Rob and Rob, and they were up for going, so we went.'

The gig was Future Primitive, of course, playing at Subteranea, with stand-in drummer Spencer Cobrin temporarily behind the kit. In the years since the question has been asked and the story told, the legend has grown up – abetted by Robin – that he watched the gig, marched backstage, told Dave, Nigel and Gavin that their drummer wasn't up to much, and landed himself the job.

'I think he probably did do just that,' Glynis laughs when asked the truth of the story. 'He's very critical of drummers!' Rob Leggatt laughs just as hard when he says, 'Yeah, that's what he did. We were watching them – me, Rob and Robin – and we were all pretty drunk, and I have to say I thought they were pretty cool. They were a four-piece and, for a lot of it, it would be the drums and three guys with guitar, and it would be all fairly heads down. But they did a couple of numbers where I'm pretty sure Gavin put his guitar down and would just sing into the microphone, so it was much more of a pop thing. And Robin quite liked that; he said it made it stand out from every other band that was just heads-down rock'n'rollers.

'He thought they were really good. He could obviously see the potential that Gav had, because he's quite charismatic, quite a performer. Robin had been in enough bands to know by then that you could have the best musicians in the world, but if you haven't got a good frontman, and someone who can write songs, then you're probably never going further than Subteranea.

'So then,' Rob Leggatt continues, 'Robin says, "I'm going backstage to tell 'em what I've seen." And Rob and I were thinking, Well, that'll be the end of that. Back to painting and decorating. But you know, he went in there as businesslike as anything, and faced the wall and came out with a job.

'I think afterwards we went and jumped on a whole load of cars, or something stupid like that, as a way of celebrating,' Rob says. 'Well, we *were* really drunk!'

Robin smiles enigmatically when asked about the fateful evening. 'I thought they were good.' A few days later, Gavin would ring him again. 'He said, "Do you want to come for an audition?" I didn't know anyone else *was* auditioning, to be honest. And he gave me a demo, and I thought it was really good. I knew I'd get the job – well, I felt good about it, anyway. Basically, I worked out the secret: when Gavin's shouting, you just hit everything harder!

'But of course I was still in Sensation,' he says. 'I had to quit to join Future Primitive full-time. Not that I was getting paid by them, so far, but there was a point of confrontation. I mean, I was getting paid by Sensation, and it was a really good band. But I had to have this chat with Johnny, and say, "Look, I'm going to go with it. It's really me. It's the first time I have been in a band and I can play like *me*." '

He laughs. 'Why this band? No idea. Because it clicked? Because there were no rules? Because it wasn't all there already? Well, Nigel and Gavin and Dave were there already, of course. But me . . .' He laughs wickedly, happy to tease his bandmates even in their absence. '*I* was the missing link between success and failure!'

K

There must be something that we can eat . . .

'Every year, at New Year's Eve, we'd all sit together at home and toast the New Year. And every year, for Gavin, we'd say, "You know, this year's gonna be the big one. It's really going to happen this year,"' Lorraine Rossdale recalls. 'And then another year would go by, and nothing would have happened, and so it would have to be the *next* year. And we'd sit there and say, "Okay, this year, it's *really* going to be the year." And I remember thinking, that last New Year's Eve in 1993, just how many years we'd been saying it. And that year, Gavin shrugged and said, "I'm not going to say it's going to happen this year. It's ridiculous saying it. Because it *isn't* ever going to happen, is it?" And we didn't know what to say. "Oh . . . yes it is, Gav, come on. It still might happen. It *could* happen . . . couldn't it?"'

It could. And it did. But not quite yet. As Future Primitive started to gel in the months just before and just after Robin Goodridge joined the band, and a record deal with a new but ambitious US label, Trauma, waited on the horizon, there were demos to make, dates to play, and audiences to find. It started to feel right.

Nigel Pulsford's friend Neil Crossley, himself a musician, remembers his impressions of the band's early days.

'The thing that really impressed me about them was the songs, because they had such strong hooks. Even before they had Spencer [Cobrin, Robin's pinch-hitting predecessor on drums] playing with them, they were doing things like "Little Things" and "Comedown" and "Glycerine". It was all kind of there already, even if we'd be going to see them at places like The Bull & Gate [a modest-sized pub venue in Kentish Town], and there'd only be twenty people there. And the weird thing is that even later when we saw them in the States – well, okay, they were a bigger band and more professional – but it wasn't much different, because back then it was already there. It had changed, but it hadn't changed that much.

'And Nigel always liked discordant guitars, and from that point of view, I could see why he was doing what he was doing. I think in terms of the actual material, it was more overtly commercial for him, so I was a bit surprised, but at the same time you could see it was a good thing. The band was a great vehicle for him because initially it was just Nigel up there playing guitar on stage, so he was able to do all this discordant stuff that he likes to do, having this sound which is almost out of control. And it was all very Pixies; of course, I remember very well being at his flat in Stockwell and him playing the Pixies; he wouldn't shut up about them.

'I remember being up at Nigel's flat in Kensal Rise in 1993, some time just before I'd seen Future Primitive for the first time, and late one night he put on this five-track demo. At first I wasn't too sure about Gavin's voice, but by the end of it I realised exactly how good it was. And I've still got the demo, in fact,' he laughs. 'It's weird, because if you sit down and play "Little Things" on the guitar, it's only about three chords all the way through; but it's such a great song. I remember thinking, he's a really good songwriter, this guy. And a few weeks after, my girlfriend and I went off on a driving holiday to California and I remember bunging this cassette in my bag because I hadn't had the chance to listen to it properly, and we ended up playing it to death in the car. I'd forgotten we'd taken it, and one day we were driving to Death Valley and my girlfriend took it out of the bag and, you know, it sounded absolutely fantastic in those wide open spaces. By the time we got back we were completely in love with it. It sounds like such a creepy thing to say,' he admits. 'You wonder if you just like it because your mate's in the band. But having said that, I've had mates in lots of bands and I wouldn't dream of taking their tape on holiday with me. I still play it occasionally – it's much more minimal than the finished album – and it's absolutely gorgeous. I can see why they got signed on the basis of that. It has so much promise, and it just *reeks* of hit songs. And I remember going to see them with my girlfriend's younger brother one time, and he said, "Oh God, they're going to be *huge*." Which sounds stupid, because everyone says that. The thing is, Patrick is quite young, pretty sussed, and he's more into dance music, but after the third song, that's exactly what he said.'

At around the same time Nigel was discovering that his new band was turning into one of the most rewarding musical partnerships he'd had, another – equally important – partnership had come into his life. That partnership would be with Judith Rose, a Leeds native who had recently graduated from University College in London and was part of Nigel's West London social circle of avid indie music fans. In fact, she worked at the Notting Hill Record and Tape Exchange while in university, along with several of Nigel's friends. She had been dating Kris Jozajtis, one of Nigel's former bandmates in King Blank, a man with whom both Judith and Nigel remain close friends. After they split up, however, gradually and almost to her surprise, Judith found herself spending more and more time with Nigel.

'I kept bumping into him around the usual pubs and places. And overall, you know,' she smiles, 'I thought he was a rather strange person to be falling in love with. Years before that, I would have expected I'd end up with some sort of cliché'd paranoid rock-type schizo; some screwed-up, heroin-chic, Iggy Pop type. Nigel was nothing like this; not nearly screwed up and strung out enough for me, although he *was* a full-on, fingers-bleeding guitarist! So I couldn't really understand what was happening, and I kept telling myself, "God, I can't be in love with him." But, I was; he really gave me goosebumps, you know,' Judith adds, eyes twinkling.

According to Judith, those first Future Primitive gigs were anything but rock-starry. 'I'm sure you've heard about the four men and a dog gig they did,' she notes, referring to the ill-fated Camden Falcon show where, as Gavin says with a wince, his dog Winston spent the whole night licking the other dog in attendance, just a few feet from the stage and in full view of the lone record company executive who had turned up. At least there wasn't any ticket money to be nicked at that gig; Judith recalls another similarly modestly attended show where in the middle of the set, 'Someone came bursting in and stole all the money they had on the door!'

Dave Parsons' mate Pete Hislop, who went to 'practically every gig they did' in Future Primitive's early days, recalls, 'I really liked them. They were quite tight, and they had some good songs. In fact, they had one song that they probably hate now, because it was the song that they really became known for.' That song was 'Honky Manchild', which never did see the light of day on Bush's first album or indeed since, but which became popular enough to win over the listeners voting for favourite band demos on a much-respected radio show hosted by Gary Crowley, on London's GLR. Live, it was always the highlight of the evening, whether the audience had twenty people or two hundred.

'It was a great song, a really good one,' Pete says. 'In fact, I really wish I had that song now. I don't think they'll ever play it again, because it was just played to death, and in a way it's probably one of those songs where the band just want to get rid of it, like James' "Sit Down". I'm sure that they eventually thought, We don't want to be known just for this song, because it seemed to be the song that everyone would sing, that everyone loved, and so they had to play it every single gig.

'We went to the first gig they ever did, down in Borough past the Elephant and Castle [in south-east London],' he adds. 'In a car park. It was somebody's party, and they'd been asked to play there, and they had a little stage and a little tent set up. And it went down pretty well.' Pete smiles at the modest circumstances. 'It was great being at the very first gig, and I think Dave had a really good time, too.

'And then they started playing quite a lot; really small gigs in pubs. I saw so many of them I can't remember all their names. The Half Moon in Putney was one, and the Powerhäus in Islington; all those places. The audiences weren't massive, but over the months they developed this fan club that kept coming back, with lots of girls who'd come and dance at the front and get people moving. And you know,' Pete emphasises, 'they never, ever stinted on their performance; they always gave one hundred per cent. That always impressed me, Gavin performing perfectly all the time; regardless of where they were, they'd all be really into it and really go for it. I was amazed, because I don't know if I could have done it, if I could have stood up there and given it everything in front of, basically, your mates and a dog. Gavin's dog,' he corrects himself, laughing.

'They had one gig at The Orange down in Fulham. It was the first time I'd ever seen it so packed for them, and a lot of record company people had come down. I think it was the first time they'd been touted as a band that people should see. And it was a good gig with great atmosphere, but for some reason they obviously didn't strike a chord with the business people. It didn't quite work. But they carried on gigging, anyway.'

And carried on trying to make ends meet, getting by with a little help from friends. In fact, Alex Tate, who had split up with Claudia, was now living with Gavin in his basement flat along with Gavin's girlfriend Jasmine Lewis, whom he had begun seeing at about the time he and Nigel began working together. Occasionally, there were even more overnight guests. In fact, Alex recalls, life in the flat in Montagu Square was 'a lot like the London version of *Friends*. And because my [ex]wife kept coming over, I guess I was Ross. And occasionally Chandler. And obviously Joey.'

Gavin, he says, did the housework. 'And then he'd complain to me and Jasmine that we were just – really bad children, basically! "You two just sit in the armchairs, but I'm going out with the dog now, and I want this flat hoovered when I come back!" I did the cooking, since I thought that was easy. And Jasmine did the shopping, because she was working [as a model] and had the money. And Gavin did the cleaning. Yeah, I was spoiled by Gavin,' he grins. 'He was like Mum, which definitely means I was always told to do more hoovering. Though, of course, all that training has paid off now, as far as my girlfriend's concerned!'

Soraya Rossdale, who is almost a decade younger than her brother, lives in London and combines an international modelling career with a newfound love of journalism. And, Gavin will note with pride, she has recently begun working as a volunteer at the homeless charity, Shelter.

Soraya, who would go on to become Jasmine's best friend, remembers her time as a temporary flatmate at Montagu Square with great affection. 'I was eighteen, and I'd finished boarding school and come up to London. I'd been bunking off before that, and wasn't getting on well at home, so I stayed at Gavin's for about three months until Gavin said I really had to find somewhere else, because he already had Alex in the front room and I was sharing it, sleeping on the floor, with [Gavin's friend] Nicky kipping in the hallway!' The main hazard in such confined quarters, she laughs, was Winston. 'I remember getting up to go to the loo in the middle of the night and Winston growled so hard I was stuck there for about half an hour. If it wasn't that, he'd be chasing you down the hallway.

'And Gavin was always doing his music, always strumming his guitar. Trying to get his attention was an absolute nightmare. It used to irritate the hell out of me.' She laughs. 'Especially when I was younger. I'd be ringing him up and the whole time I'd be talking to him about not getting on with my stepfather or not being allowed to go out in the clothes I wanted, he'd be strumming away and I wasn't even sure he was listening. But eventually he'd come out with something philosophical, and it would always come around to me having to do some work!' She laughs, and notes that last Christmas her gifts from Gavin were 'a really nice skirt – and typing lessons! Still, he's the best present buyer in the world. Whatever he bought me when I was younger, I loved. I always used to look forward to what I was getting from him more than anything else.

'I wasn't sure what to say about him for this book, you know,' she confides. 'I'm a Scorpio, like Gavin, and if anything I'm very similar to him. He's got a very dry sense of humour, which is okay when you get old enough to understand it. And kids are completely drawn to him. When I was at boarding school, I had tapes of his music, and everybody else would listen to Bros or that sort of stuff, and I'd listen to my brother's music. My earliest memories of him, in fact, are about being seven or eight and him coming down to my school to visit.

'I always loved Gavin; he was brilliant with me. Even as a teenager, he was the person I always wanted to be with. And as I grew up, he became my idol. In fact,' she laughs, 'I wrote him a poem when I was fourteen, called "Idolatry".' The final verse runs: *"I felt and I cared for you/As I still do/I loved and admired you/But that you already knew."* 'Remember I was only fourteen when I wrote that,' she cautions. The sentiments, however, remain the same.

'Everything he did would absolutely amaze me, even when he was just painting houses and everyone else seemed to think he was just dossing. In my mind he was great, even if everyone said, "Why on earth do you think he's so amazing? He's just a painter and decorator!"

'I'd go round to visit, and we'd hang out, or we'd go to music shops. He took me to my first French film, in fact, because he decided I needed a bit of culture. During my teenage years, whenever I'd run off, everyone knew where I was; at Gavin's. We'd take long walks across the park to Kensington High Street to get a

CD, and when we passed someone who was homeless, he'd always find a pound.' It is, she adds, what has inspired her own charity work. 'I've been doing that for the last few years, and my life has really changed.

'Gavin's very hard to pin down,' Soraya says thoughtfully. 'I have to think about what I'm going to say, and then I'll call him. Recently I've had some good conversations with him in which he opened up a little bit, but not a lot. He's always been very closed. I always think, if I could walk into a room and hug him and give him a kiss, it would be great, but he's not like that. I remember one of the first times he came to see me and said he loved me, said, "Yeah, love you lots." I was so shocked. And I thought, Maybe I don't know him at all. I think Gavin's really intriguing, because however much you think you know him, you don't.

'Eventually, over the years, I got to the point of thinking, Hmm, he's got his faults too. I kind of found my ground. Not that he did anything wrong or was particularly mean, it was just a case of accepting how Gavin was with people. It's his lack of ability to be more open and loving. I used to resent that, because that's what I wanted more of. I'd love to go round there and get a big hug off him.'

Meanwhile, back at Montagu Square in the Before Bush Success era, Gavin was displaying the same determination he'd always told Soraya was important. Even if gigs were few and far between, and even if they often meant trying not to think, as Alex recalls, that 'one of the audience might be an A&R man and could change your life.' And, he goes on: 'That you've been waiting for this gig for two months, being relatively anxious, and now here it is and the PA costs you thirty pounds and you spend the gig wishing you had enough money to spend fifty. So yeah, there's pressure.' And, says Alex, as always, money was tight. 'Sometimes honesty was too painful and denial was easier. We got to the point where I owed Gavin some money and he couldn't pay the rent and neither of us had a quid to our name. And there we were, staring at an empty cupboard,' Alex adds. The very same empty cupboard that would turn up in 'Little Things', perhaps. 'But of course at no point,' Alex insists, 'did we think we should do something different!'

Occasionally, says Alex, things would look up. 'I'd get a promo [video] to do in Spain, and I'd get Gavin in on the production side, or Gavin would get some deal and rope me in, or Jasmine would ring up and say, "Okay, there's some work, so you two be here at this time." It was nice, really; I don't know why we decided to look after each other, but maybe it was because we had family backgrounds that were a little problematic. And Gavin was the first one to say, "Come and stay at my flat." Although I gave him a job here and there, there was definitely nothing in the contract to say that I had to reciprocate! Of course, neither of our families were that far away, and even though we felt that we were fully-grown adults, and that nobody could tell us anything, Gavin would come back from his mum's with stuff to eat, and I'd come back with huge bags of pasta from mine.'

Gavin's mother Barbara recalls, 'Oh yes, Gavin would come round and have dinner and he'd raid the fridge, knowing that Alex and Jasmine were waiting excitedly to find out what he'd got. So whenever I knew he was coming by, I'd just go and get some provisions and make sure they were in the flat when he arrived. Those were about the only things I was allowed to do, though,' she adds. 'Nothing major. At any point he could have picked up the telephone to his father or to myself and said, "Help me out," but he never would. Of course by then we all wondered whether it had been going on so long that there was no hope. I remember I asked, "Gavin, is this really going to work?" And he said, "Well, I'm going to give it one more year." And I thought, Well, we've come this far. What's another year? She laughs as she notes, 'I think it was actually a year and a half from then, but there you go.'

Meanwhile, back in the dire financial straits at Montagu Square, there was plenty to talk about even when the cupboards were empty. Alex enthuses, 'Finally, I'd met somebody who could talk about things of interest. He had a great record collection, and he knew enough about film that we could talk about that. And so, although we didn't have the money to go out, there was enough interesting stuff between us to keep us occupied. I must have wondered if he was ever going to be rewarded for his work, but I never became cynical about him, because he seemed to be progressing. I'd be sitting about moaning, "Oh, God, am I *ever* going to find a screenplay I want to work on?" Meanwhile, Gavin would be hammering his guitar, plucking his fingers to bits, trying to work out something in a song. Once I remember him working on a drum pattern at seven in the morning, and I'd only got in at four. And I'm like, "Gavin, man, I need some sleep!" And he says, "Yeah, but I've got this idea and I have to work it out," and that was it. I had to suffer. In fact, with Gavin, he's going to have to get it right,' Alex laughs, 'or we're all going to have to suffer until he does!'

Significantly, Alex says, Gavin's adopting Winston, the faithful Puli hound who still accompanies him everywhere, 'gave a structure to his time that he never had before. That's when his songwriting really came together, I think. Going out, walking the dog, feeding the dog, and then writing songs, and then walking the dog at the end of the day was all really good for him. And I suppose Jasmine was away a lot too, but she was in the picture, so he didn't have to use up his energy going out to pull girls all the time!'

As it happens, before another New Year's Eve had come and gone, Jasmine Lewis, Alex Tate [billed as Alessandro Tatteo] and even Winston the Puli hound would all be notching up backing vocals on a debut album they perhaps didn't imagine Gavin Rossdale and his bandmates would ever make. But make it they did.

L

'Let's say it was just a chance of fate, the way it all happened. Think of it: twelve years of sitting outside people's offices, waiting for them to come back from lunch to give you a little bit of free studio time. And then finally getting a bite of the apple. And not only did it all take off, it just *exploded*!'

Gary Crowley shakes his head. Looks over at Simon Halfont. And they both grin like Cheshire cats.

In the music business, the successful bands you can link to your own name stand as your regimental rank, your trophy shelf, your deck of cards that all, to hear 'em tell it, came up trumps. Claim a part in someone's success, and you're a somebody. The industry is full of people who will look you in the eye and tell you that it was they who discovered, shaped, signed, shopped, 'worked', A&R'd, or 'broke' – note that this means 'made very successful', rather than 'accidentally smashed to bits' – an act. In other words, that they were the person without whom the rest of us would never have heard of the band in question.

Gary Crowley and Simon Halfont probably have more right than most to dine out on an 'I was there when Bush got their shot' story. Funnily enough, it doesn't seem to have occurred to them to boast. But get them talking, and they've got quite a story to tell.

Influential London-based DJ, occasional A&R man and genuine music fan Gary Crowley has a tangential involvement in the Bush story that starts more than twenty years ago, when he was in the unique position of having given Bush manager Dave Dorrell his first and perhaps only job as a poet. Mind you, they were both fourteen at the time.

'Dave and I both went to Rutherford School just off Bell Street, off the Edgware Road, although it's now called North Westminster School. I was in the year above Dave. We were in perfect place for experiencing punk, really. The Sex Pistols' Steve Jones and Paul Cook had a flat at the end of Bell Street, and Bell Street joins Lisson Grove, where The Slits and The Clash used to sign on. So here we were, these fourteen-year-old school boys who were not only into punk in a very, very big way, but seeing these people during our school lunch times.

'So we became friends, and it was kind of a small, select band of myself, Dave and a few other pals. I remember going to see The Clash once, six or seven of us turning up in school uniforms, and their roadies saying, "What's this? A fucking school outing or something?" There couldn't have been a better place for us. We took over our school magazine and turned it into a punk fanzine. We only printed about twenty-five copies. I was Editor in Chief, and Dave was the poet. The fanzine was called *The Modern World*, 'cause I was the editor and I had the say and I was the biggest Jam fan in the world. Then we left school and went off in our different directions, and we'd see each other at gigs and clubs over the years, too.

'I was first aware of Gavin in about 1983, I suppose. I remember going to see Midnight at The Players' Theatre in Villiers Street, a wonderful old atmospheric music theatre. At that time there weren't gigs as such, there were happenings, there were events. It was the 60s all over again. I think I met him at clubs a few times after that, too, probably fell over him at The Wag or The Dirt Box or those kind of clubby-type places.

'Even then I thought, What else could that guy be, you know, but a frontman? It sounds cheesy, it sounds corny, but he had it. Whatever that sort of x-factor is, that sort of special something, he had it. He certainly looked the part, too – all that hair, pre-Raphaelite locks down his back. And the band? It was very early days. They were quite rocky, out of step with what was happening at the time, because it was much more of a dance time – he was always a rocker, I suppose, was Gavin. So I thought the band were OK. Maybe a bit of a case of style over content; I mean, they looked great, but they weren't completely convincing, musically. They didn't completely pull it off.

'Could Gavin sing?' Gary laughs. 'Well, he could sing OK. I don't think there was anyone running for cover!

'Then we kind of fast forward a few years,' he continues. 'And at the end of the 80s, I was doing A&R for Island Records, and Gavin then had a band called the Little Dukes, and he turned up, or maybe I met him with [bandmate] Emil. Those two were like a double act, certainly at the beginning. When I was with Island they came and played me some demos.'

'I must have met Gavin around then through Gary,' says graphic designer Simon Halfont. 'He asked me to do some little logo things for his band, and of course he played me some stuff.'

'He was kind of playing his demos to everybody during that period,' Gary agrees, and then adds, with a twinkle in his eye: 'What was that great quote we used to use? If it wasn't for us, he'd still be waiting outside [former EMI head] Clive Black's office.'

'Yeah. He'd be waiting for Clive Black to return his calls!' Simon adds.

'Gavin was always sort of – around,' Gary continues, 'but I suppose he never seemed to be getting anywhere. Still, he so looked the part. I remember him coming into the office and all the girls in A&R going, "Who was *that*?" '

'I also remember walking with you down South Molton Street about the same time,' Simon adds. 'We bumped into Gavin, and we saw heads *craning*, just to get a look at him. It was probably the long hair . . .'

'Sasha was still in the band then,' Gary continues. 'And so was Emil. They came in to see me a couple of times, and I thought there was something interesting there. Clive Banks, who was head of Island then, was a fan, but Barney Griffiths – head of A&R – wasn't convinced.

'I could see Gavin's work was getting better, though. It was a lot rockier compared to what he'd done with Midnight, two or three years before, but it was still evolving. We went down to see them rehearse a few times, took them out to lunch. At one point it really looked as though we were going to do it. But Barney still wasn't sure, and we passed on it. They'd still come and see me every month or so with a few new songs.

'They were persistent. But to be honest, there weren't really that many other people taking an interest at the time. They were always guaranteed a free lunch off yours truly, or certainly a drink. And then they went away.'

When Gavin returned from Los Angeles and found himself in a new and rather different musical situation, he rang Gary again. 'Gavin came to my flat, and said, "I've got something new here." And you could tell by the tracks they were working on, this band Future Primitive, that something had changed for Gavin. There was a song called "Honky Manchild", which I played on my radio show on GLR at the time, on the Demo Clash spot. And for a couple of weeks, it beat everything it was up against.'

Live, too, Gary thought the band were a surprising leap forward. 'I remember seeing them at the Mean Fiddler with Nigel on guitar and Dave playing bass. And of course the guest list out-numbered the paying punters – there must have been twenty-five or thirty people there maximum – but I could just see the whole thing had gone up incredibly compared to when I'd seen Gavin playing with Emil. They were very ambitious, but they weren't quite pulling it off. This time it was obvious: this was a very tight combo. It went up a few gears, and more. I remember thinking, Jesus, this could do really, really well if the right things happened.'

'And then Simon moved to Los Angeles,' Gary concludes, nodding at Simon.

'I was very good friends with Rob Kahane,' Simon begins. 'When I went to Los Angeles, I stayed with Rob and he found me a job. The connection was that I was designing George Michael's record sleeves at the time, and Rob was managing George. And one of the deals he'd done, which was one of his many deals, was a label deal with Hollywood Records. He asked me if I knew of any acts, because he didn't have anybody. So I rang Gary, because I knew he was doing A&R. "Got any scraps off your table?" I asked, joking.

'And Gary came up with this immortal, hysterical line,' Simon says, giving the words the correct comedic pause. 'He thought a minute and said, "Well . . . there's always *Gavin*."'

'Not in a nasty way, of course,' he hastens to add. 'Because I was a fan of Gavin's, and obviously so was Gary. But we knew that no one in the UK music business was ever going to get the kind of music Gavin was making. So I came to London, met Dave Dorrell, and explained the Rob situation to him, gave Rob a bit of a sales pitch: "Yeah, a new US label, maybe it's the way to go."'

'Dave gave me a tape with about five or six tracks, and a videotape of the band playing live on [Channel 4 music show] *The Word*. And I remember going back to my mum and dad's here in London and playing it, and thinking, There's *definitely* something here. A lot of the things on that tape turned up on the album, in fact: "Glycerine", "Comedown", "Everything Zen". So I rang Rob. Knowing Rob and how to tease him, I said, "You're never going to believe what I've got!" He got excited, so I said, "I don't want to tell you anymore about it, I want to play it to you and show it to you." But even the video, I felt, didn't do them justice.

'Rob loved it, but I still asked Dorrell if I could shop the tape around for him in the States. It was obviously such an American thing.'

'And in America, the band would have a clean sheet,' says Gary. 'None of this perceived baggage from before, from whatever Gavin had done that hadn't been successful, or from Dave being in Transvision Vamp.'

It's easy to think that Gavin's claim – that the UK music business saw him as used goods – is the sort of exaggeration brought on by insecurity in a phenomenally insecure business. In fact, Gary suggests, it wasn't exaggeration at all.

'Oh no, he's absolutely right. He was a lovely guy, but no one was biting. Remember, Gavin had been shopping himself and his music around for, like, a decade by then, since he'd been a teenager in Midnight. And you know what A&R guys are like.' Crowley, ex-A&R man, knows whereof he speaks. 'This was the early 1990s, too. We'd had Manchester, we'd had shoe-gazing before that, Britpop was coming . . . As for the music press, it's very true that A&R guys listened to what they said, and this band certainly weren't getting written about at all. They weren't making an effort to be trendy. They weren't hanging out in Camden, going to the right pubs.'

Simon continues. 'The next step was for Rob and I to take the music to Hollywood Records. Peter Paterno [Hollywood president and longtime heavyweight music industry attorney] was running it at the time. I've met Peter subsequently to that and he's a nice enough guy, but it was the opening baseball game of the season and he was sitting there watching it on television while we played him the music. I was furious: "What's up with that guy?" When Trauma's deal with Hollywood went sour, and Rob was no longer managing George Michael, Rob was in a no man's land, not really having anything going on, for about,' Simon grins, 'oh, a minute and a half!

'But the next thing we knew,' Simon continues, fast-forwarding past the part of the Trauma story in which Rob Kahane and his partner Paul Palmer found a new distributor in Interscope, 'Trauma had gone with "Everything Zen" to radio in the US. The thing with Rob, because of his time with George Michael, was that he knew how to get people interested, knew all the radio people, and he's very hands on. Suddenly, "Everything Zen" goes to radio and the fucking thing just exploded.'

'It seemed to happen very quickly,' Gary recalls. 'I was in London, and Simon was in LA, and he'd be telling me that the record had been picked up by KROQ! We were so excited. "We'd always said America would get it! We were right, we were right!" '

'You'd be driving around and it was virtually every other record,' says Simon. 'You'd hear it two or three times in the morning, and think, Fucking hell! In those days, KROQ were so specific about what they played, very regimented. Depeche Mode, The Smiths, Morrissey and The Cure. That's what it was at the time, very retro. Somehow, this record just slipped through. And KROQ is a hugely influential radio station; if it's a hit there, it's a hit everywhere. I remember calling Gavin and telling him it was all over the radio, but I don't think he really took it in. He couldn't actually hear it for himself. He was probably like, "Yeah, sure it is." When he came out to the States I think he was quite taken aback.'

Ask Gary and Simon if they know of another artist who, like Gavin, would have stuck at his music for so long in the face of setbacks, dismissal and indifference, and they shake their heads.

'No. No one else,' Gary says. And then he laughs. 'But what else could he do? He had to do this – I can't imagine him doing anything else. Sooner or later, he was always going to be a rock star.'

'And he was still young enough to enjoy it and appreciate it,' says Simon. 'It's a bit of a fairytale, really. Sometimes you hear of bands who have done two gigs and put a single out and it's a huge hit. This is more poignant, more special. Gavin had been trying so hard for so long, and you couldn't help but think, Hats off to him, he's paid his dues.'

M

Starting to deserve this . . .

The last studio Bush had recorded in was hardly the big time, located in dreary Harlesden in north-west London on a particularly grim council estate. Where, as Dave Dorrell joked, you couldn't even be sure it was an eight-track, because someone might have nicked at least one of the eight. Still, Trauma Records' Rob Kahane, who had travelled up to this location in a limo, had heard enough to convince him to sign the band. In January 1994, just a few months later, and standing in the slightly more upmarket – if by no means luxurious – Westway Studios, perhaps even the wary Gavin Rossdale felt, to paraphrase a line in 'Machinehead', that he was starting to get what he deserved.

A decade after he had started making music, he was finally being given a chance to make an entire album: unlike his bandmates Nigel Pulsford, Dave Parsons and Robin Goodridge, *Sixteen Stone* would be his first. Once the deal had been signed, the only issue remaining in the weeks leading up to making the record was who they could find to produce it, given that the music they made was out of step with practically every other UK band. Or at least the bands currently being touted as the next big thing.

Perversely, Bush found their man (or men) in the least likely place of all. Legendary British production team Clive Langer and Alan Winstanley had worked with some rather sizeable names in UK pop music in the preceding decade, from Elvis Costello and Madness to

The Teardrop Explodes, Dexys Midnight Runners, Aztec Camera, Lloyd Cole and The Commotions and Morrissey. Not, perhaps, a natural choice for a rock band, and one influenced by American underground and independent music at that. But here they were.

Clive Langer recalls, 'It's funny how it came about. I think the reason we got the job was that I was having dinner with a friend, Ben, from Boilerhouse and some American record company people. Ben was a big fan of Dexys, and he suggested to Dave Dorrell that myself and Alan might be good for Bush. I think he could hear the pop side of Bush, and we weren't averse to rock music. So then I met with Gavin and Nigel and they played me their demos – although we'd already met Gavin in about 1983, I think, when we were working with Haysi Fantayzee and Gavin was hanging out with the whole gang. Gavin was very young then, and I think he was quite shy.

'This time things were different; he was much more confident. The first thing that really struck me was the intro to "Machinehead". That was that, really. I'd just been to the States and I was listening to grungy bands like Brad, and all of a sudden we're off with this UK grunge punk band. It kind of fitted into place, and we got on really well, and we got on with it.'

'There are two reasons I wanted to work with Clive,' Gavin suggests. 'One was the fact that he'd written "Shipbuilding".' This of course, was the hauntingly pointed anti-Thatcher elegy Langer co-wrote with Elvis Costello. 'Obviously, if he'd written that song, he's got really good taste,' continues Gavin. 'The second was that he was English. Those were the only two criteria that I considered. We all met him for lunch in a pub in Camden, and we saw immediately that he's the sort who just wants to take over and ask about your life. He's really nurturing, and he just satisfies things in me – makes me feel good.'

Gavin laughs. 'On that first album, it was a case of Clive and Alan making us feel comfortable so we could express ourselves and be free and not weirded out. It's quite difficult going into a studio to make a record, and if there's people there to look after you, it's a lot easier. It was like a little teething period, before things slipped into place.'

The teething period wasn't without its cuts and bruises. The day before going into the studio, Gavin's penchant for football had landed him with an elbow in the mouth. It wasn't the best place for a singer to get hit right before beginning an album.

'My mouth was cut completely open, cut all along one side and just hanging open, so I looked like I had the biggest cold sore in the world. My whole lip had turned into a crust. Ugh! It was a terrible way to turn up and make a record.'

Much more seriously, by the time the band was ready to enter the studio, Nigel's father Kenneth was seriously ill, and would pass away during the recording. In fact, *Sixteen Stone* is dedicated to him and to Gavin's stepfather, who died just as the record was completed.

Nigel recalls, 'My dad was taken really ill a few days before we were due to start, so I had to leave to look after my mum and spend time with Dad. I came back ready to go in the studio on Monday and got a phone call on Saturday night from the hospital, saying he'd been taken ill again. I went straight there and he died a couple of days later. So even when we went into the studio, I didn't really enjoy that first album much; I didn't have the energy to argue my corner on anything; we started just forty-eight hours after my dad died.' Even now, Nigel has said, he finds it difficult to listen to *Sixteen Stone* because of those associations.

Clive Langer remembers that the difference between the band's musical interests and his and Alan Winstanley's wasn't as great a hurdle as might have been expected.

'After the first few days I think Gavin thought, What am I doing in a studio with these guys? They haven't listened to any PJ Harvey! So he brought all these records in and I pacified him a bit by listening to them.' He doesn't, he adds, see as great a gulf between pop and rock as others claim exists.

'When you break a song down, it doesn't matter how it's dressed. If it's catchy and has a chorus and a bridge and a verse, to me it's a pop song. It can be the heaviest thing, or drum'n'bass or reggae or whatever. There's a song there, and Gavin has chosen to dress his songs the way he feels comfortable, and I like that. I used to be a guitarist and I used to enjoy making a lot of noise. It's power. The guitar is such a physical thing. It's good that he's not just a lead singer.

'Gavin's playing has improved a lot over the years I've known him,' he adds. 'I remember on that first album we spent ages doing his guitar and then one day we got a much better sound and then he just did them all again quickly. You know, when songwriters play their own songs on the guitar, there's a unique and compelling way they do it, and you can get the greatest professional in the world to copy it and it won't sound the same. That's why people like Neil Young are so attractive.

'I think Gavin enjoys the whole process of making a record,' theorises Langer. 'He even enjoys the worrying. It's in his make-up; he's not going to stop worrying even if it's brilliant. He's quite changeable as well. One day it will all be great, and the next day it won't be. Actually, I get worried when he thinks things are really good, because you know it's going to turn the other way in a day or two. There are a lot of artists like that, and I've worked with some of them – Kevin Rowland [of Dexys Midnight Runners] and Morrissey especially.

'I think Gavin always really wanted Steve Albini to produce Bush, even on the first album, but it wasn't going to happen right away,' he continues. 'We weren't doing much work at the time, so we did it quite cheaply for them. But it worked out well, the balance between our inclinations and theirs. I think we were lucky we met when we did. I was brought up listening to Hendrix, Cream, loads of heavy music, blues, and it's really the same language. When I listen to Nirvana songs I hear melodies from Cream songs. It's all the same old stuff.

'I think Gavin's always been ambitious,' Langer adds. 'And you could see he was getting fed up with not making it. I think they all were. Except for Dave, who *had* made it, to an extent, having been in Transvision Vamp. I don't think anybody expected Bush to sell millions of records, though. I thought it would be great if they sold a quarter of a million. I admit I was shocked by how well they did with *Sixteen Stone* in the end.'

But not, of course, right away. 'That record took about two and a half months to make,' Langer recalls, 'but it wasn't released for about a year. I usually never play records after I've worked on them, but I remember when I listened to it in the summer after I made it, it did sound really good. Anyway, for quite a few months I thought it was a forgotten thing but, during that year, I went to see the band playing in clubs in London. They were good, but they weren't the best or most charismatic band I'd seen. They were just good, which is why I'm quite amazed when I go to see them play now. I think if you put them in a club now they'd be pretty good,' he adds, lifting an eyebrow to indicate a massive understatement. 'I think they'd be pretty intense.'

'We were probably under-rehearsed,' Gavin says of the recording of *Sixteen Stone*, which was delivered to Trauma in early April

1994 (by a strange coincidence, on the day Kurt Cobain died). 'Maybe it was just feeling the whole pressure of making a record, especially if you'd never had the chance to make one and you'd been a musician for a while.

'And, yeah, it was strange to work with producers who'd never done rock music. Maybe the fact that they don't know *how* to do rock music was the best thing. It did start off really badly, because Nigel wasn't around. We had to stop and start the record about four times, because of his father. And I remember thinking it was just crap really, that it wasn't happening. It's always like that: friction and weirdness and somehow then it just kicks in. And the fact that Clive and Alan didn't come from where we came from probably helped, and it seems so brilliantly ironic now.

'I remember, as it was coming together, that it began to dawn on me that people might actually hear what we were doing. And how weird and great that was. Whereas before it had always been that situation of making a demo, which you play once to your friends and then put in a drawer. And you might play the songs every now and again in a pub somewhere, but you don't really think about it beyond that. And I really vividly remember thinking about "Glycerine" and, for some reason, at that moment I thought – although I didn't know her – I wonder if Courtney Love would like it?'

And, although we're getting ahead of ourselves in the story by a few million records, Gavin continues. 'Which is why it was so strange, two years later, to be singing it on *Saturday Night Live* and Courtney came to watch me singing it.' He shakes his head. 'It's astonishing what life can do for you. And she told me she cried when she watched it.'

It's almost as weird, he adds, as the fact that *Sixteen Stone*, which would go on to sell eight million records, was considered to be rather a waste of tape by Hollywood Records, Trauma Records' distributor at the time the album was delivered. Gavin recounts the now-famous anecdote.

'The funniest thing was when we delivered it to Hollywood Records and they said – I'm sure you know this story by now – that not only were there no singles on it, there were no album tracks, either.' He shakes his head. 'It's amazing. I guess it's funny. But it's also why when we finished the record, it wasn't released for seven months and why, after all that work, we went back to painting houses.'

But they were proud of the album all the same. And, Gavin adds, 'Clive and Alan were proud of it, too, I think.' He smiles mischievously. 'It changed everything for them, too, changed the bands they worked with.' He laughs triumphantly. 'We ruined their lives!'

N

'All the songs on that first album were written before I ever knew we were going to get signed, or before I ever thought anyone would even hear them. For me, "Everything Zen" was just another song I was writing for the league of unpublished songs, on the longest list of unpublished songs ever written in north London.'

Sitting in the kitchen of the tiny flat at Montagu Square, working after Alex and Jasmine had gone to bed or before anyone else had woken up, Gavin wrote the songs that eventually made up *Sixteen Stone* over a period of a year and a half. Even though, as he says, he couldn't be sure they would become more than songs on demo tapes. And he already knew what happened to demo tapes.

'Until then, demos I'd made always seemed to be for my friends. And playing stuff to them was part of it. But of course, you make a demo tape and you'd only play it to your friends once. It would be the greatest thing ever when someone heard a song I'd done and asked, "Can you play that again?" That probably only ever happened to me about twice. And that's why I remember it!'

Of all the songs written for what would become *Sixteen Stone*, 'Comedown' would be the first. What's more, it was the first really Gavin Rossdale song.

'I can remember sitting there writing this song. I know exactly where I sat in my bedroom and everything. It's about Suze [DeMarchi], who I was seeing then. And writing it was just like unlocking a door. It was the first time I'd written a song on my

own. And it was just like . . . a dream state. A really quick song to
write; the kind where you tap into some kind of creative flow. It's
really cinematic to me and when I look at it now and read it, that's
exactly how I wrote it. I didn't change one word. It's weird.'

He pauses. 'Yeah, it's all that . . . paranoia about the future.
About feeling weird. I suppose it's my first low self-esteem
workout. It's funny; I've always managed to get myself in situations
where things just don't seem to work out that easily. That was a
scary time, that was an awful time. There I was, with nothing. And
I can see that's why it just flows. It seems so vulnerable to me, as
if that intense happiness we all long to feel is so temporary. The
verse is much more pensive and introspective and it's about the
time when I was away from everyone, whereas in the chorus you
can feel a release; the power of taking solace in the good things and
finding all the positive things. And it just fitted having that Billy
Cobham bassline, which made it groovy and to me totally unrock.
That was the first song I demoed and first song I played to Dave.'

Looking back, he says, he still feels like the same person who
wrote those words.

'It's a different time now, so I don't think I could write like that
or want to. It's strange, though: different things go on now, but
basically I just write about myself and how I feel and what I see
around me. So in some ways, it hasn't changed. People ask, have
you changed over the years? And you can; you can betray yourself
by changing. What's weird is, I know the mood of this song. It's
not so much the lyrics . . . just that I *know* that mood, if that makes
sense. A mood which I still totally feel and I love to be able to
continue having.'

'Comedown' was not only the first Bush song, it was the first step
on a path on which Gavin would begin writing by himself, without
collaborators, and set the course for his future band.

'I guess writing exclusively by myself has that old school thing
about it. Which sounds strange to say, since I came to it late. But
the first couple of bands I was in really didn't do it, didn't make
it.' And when the bands split up, as they did, he says, 'Every time,
I was like the last date standing at the bus stop. Everyone has left
me, my whole life,' Gavin emphasises. 'Which is probably why I
don't write with anyone anymore. In my first two bands I would
rely on the others to write; I just used to give my opinion of what
the music should be like. When I wrote "Comedown",' he adds, 'I
thought, My God, what have I done?

'Who wouldn't want to be, I don't know, Supergrass? Who wouldn't want to be handsome?' he asks with a grin, acknowledging that from 'Comedown' to the present, his songs have ploughed a furrow darker than the pop mainstream. 'And that's why I don't write with anyone anymore. It might go brilliantly, but it's hard to fight the fear that next week, suddenly they might not want to work with me. Obviously, I wouldn't turn something down if a bandmate came up to me and said, "Have a listen to this – it's called 'Black Hole Sun'." I wouldn't turf it out. I'm not an idiot. I just didn't want to give the impression that I was dependent on people; I think I have a terrible phobia about it.'

'Everything Zen', which Dave Dorrell recalls was no one's first choice as a single except the band's, and which even Nigel found 'a bit rocky', would go on to become the electrifying calling card that took Bush from nowhere to everywhere, via a playlist add at KROQ and massive listener response before listeners knew the slightest thing about the band responsible for it. Since then, it's been assumed that its savvy, *Zeitgeist*-surfing catchphrases like '*I don't think so*', and '*We're so bored/you're to blame*' and the ever-popular '*I don't believe that Elvis is dead*' are exclusively a comment on the America Gavin discovered in his months in the LA wilderness.

Instead, and rather unexpectedly, it was inspired by a magazine interview with Suede and David Bowie. 'That was about all the infiltration of Britpop,' Gavin insists. 'And mentioning Minnie Mouse is obviously a reference to David Bowie. That article came out when Suede were the greatest band in England, and they did that interview with Bowie. And it was just so . . .' The man who risked torment at school for liking David Bowie – and therefore risked his masculinity – shakes his head. 'Obviously I was jealous, but it was sickening. When I read that, I just felt so far away from ever having any career in music. This is my country . . . and *this* is the kind of music people are championing? And here I was, doing music that was 180 degrees away from that. That's what the "*kissy kiss*" part refers to – Suede and Bowie really getting on, being mates, and Bowie going "and it's just amazing how advanced your songs are for your first record". I wasn't angry with Suede,' he adds. 'But it just made me feel very far from ever resolving anything for myself.'

In between, of course, there's a host of other references to icons and touchstones. ' "*Raindogs howl for the century*",' he points out, 'is my two favourite people, Tom Waits [and his album *Raindogs*] and Allen Ginsberg [whose seminal poem *Howl* was the anthem of the Beat Generation]. I suppose the song is about youth culture – or just culture. Something that people search for or try for. And just how short you can fall and the mistakes you can make.'

Not everyone considered 'Everything Zen' a mistake, it would transpire.

'On that first tour, Lydia Lunch came up to me in a club in Los Angeles,' Gavin recalls. 'She passed me a bit of paper where she'd written "There's no sex in your violence – nice twist!" And she just walked away. I never even spoke to her.'

It was, as Gavin acknowledges, quite a moment to receive praise from another wordsmith, and a famously unsycophantic one at that. 'It was fantastic. Especially because as a song, it's a statement of intent.'

'Bomb', a popular live favourite, is frequently cited by Gavin, along with the album's title, as evidence of the UK-specific side to a band often thought of as exclusively American-influenced.

'That's to do with growing up in Kilburn,' he acknowledges of the song's subject matter, an IRA bombing in Covent Garden a year before the song was written. 'All those pubs in the area – The Cock Tavern, and Biddy Mulligan's, were famous for the IRA. And whenever we went to watch bands at the Kilburn National, Biddy Mulligan's was the first pub we went to, and there was such a weird energy about being around all those kind of people. You knew they were there.

'The hardest thing about writing a song like that,' he says, 'is that if you have feelings about these things, about political issues, how do you write it? Besides just saying, sure, war is bad?' In the end, Gavin settled on the politics of the personal. 'I just thought of the people who were in that bombing. I thought of a guy who was in the Convent Garden bombing so I just wrote it from his perspective; from the point of view of some man who's gone out shopping for his wife, and gets caught in it.'

'Testosterone' would become another enormously popular live track – though possibly, as Gavin admits, one whose critique of machismo, married to a ferociously rock-driven energy, might be overlooked by many of the people singing along.

From '*I'm real proud of my manhood*' to '*Got a big gold gun*' it is, he says, 'a totally straightforward view of maleness. It's a catalogue of all the things men are supposed to believe; a stereotyped view of how men look at themselves. So you have to talk about your dick, about your sexual prowess and all the coke you can do, and how we never cry, we just ball. About how you're never wrong. I think it's really funny,' he adds with a grin.

'It's always been such a big track live. And the whole thing is that it's good to have a bit of a laugh as well. It's also perfectly serious. And the funny thing is, I've probably suffered at the hands of the sort of person the song is about, and the guy who's singing along might be the kind of macho guy who likes staring me out in the pub. It doesn't happen now,' he notes. 'Maybe because I've gotten really good at deflecting people's stares, and I'm used to it. But it was just good to have a serious comment, but in a funny way, especially because I'm in a rock band and the comment is encased in a really big rock song. It's the same thing as when Gwen [Stefani of No Doubt, now Gavin's girlfriend] is singing "*I'm just a girl*", and she's making boys sing along.

'It's always strange, though,' he admits, 'when you're playing it and you're looking down and wondering if there's anyone out there who just doesn't get it. Whether they're just taking it at face value.' It's something he would consider even harder, he says, when Bush began touring and found themselves in places where having a big gun was particularly commonplace. 'Yeah,' he nods. 'Going to Arizona and places like that, where all you need is a driving licence to get a gun. And going into a shop where you've got Cheerios and Graham Crackers on one side, and guns on the other.'

'Glycerine', the album's gentlest song and a showcase for Gavin's voice and a rough/clean acoustic guitar, would not surprisingly become the track on *Sixteen Stone* that found its widest audience. In industry terms, its success had a simple explanation – which was that other demographic groups (girls, grownups, anyone widely supposed not to respond well to noisy guitar) found 'Glycerine' more to their taste than, for example, the harder-edged 'Machinehead'. Then again, 'Glycerine''s success might be because its devastatingly simply-put sketch of longing and loss is universal. Because, as Gavin says, 'It's like life: an unexplainable high and an unexplainable low. Because it all comes round. Because it's desperate and fragmented, and that's part of everyone's life.

'I really hate generalising,' he expands. 'Because everyone says that guys tend to like the guitar – or that's what they say they like – and with the girls, it's the lyrics. Well, that's not always true,' he smiles. 'I had a kid come up to me in CBGB's and he told me that

"Glycerine" was the first time he stopped and listened to the words in a rock song. And he told me this really quietly, almost conspiratorially, as though he didn't want to lose his cool. It feels really good when something like that happens.

' "Glycerine" was one of those ten-minute songs. Sometimes they'd just flow like that, and it felt brilliant to be able to write that way. It's such a good purging. It's a song about the impossible – about things that can't work out; about when you really want things to work, but you know in your heart that they can't.'

Considering the suggestion that its lines *'I'm never alone/I'm alone all the time'* were a strangely prophetic look at the up *and* down sides of fame and the isolationism at the core of his songs from then until now, Gavin insists, 'Yeah, but it was pertinent even then, for me. It wasn't projected, it was just how it was. How it's been, and how it probably will continue. It's a necessary part of my own makeup, I think. My blood flow. My DNA. My genes.

'There's a lot of fear in me,' he continues. 'But fear's just mortal, isn't it? Maybe it's about the dangers of being too aware of everything. It always seems that the people who are most careful are the ones who have the most accidents. I dunno, there's a sort of mad anti-logic to it – like the heaviest smokers and the Guinness drinkers living until they're ninety.

'It's funny,' he concludes, scanning down the page of lyrics to 'Glycerine'. 'At the time, they weren't even sure if they were going to release "Glycerine" [as a single to radio]. But when they did, things just flipped. I'm sad it didn't really get on the radio here,' he adds, gesturing to the country that lies outside his window. 'But I really enjoy singing it live and performing it solo. It's a weird sort of perverse test, a nightly test. To see if I can do it.' Ask him about the vulnerability at the heart of 'Glycerine' – and arguably at the heart of everything he's written – and Gavin replies, 'I've basically always written the same lyrics. I think maybe one of the first song lyrics I ever wrote had a hopeful theme – or maybe just that hope that love wouldn't fuck you over, or fuck you up or something – and then I thought, God, there's nothing more boring than hearing about that. If you feel that, why write a song about it? When I feel good, I don't bother to write any music. I go out and have fun. But in a way, songwriting seems to be a way to appreciate all the good things. Life is relative, and if you don't explore and embrace all the weird things you feel, how can you expect to fully get the enjoyment of it when it's great? There'd be no perspective if you didn't. I guess I don't understand those unbelievably easy, cheery people who are happy all the time. Especially when so many things are so frustrating for everyone, every day.

'I'd love to be able to write a "Michelle",' he says of the Beatles song. 'And I think that will come. My songs have a kind of sadness at their core, but with "Glycerine" or any of the slower calmer songs, they also reach out to people. Even with the bitterness of "Comedown", I did want to be sweet to her [Suze] as well. I just think about what I haven't managed to achieve yet,' he says of his lyrics, 'and I just don't know if I'm good enough yet to write a song, top to bottom, without any conflicts in there. I know that I'm fragmented and my mind changes. And if I could just not drift through a song, if I could have a top to bottom love song, I would try and go for it. But whenever I'm in the process of writing a song, it just doesn't seem to come out like that. I have to temper everything with its opposite.'

'Plus,' adds the former teenage punk, 'I hate not being able to play my music next to something by Johnny Rotten. I want to be able to play "Bodies" [by the Sex Pistols] next to my records. Whenever I get kind of stuck, I think of that; I think, Come on, get a grip.'

In the meantime, the twelve songs Gavin Rossdale had written for *Sixteen Stone* would – although he didn't know it then – go on to find about ten million people ready to get to grips with them.

Once *Sixteen Stone* had been completed, all it needed was a title. One came to Gavin as he sat in the Duke of Westminster pub in London's Crawford Street hearing a friend's anecdote about an encounter with a woman who'd billed herself as a seductive Swedish blonde. In the flesh, there was rather more Swede than he'd expected. Sixteen stone – that's 224 pounds – worth, to be exact. But if there's a joke in there about things turning out to be bigger than anyone could have predicted, the punchline wasn't due to arrive just yet.

More pressingly, Future Primitive – the band name no one but Brian Eno liked – had finally become Bush, egged on by the album's graphic designer David Carson, who thought a nice four-letter word looked much better on a CD than Future Primitive ever would. A side benefit, of course, was that future interviewers around the world would have endless opportunity to speculate as to whether the name had anything to do with Shepherd's Bush in west London (which it didn't, particularly). Or with *Cannabis sativa* bushes (which it might). Or with a rather affectionate nickname for pubic hair, either male or female (which it probably did, some days, depending).

But there still wasn't a record with Bush's name on it anywhere it mattered: to date, the only recorded and distributed proof of the band's existence was a lonely seven-inch single by Future Primitive, 'Bomb', backed with 'Bud', on the band's own label.

In the meantime, just as the album was delivered to Trauma and thence to its distributor Hollywood, one of the heads of Hollywood Records, Frank Wells, died in a helicopter crash. Wells had been Trauma's and Bush's supporter at the label and, after his unexpected death, the new movers and shakers at Hollywood reacted to the delivery of *Sixteen Stone* with something less than enthusiasm. Soon, Rob Kahane and his label were an idea with nowhere to go, or at least without a distributor to get them there.

In retrospect, Dave Dorrell insists that the dark days between April and November of 1994 weren't quite as dark as all that. Well, possibly just a little tiny bit dark around the very edges, maybe.

'Yeah, I'd been in that sort of position before, and I thought exactly that, that the record might not come out. But we'd made an album, after all. So it seemed stupid for it not to come out *somewhere*. And Rob Kahane was very keen to find alternate means of distribution. So that's what he did, and [before Interscope turned up] he talked to Indie, which was the largest independent distributor in the States at the time, so there was always the belief that somehow we'd get the record released.'

Neither he nor the band, he says, ever completely felt that Kahane had thrown up his hands, or indeed washed his hands of Bush. 'There were a few times when I might have thought about it, but I suppose that we were all naive enough to kind of think that, one, the record would get out, and two, it would probably sell a few copies. There was certainly a sense of frustration, but it was fate that dealt cruel cards. None more than the ones dealt to Frank Wells and his family that day,' says Dorrell. 'So we were, I think, keeping some perspective on things.'

The band didn't play much during that time, he confirms. 'Just a couple of gigs. We'd run out of money, and the record company didn't have any. We weren't going to play our stuff until we got distribution.'

In the meantime, there were still bills to pay. Nigel continued to work at his audio-visual job, trying to pay off his debts, and remembers being more than £12,000 in the hole before the band would eventually go on tour.

Gavin, for his part, still had the odd offer of work, though not always what he'd had in mind. He'd already turned down one opportunity to ditch Bush and pursue something else months earlier, when producer Butch Vig was sent a tape of Future Primitive's material. Vig didn't necessarily want to produce those songs, but he liked Gavin's voice and he was definitely looking for a frontperson for his new band, Garbage. In the end, Gavin laughs, Vig found Scotswoman Shirley Manson to sing 'Stupid Girl' instead . . . though the chorus Gavin sings by way of illustration suggests that he could have made a fist of it all the same – even if the frocks might have had to change size. In any event, a slightly different musical offer would come his way in the middle of 1994. Gavin recalls, 'I got this call from a friend of mine, Clive Black, who was the head of EMI. He'd known me for years and helped me, given me demo time, but never signed me. He'd seen us play a gig during that time – getting some friends down, trying to make it look like things were happening – and then he gave me this call. He said, "I've got this project. Have you got any pictures of yourself?" And I was like, "What do you mean, it's not about the band?" Anyway, I sent him a holiday snap and a larger photo. And when I asked what it was all about, it turned out to be a side project involving Nick Rhodes from Duran Duran and Warren, his guitarist.'

Gavin wasn't interested. 'But they had my photos, which I really wanted back, so I went round to meet Nick. And he had a huge [home studio] rig in his house in Fulham that must have been forty-eight tracks, about the size of those desks here,' Gavin says, motioning to the Westway studio desks from behind which he recounts the story. 'And he spent about forty-five minutes trying to turn it on. Anyway, he was really nice and I had a good time. We jammed a while in his studio, and it was cool.' But it wasn't exactly what he, let alone the rest of Bush, had in mind.

'It was very frustrating,' Gavin confirms of the unexpected hiatus between the album's completion and anything happening, 'because it just seemed as if that crazy leap of faith we'd taken in signing to a new label was, like, majorly in vain and we'd majorly screwed up. That was the worrying bit, realising we therefore didn't even have the chance to sign to, say, a [small] label like Food. And Trauma couldn't bring the record out, either. So that was tricky,' he says, in a triumph of understatement. 'We only played twice at that time, because it was just horrible. We played once at the Marquee, to 200 bored people. It was a nightmare.

'The worst thing was going back to [painting and decorating] work after I'd been so sure that wasn't going to happen, and having done that youthful, escapist thing of thinking, Nah, that's it, we've done that. And the very last job I had was like the ultimate

Groundhog Day job: I had twelve offices to paint, all exactly the same, so that every day was the same as the day before. You couldn't help but think it was symbolic. You can imagine: each one the same, and twelve of them. Each one took about four days. So by the time you finished one, oh great, there's only eleven more to go. People do that all the time for a living, and I can't complain about it,' he says. 'But it was just that, after the excitement and hope of doing my record, I wondered whether that was a small sign of the treadmill to come . . .'

The only consolation at the time, Gavin adds, is that the band hadn't actually heard Hollywood Records' famous quote that the album had no singles on it and no album tracks either. 'That, at least, we were spared. Though I think we had figured out that they didn't like it.

'In the end,' he confesses, 'I did that typical thing of getting a totally shitty publishing deal to keep Nigel in the band. He didn't want to leave, but he just couldn't physically afford to stay without some form of money. For seven months I tried to not sign; I was pleading with him not to, because I didn't feel we had to. In the end, it cost me about . . .' – his eyes widen at the ridiculous sums – 'four million dollars to buy the publishing back.' He shrugs philosophically. 'But it's just the way it is, isn't it? It was just what was needed at the time. It was no good, and it was very unfair. Obviously other people get really ripped off, and it wasn't like I got ripped off *per se*, it was just they got a much better deal than would have been the case if I'd been able to wait. But obviously, I kept Nigel and that's the way it goes. You can't lose sleep over it.'

And, in the end, even his *Groundhog Day* job has subsequently given pleasure to the inhabitants of those offices, to hear John Black – the man who gave Gavin the work – tell the story.

'Oh, yeah, the people in those offices – Harley Street dentists' surgeries – still talk about it. I worked there recently, and they still laugh and ask, "Have you seen anything of young Gavin lately? I remember him painting that wall for me." They tend to add, "I suppose he pays someone else to do that now." '

Over in Notting Hill Dave Parsons, who had managed to eke out his money from Transvision Vamp, was also running out of savings. What did he do to pay the bills?

Dave grimaces, faintly embarrassed. 'I don't know, all sorts of things. I'd drive someone to the airport for twenty pounds. Or I knew this girl who was a stylist and I'd drive her around. You know, just whatever I could, really. I worked on my friend's stall in the market for a while. Paint someone's flat . . . Same as everyone else really, though of course Gavin and Robin had been painting for quite a while, so they were a bit further up the ladder. My skills in that sphere were pretty poor, so I just got really crap jobs!'

Pete Hislop recalls Dave having a rather less enjoyable job, in telesales, as well. 'He absolutely hated it. It was exactly the worst sort of job for him. And it was one of those jobs you'd really only do if you were desperately short of money, where they say, "Right, come in for two weeks, we'll give you £200 and then after that, you make your money on what you sell." It's one of those jobs where you have to sit by the phone, and you've got someone talking in one ear telling you how to sell while you're on the phone to someone else. Dave's not a salesman, he never will be, it's not what he's about, not at all. And a lot of my friends had worked there, and they were doing quite well, because they had gone off into other aspects of that business. But it really wasn't Dave. So he lasted two weeks and then that was it. He couldn't do it anymore.

'In the meantime,' he adds, 'Dave just kept practising. My wife had moved into the flat we shared after we got married, and she was finishing her thesis. She'd be out in the little hallway on the computer, and Dave would be in the bedroom, and she said all she could hear was Dave going, "ding ding ding dum, ding ding ding dum", practising and practising until he got it right. She was on the computer just getting madder and madder, but somehow they both got through it without killing each other.'

At the same time that Dave was going through one of the worst patches in his life financially, things were looking up in another, and at least as important, area. Sarah Chope – a freelance accountant, another committed Notting Hill resident and Dave's girlfriend since 1994, explains.

'I'd seen Dave around, and knew him from the area. His friend Ben was the mutual acquaintance. We shared the same local pub.' (Dave, in a separate interview, says, 'I fancied her for years, but I never knew that I knew anyone who knew her. And then I finally met her . . .')

'I was getting to know him at the time just before things began to take off,' Sarah continues. 'And that was when he was really, really poor. In fact, that may be why it took a little longer for us to get together – he just didn't have the money to ask me out! Anyway, he was down the pub, probably making a couple of drinks last all night. He's never lived off anyone else, and I'm sure he didn't go in if he didn't have the money, because he wouldn't take a drink from anyone else if he couldn't buy his round. I lived two minutes away from the pub, so naturally I started sticking my head round the door a little more often, and ending up going in, the way you do when you start being interested in someone.

'No, I didn't worry about what he did or think that we wouldn't be compatible. And yes, maybe some of my friends did say, "Oh, Sarah, not a bloke in a band – when are you going to go out with someone who has a job?" Because we've all been through that. We really got together around the time of the Notting Hill carnival. I remember thinking that I should pace myself and maybe be a little bit better behaved and not quite so outrageous as usual. But the day of the carnival we were up on the roof of a friend's flat, and I remember dancing away madly in just my bra and shorts and running about and then thinking, Oh my God, have I blown it? So much for pacing myself . . .' She laughs. 'But I don't think he seemed to mind, actually.'

Fortunately, given that there wasn't a lot of money to go around, the two had plenty to say to each other. 'We just talked a lot, and discovered we had a lot in common – "Oh my God, you like that as well?" We talked about music and politics, I suppose, mostly.

'And of course, luckily for him, things with the band started to pick up quite soon after that,' she adds. Of course, neither Sarah nor Dave – nor, indeed, the rest of the band – were to know that at the time.

And finally, Robin Goodridge was doing the odd studio session. And, as always, painting. His longtime friend Rob Wells recalls one job that would, unexpectedly, be abandoned when – against all odds – Bush did finally break out of their *Groundhog Day* situation.

'Robin had been kipping at our house [in London], and he was painting our kitchen because he was still around and the band still hadn't taken off. Of course, then he went away on tour, and didn't finish the job. There's still a big mouldy patch on one of the walls, so I always think of Bush when I look at that patch. Mind you, I'm not bitter,' he laughs.

We can only assume that Julie Walters, stage and film actress and the star of *Educating Rita*, isn't bitter about her walls either. Her house was the last painting job Robin Goodridge would undertake. And he didn't finish that one, either.

'A really lovely woman,' Robin recalls. 'And I remember telling her the story about the band I was in while I was painting her house. I was getting these calls from Los Angeles, saying, "It's happening!" and telling me we'd be off to New York. And of course she said, "Oh, good, I really hope it goes well for you. But if not, you can always come back and do the bathroom!"

'I bumped into her a few years later and she was really happy to hear that it had gone well. You know, her career didn't take off until she was thirty – *Educating Rita* was her big break. I actually finished the kitchen, but never got to do any of the other rooms.' Which enabled him to give one of the more inventive excuses offered up by a member of the painting and decorating fraternity, he jokes. 'Yeah, something like, "Well, I've just gotta leave, 'cause I'm in a really successful band now. So I'm out of here, bye!" And then slamming the door.

'But seriously, there were no hard feelings, I think. After all, I'd enjoyed my work there, and I had a professional attitude. I was clean, courteous, and punctual. Actually,' he winks, 'punctuality wasn't really my strong point. I did like to start around ten . . .'

Robin was about to undertake a job that had even less to do with nine to five. And not very much to do with gloss paint, either.

P

'People, some of them, say they always believed I would make it. Well, it's nice of my friends to say so. But I don't believe them. It's unfair of me to get into their minds, because obviously they know how they feel more than I do, but I think it's a little selective, because there was more chance – I mean, far more chance – of it never happening. They would have had to have intense faith in me. Even I didn't know it was going to happen. In real life, this doesn't happen. No, I take it back. I'm just impressed by their having been so sure.' – Gavin Rossdale

Against all odds, it looked as though the record that almost never was was almost ready to come out. In November of 1994, some seven months after *Sixteen Stone* had been completed, Bush went to New York to make a video for 'Everything Zen', and then to Los Angeles to play an industry showcase at a club in West Hollywood, The Dragonfly. 'Everything Zen' had been on the radio in LA for four to six weeks, and Trauma would have all the requisite industry types – press, radio, television – in attendance.

So far, so good.

'Oh, yeah. We'd been out to dinner, we were on expenses, we'd been introduced to heads of record companies and there was a production line of Interscope people who'd flown in from all over America to see us,' Robin recalls. 'I remember me and Gavin standing on the balcony of the Sunset Marquis Hotel in Los

Angeles, laughing at how funny it all was. We'd been in New York all week, doing the video and general bullshit. It was the first time I'd been to America since I was a kid, and there we were being told we're fucking huge – or we're gonna be. And of course I was thinking, That's bullshit, everyone says that. It's just what Americans do, blowing it up way beyond all proportion. That's what you think, being English and still having that sort of anti-American attitude that you have when you first visit. Once you've been there a while you realise they're all right, and you know how to deal with Americans being American. Not that it's a bad thing, but it's different from English people being English. And it was the first time I'd come across American businessmen in the music industry. So there was this whole thing going on . . .

'And then we go and do this gig. It was a nightmare!' Robin laughs. 'And they'd hired this idiot, the soundman, to set up the PA, and he didn't get the power sorted out. So every time we started playing, the fucking power went out. And it happened four times. We started the set and everyone's screaming, and two minutes later, *thud*. No power. The funny thing was, all of us are standing in the dressing room going berserk after the third time. You've got all these people flown in from all over the world to see you, and you can't get fucking electricity sorted out. What kind of idiot is in charge of this whole fiasco?

'But we had this guy in the corner saying, "You guys are a really good band." And it turns out to be Kevin Weatherly from KROQ. You know, most people are begging Kevin Weatherly to play their records, and he's in our dressing room begging us to carry on playing. To go back on after the third time, you understand. At the time I didn't know who the guy was, I was just sitting there really pissed off. I felt so uncool. You know, when the power goes off, the one thing that doesn't stop is the drums. So everyone has stopped and I'm sitting there still playing, and my head comes up and everyone's standing around. *Three times*. In front of all these people who have flown in to see this English band, who are allegedly going to be huge. It was a ridiculous setup. In the end, it was sorted out by a friend of ours called Hein Hoven who was at the show, and we went back on.

'Funnily enough, you know, it all worked out brilliantly, because the Americans thought all English bands were like The Stone Roses, and had this huge attitude – the "we might play and we might not" thing. And because we kept coming back out each time, we blew

that whole preconception away. So maybe they thought, At last
there's an English band behaving like an American band. We were
a band that had a professional attitude and showed some knob, as
opposed to being all temperamental, Oasis-style. It was a great
outcome; I mean, what a buzz, you've got heads of record
companies wetting themselves over it. You can't lose in that
situation.'

Meanwhile, 'Everything Zen' was on its way to being a bona fide
hit, thanks to the influence of KROQ, one of the country's oldest
commercial 'alternative rock' radio stations, and the station to
which others in the format looked when setting their playlists.

Of course, no one could actually buy the record, because
'Everything Zen' – not unusually for a first track from a new band
– had been taken to radio in advance of the release of the record.
So, at the time, radio listeners had no idea who Bush were, what
they looked like, or even where they were from. They just liked
what they heard.

'In a way,' Robin theorises, 'the biggest marketing fuck-up – the
fact that the record wasn't even out – actually turned out to be the
smartest move. There wasn't any version of the single available in
the shops. The day it was first played on the radio, nobody had a
copy except KROQ. So the vacuum it created obviously helped us.
It could have fucked up completely,' he adds. 'You'd never have
seen us again and we'd never have this conversation and I wouldn't
be drinking in the afternoon. I'd still be at work covered in
semi-gloss!'

According to Kevin Weatherly, programme director at KROQ,
the decision to add 'Everything Zen' was simple.

'It's intuitive. First and foremost, it's got to be a piece of music
that we're passionate about, and if we're not, then we need to have
it proven to us. But yeah, we still kind of do things the
old-fashioned way where we hear something and, if we really like
it, we play it. And yeah, I had heard that they were nobody in
England, and it kind of figured because, as cynical and cliquey as
the music business in America can be, I know it's even more so over
there. So I knew they weren't a big deal there. And I didn't *care*.

'I would say that Bush have become one of the most important
bands of the 90s for KROQ, from the first time we played
"Everything Zen" and how that first record took off, all the way
to five tracks deep off that first album. "Everything Zen" did great,
"Little Things" did a little better, "Comedown" was probably the

biggest song on the album for us, and "Glycerine" and "Machinehead" were both huge. By the time we got to "Machinehead", fifteen months later, the band had gone from being one that no one knew about or cared about to probably the biggest band on the station during that time.' It's not just a little unusual, he adds, to play that many tracks from one album. 'We get maybe four or five of those albums a decade,' he says.

'Gavin's a star,' adds Weatherly. 'But the star-making process is kind of like connecting the dots. At first you hear the music and you like it, and you see the band and that takes you to another level. But first and foremost it's the music. We knew that Bush was potentially going to be a band that we were going to embrace, who could be more than just a song on the radio station. They could actually become one of our most important artists for that time.'

But that was still to come. In the meantime, Kevin Weatherly was still back at The Dragonfly, urging the boys to go back out and play.

'It takes a certain amount of guts to get through something like that and pull it off. It was a typical LA industry crowd that sits there with their arms folded saying, you know, "show me". Then the sound goes down. To overcome it and still win everyone over. Which is exactly what they did. And they were really super-nice guys, and I remember that when they finally got it going, it was electric.

'At the time, there was a lot of cynicism in the business, and the whole grunge movement was in decline, and so there were a lot of people who, you know, were assuming that they weren't "real". Or that they weren't "credible". It was all BS. At the end of the day, it's not the critics and industry cliques who decide what's cool and what's not. It's the kids, and they connected with the kids. They are definitely a people's band, went on to be the hardest working band in show business. Gavin's charisma and charm and the band's ability at performing live is what won people over.'

'Quite honestly, I think I'd never felt tested before. I never felt pushed by anything until we went on tour. Because if things were pushing me when I was younger, I just didn't care about them. I'd just be a punk about them. What's it like out there? It just makes you delirious. You know, you just feel like a warrior. I felt like Kurtz's sidekick. I'm just so happy that we could go into proper warfare. It's not like a two-week pissy tour around Belgium, it's really hardcore. It's a war, and you're in it.'

Gavin Rossdale found what he'd been looking for. Welcome to the *Sixteen Stone* tour of duty: 230 dates in 16 months.

24 JANUARY TO 25 APRIL, 1995

New York, Miami, Tempe, San Diego, Sacramento, Palo Alto, Seattle, Portland, San Francisco, Los Angeles, Reno, Salt Lake City, Denver, Lawrence, St Louis, Minneapolis, Madison, Cincinnati, Chicago, Detroit, Cleveland, Toronto, Providence, Boston, Los Angeles, Washington, Philadelphia, New York, Virginia Beach, Atlanta, Augusta, Orlando, New Orleans, Houston, Austin, Indianapolis, Milwaukee, Springfield, Memphis, Nashville, Dallas, Zephyr Hills, Miami, Paris, Milan, Madrid, London, Antwerp, Amsterdam, Cologne, Hamburg, Stockholm

When Bush turned up in New York City in January 1995 to play CBGBs, the venue whose name is probably required by rock and roll law to be prefaced with 'the legendary', they were obviously excited. CBGBs is, after all, the birthplace of New York punk. It's also a rather small and shabby venue, with legendarily shocking toilets and a dressing room in name only. But for a fledgling UK act beginning its first North American tour, you'll do well to fill it, no matter how many tickets their record company buys to give to whatever industry and media types can be bothered to get down to the Lower East Side to see the latest hopefuls.

Michael Pagnotta, the band's US press officer for both *Sixteen Stone* and *Razorblade Suitcase*, remembers that everyone was in for a bit of a surprise at Bush's CBGBs debut.

' "Everything Zen" had been on the radio for maybe a month, but to be honest there had been almost no press about Bush. Maybe a few mentions here and there of the single, and those were pretty negative. The record hadn't even been released commercially.

'But we turned up, and there were lines around the block. The place was packed with sweaty-bodied people, and the band were absolutely great. I mean, CBGBs is a very small room, and if you're fraught, it shows, you know.'

'I definitely remember the huge lines outside that gig,' Robin says. 'And imagine, we actually sold out our first gig in America. And it was absolutely packed!'

'When we'd been to LA for the showcase, and heard "Zen" on the radio, sure, it sounded brilliant,' Nigel said. 'But coming back over for that first tour, it was hard not to think, Jeez, I hope it's still happening. I hope they're still playing our record. I was very anxious. You end up having to buy *Billboard*, because you don't want to believe what the record company are telling you.

'So when we arrived to play CBGBs, we had to go out to Tower Records to do a signing and, to be honest, we thought there probably wouldn't be anyone there. But it was packed. And CBGBs was rammed. It took us twenty minutes just to get to the stage.'

And then it was time to hit the road to Miami, and a three-month tour that would, unbeknownst to the band, only be the start. Supported by a skeleton crew of four – tour manager Gary Basil, sound engineer Razza Sufi, bus driver Guy 'Bone' Johnson and technician Clint Letulier – the band would see some of the hardest, least glamorous and most gruelling tour action of their careers. They didn't know it yet. They also didn't know they would be doing it for nearly two and a half years without much of a break, even when they stopped to make a second album – but that's getting ahead of our story.

Bone, a former St Louis Blues defenceman and later a trainer/sports therapist before he was drawn into the world of rock'n'roll, remembers meeting the band at the beginning of the tour.

'I'd been driving a tour bus for probably seventeen years and I was very fed up with the business. I'd had my own bus for years, but I was at a place where I was very willing to quit, and I told the boss when he sent me on this pickup, "If I don't like this lot, I'm not staying. I'm on the plane. I've got two million miles on the road and I've been everywhere. There's nothing to keep me here unless I like these people." ' As it happened, he did. And then some. 'The thing that was so brilliant about meeting them at this time is that they needed me, and it was a while since I'd been needed.

'We had a bus full of people. And equipment. I was driving the bus and doing loadins. It was basically the band and the crew – me, Clint and Razza – and not only would I drive six or seven hundred miles a night, but then I would get them bedded down, go to the trailer for a sleep, go back to the club, and then sleep for another two hours.' Bus drivers aren't usually supposed to do all that. 'Yeah, but that's just the way things developed. We were very short-handed and they were very new to this and it took everyone's work to make it happen. And we grew at such a massive pace; we went from clubs to three thousand-seaters on the first tour and we were undermanned the whole time. And, for the better part of the three years, I did security, too. I did it because I wanted to, and because I didn't trust them with anyone else.

'It was difficult. You don't know how difficult it was. Money? There was no money. We got twenty dollars a day *per diems*. We had enough to buy two cheap hotel rooms so everybody could have a shower, and if somebody wanted to watch something on TV there'd be ten guys in one room. There was no catering at shows of this size. We'd have to ask the club owners to get us a decent meal from McDonalds.'

It wasn't something Bone had to be doing, by the way. 'I'd just come off a Guns N' Roses tour, and then Paul McCartney, all shrimp and lobster catering. Doing this kind of tour with Bush, I was doing something that I hadn't done in years, but it was something that I had to do. And there's been many times since then that Dave [Dorrell] has told me to quit working so hard, but it's just not in me. If someone says, "Stop, I'll do that for you," I'm never going to enjoy my meal because I'll be wondering if it's been done.'

But it went well. No one went home, no one got too sick, no one ended up in jail. 'Oh, God no,' Bone laughs. 'Not even Clint. Of course, it's not all love and kisses. There's the fatigue that comes from playing five nights a week and sleeping two hours a day and not having the right food and shit conditions and lousy rain and it all affects you. There's days when we love each other and days when we'd rather not be in the same room. But it's never lasted longer than the incident. Sure it was hard as hell, but everybody knew that's what had to be done at the time. They had a goal and that was to show North America what they could do. And I think they had something to prove to themselves.'

And prove it they did. Dave Parsons – master of understatement and, with Transvision Vamp, the only member of Bush to have toured America extensively before this expedition – says, 'America is a really tough place. It can break bands. Destroy them. Finish them, because those tours are really, really, really hard work.

'You can turn up in Cleveland, and nobody's ever heard of you. It's quite demoralising to drive and drive and drive to find you've got a difficult audience, or maybe you have an audience but they've never heard your songs, somebody's just done a good PR job.

'You need to be hard. The first tour started off well and kept going well, and we could see that it was getting bigger and bigger, with each town we hit. Remember, it was February, the middle of winter, and we were heading across the mid-West. We were all on one bus, us and the crew, and pulling the gear in a trailer behind us. Since it was a club tour, you wouldn't go on stage till eleven at night, and you would have done interviews all day.

'We used to get off the bus and just do interviews, starting at about ten in the morning. Someone would go to a radio station and someone else would do a phone interview with the local paper. The problem is that for any record company or promoter, when a band is ready to work hard, if you look at their schedule as a bit of paper it's easy to say, "Okay, from half past one to half past two this afternoon you're not doing anything in there" and they fill it up. It's fine on paper but the reality is that people can only take so much. Especially when you finish playing at midnight, the crew finish loading out at half past one and you have to wait up for them before you can get on the bus and go to the next town.

'It got so that by the time we got on stage every night we were streaming with colds. It had become the 'flu tour, really, by the time we got to Cincinnati. As soon as we finished the gig that night, we all got carted off to Chicago and the girl from the record company came and met us and took us straight down to the hospital where we all had people sticking lights down our throats and in our ears and giving us 'flu jabs. That's what *that* tour was like.

'And of course, no matter how you feel, you can't take a day off. I don't think we've ever cancelled a gig for anything like that,' he adds. In fact, as the band's US agent John Marks and European agent Mike Greek confirm, Bush have never cancelled a date due to illness which, with the sort of schedule they have had, is practically unprecedented.

Dave continues, 'Everyone in the band has just been absolutely determined. You know, you just do it. And that's important for band morale, for the sense of being in it together. If someone feels bad, then everyone else covers for them, gives a bit more. I mean obviously it's harder with Gavin, because he's gotta sing it every night. But, you know, we're tough.'

Even so, fatigue can do your head in. Or at least prevent you from getting to the lobby.

'I remember one gig on that tour where we were staying in some little tiny hotel/motel and we were all supposed to leave at seven in the evening to get to the gig. We were just knackered. So we're waiting for the bus driver, who brings a huge cooking pot with him, puts it in his room and cooks himself up stew every night. Anyway, we all get in the lift and stand there, asking each other things like, "Oh, did you sleep?" "No." "Did you watch *Star Trek*?" "Yeah." We kept talking and it took about five minutes to realise that we weren't going anywhere. The doors are shut and we're just standing there like sheep, patiently waiting to get where we were going, but no one had remembered to push the lobby button.

'Why did we try so hard?' he muses. 'Because we spent so long waiting for it. We spent what seemed like years trying to get a deal and trying to get something to happen and really believing in what we were doing, when really very few other people believed in us. And finally we got a record deal, got that album finished, then the whole Hollywood thing fell down around us. And that last year we were really, really poor. I was more skint then than I've ever been in my whole life, even when I was seventeen or eighteen. I had less money and owed more money than I ever had. So when we got given this opportunity, this little beacon of light at the end of the tunnel, we knew how long we'd waited to get that opportunity and there was just no way we were gonna let it go. I guess that's what they say about people paying their dues. I wouldn't say that everyone had to be in that situation before they could be a credible musician. You might be lucky enough to step into a band and have everything go perfectly well for you. But then you're very, very lucky.'

The good side to the 'Flu Tour Without End, however, was that things were going well. With 'Everything Zen' the band's first US radio number one and four more tracks from *Sixteen Stone* – 'Little Things', 'Glycerine', 'Comedown' and 'Machinehead' – waiting in the wings, America was starting to realise it would be a long time before it had had enough of this band.

'It started off for about a month,' Dave relates, 'and they said, "This is good, we can put on some more dates." And about three weeks into that it's, "We can put another five weeks, then." So we do it and then it was yeah, yeah, let's not stop, 'cause you don't want to miss your chance. You don't wanna blow it. And eventually we did three months solid, from January through to April. And you do have times thinking, What am I doing? But you do know what you're doing, and you're glad you're doing it. It's a job, and how can we moan about a job like ours?

'I think it's important to try harder,' he adds. 'The moment you stop, the audience starts to care less.'

In fact, according to Nigel, the audience may sometimes have cared too much for its own safety. He recalls playing Cleveland on the first tour 'and staring up in horror at a kid climbing along the girders of the roof. Everyone stopped and watched him, and no one could do a thing, and then he fell. Must have been about fifty feet down. Fortunately he was okay; it might have helped that he was drunk. Still, it was really horrible, and everyone freaked out'.

Sometimes, it was all merely unnerving, especially for a guitarist whose previous experience with determinedly alternative acts had not prepared him for the youthful enthusiasm of the crowds that would greet Bush Stateside. 'I remember playing in San Diego with Elastica supporting us. It was a local radio station's free gig and I remember going up on the stage to the sound of an entire audience screaming. I looked out, and I swear everyone out there was fourteen! And I'm onstage thinking, That's it, I'm going home. Bloody hell! I'm thirty-one years old! I can't deal with this. I was happy at the response, of course, but I was also pretty bemused. The thing is, though, you don't choose your fans. You always imagine your fans will be people like you, your own age or your own kind of person, and then you get there and find out they're not. But you realise that you don't choose your fans, they choose you. And it's brilliant that they're there.'

Robin Goodridge, whose intensely physical job as drummer is arguably the hardest and most demanding of all, thinks back to that first tour and says without hesitation, 'I loved it.

'Think of it. You're sitting at home in England in your little house, and suddenly you're transported to the sort of places you'd never go as a tourist.

'And as we were doing it, after the first month, it just started to explode.

'I remember playing a bar somewhere in the South. After a few shows, we'd had to start asking the promoters to put a barrier in front of the stage because things were getting so crazy. What was happening was that everyone in the front row was landing on the stage, and the mics were falling over and everyone was standing on me and Gavin's trying to sing, and it was like, oh God, we've got to do something about this. We all end up with two yards of the stage we couldn't use because there were kids landing on it. So we sent this letter out to all the promoters, asking for a barrier and saying, yeah, it might seem dumb, but trust us, there is a reason we're asking you to do this. So we get to this gig and it's a bar. A bar at one end and a big long stage at the other. And there was a carpenter there when we arrived, and he was making a crash barrier out of slats of wood. We looked at it and said, "Are you sure?" And he said, "Yeah, sure, that'll hold."

'We weren't so sure, of course,' he laughs. 'But we didn't really have a choice; we had to get on with the gig. And within about three songs, it all crashed and there were bits of wood everywhere that the audience kept handing back to us up on the stage. Eventually, the venue manager ended up calling the Sheriff because it got so crowded. It was just ridiculous! And so this guy comes up onstage – gun in a holster, the lot – and it was like, "Alright, you all know who ah am. These boys are down here playing a show for you and you've all got to move back. Move back, now!"

'We couldn't stop laughing, because he was such a *Dukes of Hazzard*-style Sheriff. It was the first moment of real middle America we'd seen and it was hilarious. But for all that, it was such a fun show. It was like being in The Who. I couldn't stop laughing. It was one of our funniest baptisms of fire, realising that now we understood what we hadn't quite believed yet.

'Other people watching from the outside probably thought Bush "just exploded", like everyone says, but from the inside we saw it as a momentum thing. Every day we did it. Every day it was another radio show before the gig, and DJs and heads of radios telling us it was the biggest thing they'd seen for years for one act. Of course, it's human nature to be cynical about it until you see it yourself, especially if you're English and you're in America, because American bands believe they have a right to make it in their country. I mean, I'd never thought about America that way. I thought it was somewhere you go on tour for two weeks like everybody else does. And we ended up with two or three years!

'Of course, there were horrible things, too,' he adds. 'I missed my brother's wedding; I was in Toronto that day – freezing, snowing and hideous – and I sent him . . . a fax,' he laughs. 'A fax. I couldn't afford to say, right, I'm going to spend seven hundred quid and fly back. We were six weeks into an American tour, our first ever, and I certainly didn't have the money. I didn't know it was ever going to last. The idea of flying home was not a possibility. Unless I was dead, I wasn't going to get away with not doing the gigs.

'That tour taught me the true meaning of insomnia, too,' Robin adds. 'We shared rooms. We had a rotation system and this night I was sharing with Clint. And I'd done a gig, of course, and I was really tired but I couldn't sleep, and I spent the entire night lying in bed reading with a torch. It was eight in the morning and I still hadn't slept, and I was getting more and more manic, reading more and more voraciously. And I just remember going to breakfast and thinking, Fuck, I've got to do something about this. That's when sleeping pills came into the picture, and it was a revelation after so many weeks of feeling horrible. I don't take them any more because they're horrific, eventually.

'Gav's quite an insomniac, too. I shared a room with him for a long time and that was difficult, because just as I'd be getting off to sleep, he'd wake up and order tea. He gets up early. Well, he doesn't so much now because he's trained himself. But at that time, yeah, it was horrible. Because your head is full of so much stuff: you're thinking, Are we happening? Are we happening? Has it happened? It's not just the gigs, it's the thought of everything else. At the time, we couldn't help thinking, Is there any point that this road ends and we land in a ditch marked The End Of Our Career? That was what was going on in everybody's minds. You're in or you're out.'

30 APRIL TO 17 JUNE, 1995

Louisville, Winston-Salem, Charlotte, Sea Bright, New Britain, Pittsburgh, Detroit, Cleveland, Columbus, Grand Rapids, St Louis, Chicago, Minneapolis, Milwaukee, Buffalo, Harrisburg, Washington, New Orleans, San Jose, San Francisco, Reno, San Diego, Phoenix, Las Vegas, Ventura, Los Angeles

The first Bush tour of America ended and the band returned home to England, where the world at large, and possibly even the band's family and friends, had no real idea of what had been happening across the pond. Even in Europe, however – where the promotion of *Sixteen Stone* had faltered when Interscope changed distribution deals and neither the previous distributor, WEA, nor the new distributor, Universal/MCA, really made headway – the band's live shows were eliciting interest.

Mike Greek of The Agency, the band's European booking agent, recalls that initial response in Europe to a road-honed band was positive.

'I remember going to see them in Paris at The Arapaho, which was a small, 300-capacity club, and I stood there with the promoter, Salomon Huzet, from Garance, one of the leading promoters in France. We both watched this band do an hour set, and were absolutely blown away by their energy. That night I remember Salomon talking to Gavin about how he wanted to bring him back to France and bring him to Bordeaux, so they could sample some of the best red wines! I think the idea was if they came to France and put a lot of effort into it, he would make sure that we played in some good wine regions.'

But there was more American beer to be faced before the band would get to the promised French wine. (In fact, Mike notes, Bush still haven't had a chance to sample Salomon's favourite wines. 'Maybe this next tour,' he jokes.) Almost before they had unpacked their bags, it was time to come back to the USA. And according to the band's North American agent, John Marks of the William Morris Agency, who was introduced to Bush via his longtime friendships with Trauma's Rob Kahane and Paul Palmer, things were going according to plan. Better than that, in fact. A man not given to overstatement, even Marks expresses surprise at what happened.

'We had had early conversations, before the band began touring, about their wanting to work hard. But often one has those conversations and the band fully intends on working hard, but just doesn't enjoy life on the road and so doesn't follow through with that game plan. Our plan, rather than put them out on a support slot, was to put them into the clubs; to learn how to work a small stage and build it up. I've always felt that sometimes the crucial mistake is when a lot of young bands get on a tour [as a support band]. They end up being good in front of 3,000 people, but they haven't honed their craft and are unable to present a really good live show on their own later. But with Bush, we worked it the other way, where they were always the headliners. And to this day in North America, Bush has never supported anyone in a conventional show. They've always been the headliners. We've billed them that way and it's worked really well. They've turned out to be a great live band, which comes of working from the club level on up.

'Bush never had an attitude at all in the early days, unlike many bands. I think they were very, very devoted to touring and getting out on the road, and I rarely heard any feedback from the road where they told me a club wasn't appropriate. They were never prima donnas, they were always hard workers. And almost all the feedback [from venues and local promoters] was really positive. Almost from the beginning, we were selling tickets. As agents, we represent acts that are only capable of selling clubs or theatres, and always maintain a loyal following at that level, but with Bush everyone could tell this was going to translate best on a big stage.

'I was on the road with them a lot. I remember one date down in Florida where I really realised that this thing was going to blow up and be huge, and it was on that trip that I talked to them about coming back to America much sooner than we thought, just to continue the momentum. I think it was then that I knew we needed to get touring and that this project was going to get there a lot sooner than even I had anticipated.'

Which is why, less than a month after the band's first tour of North America ended, they were back on the road again.

Dale Meekins, guitar technician and Los Angeles native, has been in the business since 1985, 'when I started helping friends because I was the only one who had a truck out of all of us. And one thing led to another'. Which is an understatement. In this line of work,

'if you're good at your job, people hire you back', which is why the
two last big bands Dale had worked for, he stayed with for six
years and three respectively. 'I'm very monogamous,' he laughs. But
even for a monogamous technician, things can change with
lightning speed, and switching bands is consequently a lot like
'changing wives'. Well, one night, at the beginning of Bush's second
tour of America, Dale changed wives 'in the space of about five
minutes'. A friend who had worked for Bush asked if Dale knew of
a guitar tech going spare. A few minutes earlier, Dale's present
employer Mötley Crüe had cancelled their tour.

'So I said, "Yeah, I'll do it." And I left that night,' he grins. 'I've
been with Bush ever since.' He turned up in Louisville, Kentucky,
'and handed Nigel his guitar. He said, "Hi, I'm Nigel." And I said,
"Hi, I'm Dale." ' And that was that.

'What did I know about them? Well, I saw part of a video on
MTV – I think it was "Everything Zen" – but I only really copped
the tail end. And that's the only thing I knew about them; I didn't
even know they were English until the night I left. When I first saw
them play, I can't say I thought they would sell as many records as
they did, but I thought, These guys are good. Oh, they were
learning, but they were good. And they're touring veterans now. I
think they were surprised – as I was – how it exploded. I've been
part of the upswing with a band, but it was always a lot slower
than this. And I've been on the other side, too, when bands went
down. But Bush just rocketed and stayed there. I think they were
surprised at it. Everyone in the world was.'

Not everything Dale would learn from Bush had to do with
career trajectories. For one thing, he would get a crash course in
English manners. 'Nigel still says thanks for every single guitar
change. Most people in bands have bad attitudes. Listen, these guys
are nicer today than when I met them, even, or at least in a position
to be more generous. But even then, they were great. Manners and
being polite. Maybe it *is* an English thing. I know bands who
haven't even had a gold record, much less what Bush have sold, and
they have the worst attitudes of all; complete assholes who haven't
been even one per cent as successful as Bush.'

Not only that, but Bush would prove to be friendly to their crew
in ways most bands don't bother with. 'They hang around the crew
a lot,' Dale insists. 'There's a group of us, the guys who've been
here the longest, and we all go out together. When they go out to
dinner, they make sure a few of us get to go, too. They like our

company and we like theirs, and I'm sure it's good, because we work harder. You don't mind working hard for anyone who's that generous. Everybody wants to do the Bush tours, you know,' he adds. 'Everybody in the business. I'm serious! Because they have such a reputation, from the most part through us, about how great they are to work with. They get phone calls all the time: Do you need this or that, are you looking for this kind of person? We all get asked. They have the best reputation.'

Bone agrees. 'One area that is completely unique to this band, in my experience, is that they have done everything they could to keep that band/crew separation thing from happening. They get to the gig early. They eat with the crew. They're not aloof or untouchable. There's an incredible bond between crew and band.'

That summer, the band would play their share of radio-sponsored band festivals in North America, and then some.

'Oh, God, we did so many festivals, so many radio tours. "Loserpalooza", they call it,' Robin cracks. 'I love that. It means your career isn't far enough down the line to do your own show or pull with just your own cred. Everybody's much of a muchness on those shows; all these new acts with one hit single.

'We'd run into English bands on these tours, too,' he adds. Still comparatively little-known back in the UK, Bush were already a more sizeable proposition in North America than their much-hyped British colleagues would have preferred to believe. When those bands saw the reality, they weren't always best pleased.

'The English bands were always really moody with us, because they just thought we were uncool. Of course, we didn't really care. You'd always get the impression they wanted to say, "You know, you're not really doing anything in England." In which case we could have said, "Yeah, but we're headlining here, you idiot!" They didn't say it, but you could tell by their attitude. Whereas American bands were really nice. We were probably the fastest climbing band that specific summer, and we ended up headlining most of those shows. The promoters would say, "I know we booked you to play this slot, but it's really not fair to have anyone go on after you. We expect half the people will leave if you don't go on last." Even at that, it's traditional for the headliner to go on second to last. But they'd beg us to close. That's when we started to believe it was all for real, because when you're third on the bill, you don't know how many people there are your fans, but when you're begged to go on last . . . One night, we didn't go on last, Letters To Cleo were last, and we were mortified after we came off to see this band setting up and everyone in the audience starting to leave. Which is really not cool because after all, they've only got to wait another forty-five minutes. That's when we realised things were going really well.

'A lot of the revelations came when we met the kids afterwards,' Robin adds. 'One of the best things Trauma did was to link just about every single show that we ever did with a local radio station. So we just ended up with massive free advertising – not to mention endless interviews, and meet-and-greets afterwards where you have thirty or forty competition winners traipsing into the dressing room. It was a big circus, but it was great, because people were just so excited to meet us, really genuinely pleased. And you know, there's a difference between being fashionably popular and having the real old-fashioned genuine kind of fans. We realised we might actually get to be around for more than one record, and that these people have given you a year out of their life and if you keep making decent albums, they'll stay with you.'

Simon Halfont, still living in Los Angeles, remembers one such radio show. 'I saw them play a KROQ radio show that summer, and again, that's when it really hit home to me. It was a charity thing, all big names, and yet it was Bush's performance that made the hairs on the back of your neck go up. There's sixteen thousand people there, and they're singing every word of every song. It's astonishing to see that happen in such a short period of time. Every band got up and did five songs, and Bush were the only band on that day who got that reaction. It wasn't even at night; it was the middle of the afternoon in the sunshine, outdoors. So to get that vibe, that amount of noise, and that number of people singing every song, that was simply incredible.'

20 JULY TO 26 JULY, 1995
Nottingham, Glasgow, Birmingham, Stoke, Manchester, London

Meanwhile, back in Blighty, not quite as many people were aware that Bush had made even one record, let alone a hit record. Nevertheless, the band returned home in July to play six dates in venues which were much smaller, it would be an understatement to note, than those they had been headlining in America.

They didn't have to do it, of course. But they did.

Dale Meekins, a man who probably hadn't worked in a venue

that size in some time himself, insists, 'Nah, they weren't upset to come back and play those places, it's just that they obviously wished they'd be as big over here in the UK. But you've got to commend the band for doing it, because they were already so huge. But when we came over and they played little clubs, they honestly put on exactly the same show for every audience. I know a lot of bands who would just stand there and be miserable but, with Bush, it's the same show, always. And the audiences were really into it, which might have been a surprise for some people. I've never seen anybody just stand there and stare at a Bush gig; everyone always goes nuts.'

Mike Greek, almost apologetically, recalls that the first show must have been a bit disconcerting for the band. 'It was a venue in Nottingham called the Clinton Rooms, which had been used by The Jon Spencer Blues Explosion and a few bands before, but probably hasn't been used much since. I remember turning up and the place looked like a Bar Mitzvah hall. They did an absolutely storming show, but afterwards when we drove back to London I could tell that everyone was a little bemused by it.'

Nigel Pulsford recalls that, 'The nicest thing about that first tour here was all the kids saying, basically, "You're not an American band, you're an English band, you're *our* band." It's a very nice feeling to be told by someone that you're "our band". When we played Manchester there was practically a riot; the kids invaded the stage. I got so fed up all night with kids falling on me, but it was great, though. When the *NME* reviewed it,' he laughs, 'the guy couldn't quite work out what was going on. It was mad!'

Dave Parsons, asked whether the band was offended by the change in venue size, shrugs. 'I dunno. I think I felt like, "They're really gonna see a gig tonight!" You know, it was more a case of remembering that, yeah, we might be here today, but we're gonna play so well we're not gonna be here next time we come through, that's for sure. Personally, yeah, you'd rather not be playing a place like that, but you just make sure you play really, *really* well and you never have to go back there again.'

Ever scrupulously honest, he adds, 'I think if we had to go back there again, maybe we wouldn't be so pleasant about it. Still, it was a good set of dates. I remember a great show in Leeds, really rammed and hot and sweaty, and the venue was so small I could see this guy and girl snogging all the way through the set in front of me. I always wondered if that should be a compliment,' he grins.

'I think it's brilliant, though. Imagine being sixteen years old and you and your girlfriend go to see your favourite band and go right down the front and snog all the way through. I mean, why not?

'We don't throw strops,' he adds. 'On stage we've always been very professional about that sort of thing. People have paid to come and see you and it doesn't matter if there's a hundred of them or fifty thousand, you still have to play a gig. It doesn't matter how bad it sounds or how bad you feel or how ill you are, you just have to do it. It's appalling to get too precious; it's important to keep the audience in mind. Otherwise, you could get really picky with your gigs, couldn't you? You could play really hard when you enjoyed them or, when you didn't like where you were, you could just say, "Oh, I can't be bothered." And once you start doing that, you're only ever gonna want to play in New York, London and LA. And you can't do that.'

15 AUGUST TO 1 DECEMBER, 1995

Toronto, Montreal, Henrietta, Worcester, Harvey's Lake, Detroit, Cleveland, Louisville, Washington, Philadelphia, New York, Albany, Pittsburgh, Chicago, Milwaukee, Omaha, Kansas City, St Louis, Cincinnati, Nashville, Memphis, Springfield, Boulder, San Francisco, Los Angeles, Dallas, San Antonio, Austin, Baton Rouge, Pensacola, Tampa, Orlando, Miami, Atlanta, Utrecht, Amsterdam, Cologne, Hamburg, Berlin, Copenhagen, Oslo, Stockholm, Lund, Frankfurt, Bamberg, Munich, Stuttgart, Salzburg, Vienna, Casena, Modena, Portsmouth, Liverpool, Leeds, Manchester, Edinburgh, Birmingham, Bristol, London

Ross Duncan, born in Scotland, resident in North Wales but a lot more frequently resident on a tour bus, has the Chinese character for 'respect' (that's 'to respect others', rather than 'give me respect') tattooed on his arm. You can call him 'Rossweiler' if you like, because most people do. In fact, he ends his stream of tour anecdotes by saying of Bush, 'I love them and I think they're brilliant. And I wouldn't say that if I didn't mean it. My nickname's Rossweiler. I do *not* kiss ass.'

Starting his career as a promoter and then moving into the tour manager's chair (if that's an appropriate term for someone who so rarely gets to sit down), Duncan has worked with more bands than you've had hot dinners, from Biohazard through to The Moody

Blues. In the last nine years, he says matter-of-factly, he's had three weeks off. It's certainly not the only reason he would be perfect for a job the fates had in mind for him a few years ago, but it couldn't hurt.

None of which he knew, of course, that day in 1995 when, improbably enough, Duncan was at home in North Wales.

'I was painting my kitchen and the phone rang and it was Mike [Greek, Bush's booking agent for Europe and the Far East].' Ross had known Mike for years, since Greek was an eager, promising placement student at The Dance Factory, a company in Glasgow where Duncan was a promoter. 'I had a bit of time off coming up and Mike said, "I've got this band coming over from America and they're going to be the biggest thing I've ever signed, and I really need your help. They're only doing a week in England, it's all shit gigs, and I know it's not the kind of thing you usually do, but could you please look after it for me?" And as it happens, I did have that week off. First of all, you never turn work down, and secondly, because of my friendship with Mike, I knew that if he needed someone to come in and run it the way he thought I would run it, then that's great. But it was tiny places – the Wheatsheaf in Stoke, and the Tivoli in Buckley – all places I hadn't done for years.'

So he took the work on, 'having basically never heard of Bush', and the week went as well as a week in pubs could go. Robin and Ross talked at each other nonstop, and Bush returned to America and Ross Duncan returned to his previous commitments on the road with other bands. 'But then Dave Dorrell called me up and said, "Right, in October, we're back out in Europe – would you do it?" Three weeks. I said, "Yeah, I'd love to." Because although we'd only done a week in shitholes with a band I'd never heard of that were doing well in America, during the course of that week I really grew to like all four of them.

'So I set it up and we went and did it. And one night, we were playing this hideous gig in Bamberg in Germany, in a venue that nobody else had ever played. It was a village hall, basically, normally used as an oompah bar. And we had, for reasons unbeknownst to me, become the unwitting guinea pigs to do a rock show there. The stage was on three different levels, too, so you had Gavin in this oompah bar on his slightly raised platform and you've got Nigel standing in a trough, basically, and Dave Parsons on the other side, who gets away with it because he's so tall. But it was kind of strange; the place was just a shambles and they didn't know how to do anything, and the catering was all wrong, and it was just a terrible day. And the band were all furious. But, you know, the lighting rig was fine and the sound was fine. So I tried to play it down and say, "Yes, we can deal with this when we get back to London and we can take the promoter to task about using us as guinea pigs, but we're here now. So let's do it." It was sold out, too . . .

'So the band go on and I'll never forget it. The only way to get the band onstage, because the crowd was so thick, was to take them from the dressing room, which was actually the pump room where all the beer barrels were, outside into a little cobbled street in this very Teutonic, almost Dracula-like town. And we're stumbling around on these cobbles trying to find the fire exit. I had reccie'd the whole thing several times, but it looked different in the dark. So we get out and, well, we really can't find the way in.' He laughs. 'It was a bit *Spinal Tap*. Anyway, I found the door after the second one I kicked open, down a passageway which was allegedly a fire exit, and it's full of bottles and dead rats. So I march the band up confidently with my Maglite [torch], and we get to the door at the side of the stage and I confidently, yet again, kick it. And the thing falls – on top of Razza the monitor engineer's head! But there's no time to stop; it's like, "You're on!" So I throw them on, pull this door back, shove it back into place and think, Well, I'd better stand here.

'So anyway, Razza rubs his head and gets over it. And during the gig, Robin just laughed the entire time. I stood out of sight of Gavin, who was not very pleased, and Nigel, who was livid, just behind the speaker stacks. Laughing, in cahoots with Robin.

'Anyhow, they come off stage at the end of the show and for the encores normally I would have an area for the band to come off stage and grab a towel and chill out and have a beer or a water. But this place didn't really facilitate that,' Duncan says in a triumph of understatement. 'So it's into the alley and, "I think we'd better be quick before we all catch pneumonia." So they go back on and do their encore, then go off back to the, erm, *salubrious* dressing room in the back. And I disappear to do the money and other things that one must do, like arguing about how many people were actually in the house – the usual tour manager thing – and then I get summoned to the dressing room.

' "Gavin wants to see you," comes the word. And I'm thinking, "Oh, here we go, I'm for the boot now." And as I'm walking in,

I'm thinking to myself, Hold on. I didn't book the gig, I didn't want to be here, I made it the best it could be, how come I'm getting the boot? So I walk into the room and Gavin stands up. And before Gavin says anything, I sort of preempt it. I said, "I know today's been really bad but, you know, we're the first people to play here and I'm really sorry about it all but we did it and it's done and we made money" . . . and blah blah blah. And Gavin went, "Just shut up. Just shut up for one minute." '

Ross pauses. 'And then he said, "We've been talking, and I've decided it's about time we had a Scottish tour manager. Are you busy for the rest of the year?"

'I think I celebrated by having a pizza from a street vendor,' Ross laughs. 'Whoooo! But that was it, and that was October 1995 and I've been with them every time they've moved, basically, since then.'

According to the admittedly territorial Bone, who would meet Ross on the band's third North American tour, the new tour manager 'fit in like an old slipper. Of everyone, I was probably the most suspicious of him. That's me, you know. Well, everybody said, "Here he is, a little Scots guy who's going to take over the whole operation and make changes. I was convinced I was going to stand back a little bit first. I didn't want to give this guy *carte blanche* with my band and my feelings until I saw what he was made of. But we talked over a couple of months before that next US tour, and then he landed in Maine, and from the minute he came off the plane I thought, Yeah, we're all right. We'd take on the entire world together if we could.'

Looking over photos from the band's third North American tour, Robin Goodridge seizes on one taken in Tampa. 'Oh, this is the one where the speakers caught fire,' he chortles. 'Our soundman loved that. We were playing a festival, and we were on after Hootie and the Blowfish. Our soundman at the time – fucking brilliant, a real laugh, an old school Tina Turner veteran – really cranked it up, and *boom*, one of the speakers caught fire. The whole time we were playing, there was this guy climbing up the speakers with a fire extinguisher, which I'm sure he didn't enjoy as much as we did . . .'

1 FEBRUARY TO 5 MAY, 1996

Portland, Bethlehem, Hartford, Baltimore, Madison, Minneapolis, Davenport, Normal, Oklahoma City, Tulsa, Little Rock, New Orleans, Birmingham, Greenville, Richmond,

Hampton Beach, Winston-Salem, Charlotte, Columbia, Dayton,
Detroit, Kalamazoo, Toledo, Columbus, Ames, Lincoln,
Wichita, Phoenix, San Diego, Las Vegas, Anaheim, San Jose,
Sacramento, Santa Barbara, Tucson, Albuquerque, El Paso,
Lubbock, Odessa, Jackson, Lafayette, Houston, Carbondale,
West Lafayette, Lexington, Knoxville, Roanoke, Fairfax,
Providence, Uniondale, New Haven, Buffalo, Penn State,
Charleston, East Lansing, Milwaukee, Bloomington,
Cedar Rapids, Fargo, Rapid City, Tacoma, Portland, Spokane,
Missoula, Boise, Salt Lake City, Denver, London,
Rock Am Ring, Rock Am Harp, Pink Pop . . .

By the time Bush returned to America in early 1996, they had gone from clubs to arenas and amphitheatres in the space of one year. Hard work had a lot to do with it; the success of 'Everything Zen', 'Comedown' and 'Little Things' had more to do with it. But the addition of one more ingredient – 'Glycerine' – was even more critical. The album's format-spanning ballad and arguably one of its standout tracks on a record of standout tracks, the reception it was afforded provided proof that Bush's audience would encompass more than the standard, male-skewed alternative rock audience.

The first hint of the song's power, and arguably of Gavin's power as a frontman, had come before Christmas at the end of the second North American tour.

Michael Pagnotta, the band's US press officer for both *Sixteen Stone* and *Razorblade Suitcase*, remembers the event.

'Bush just kept getting bigger in 1995 and into 1996. Bigger, better. But the biggest moment of validation for me, and I saw it in Gavin's eyes the moment it happened, was when he played a Christmas ensemble radio show in New Jersey at the Meadowlands Arena, which is now called the Continental Air Arena.

'The band had finished their second tour and they were on their Christmas break. "Glycerine" was just exploding at this point, and it was kind of a Gavin solo thing anyway, being acoustic, so it made sense for him to do it even without the band. So Gavin gets onstage with just his guitar, and he does "Glycerine" solo, and the place goes . . .' Pagnotta searches for the right words. 'Absolutely fucking bullshit mental. Now, he had never played solo at an arena of this size, at least not that I'm aware of, and certainly had never received that kind of love and approval from an audience. Kids screaming, I mean, *screaming* like New Kids On The Block screaming, which is unusual for new rock stuff to say the least. And he came off the stage after that one song, and his eyes were completely glazed over, and all of us were practically near tears. You rarely have that; you rarely see the moment when things go from being ordinary to being truly exceptional. It's that *A Star Is Born* kind of thing. And that's the moment it happened for Gavin. And shortly thereafter we did a cover story for *Rolling Stone*,' he adds of the issue that would become that magazine's biggest seller in 1996. 'We did *Saturday Night Live*, we did the Howard Stern radio show . . .'

Dale Meekins remembers the screaming, too.

'It was so loud, it hurt your ears. And Gavin doing it himself out there in front of all those people just stole the show. And I thought, Wow, this is huge. I was very, very impressed by that, because until then Bush hadn't gotten there yet, but they were sure getting there now. It was so massive after that.'

And, as you might expect, what that meant was . . . more tour dates.

Ross Duncan recalls, 'Well, we went out for a month in America, that was the idea. We went out for four weeks . . . and we ended up playing seventy-eight arenas; we just kept going. We started with production rehearsals in Bangor, Maine, which is where Stephen King is from, and we all tootled round past his house and spent a couple of days shivering our proverbial bollocks off in some sub-zero temperatures. We rehearsed in this hideous place and then went and played a gig in – Portland, I think was the first show – and they served us lobster. And from then on, every show was sold out. We went over to do a month of ten thousand-seat arenas, and then it suddenly just took off. And off.'

It was definitely 'Glycerine' that made the difference, Ross insists. 'Oh yeah. All through the European tour at the end of the year, Gav was completely preoccupied with the "Glycerine" video because it was his deal. Let nobody tell you anything else. It was Gav who was on my mobile phone – I have the bills to prove it – calling Rob Kahane every five minutes making sure it all went right. Not in a megalomaniac way; it was just that he knew exactly how he wanted the video to be. And it subsequently was the massive hit that it was.

'The tour calendar we had hanging at the front of the bus was the funniest thing. 'Cause when we got on at the beginning, there was one month's calendar with all the dates on it. And by the time we finished the thing was as thick as Roget's *Thesaurus*. It just went on and on and on. But it was great because the boys were successful, they were loving it, the Bush machine was by then the machine it is now. We have seven trucks; we have four buses; we roll in, we roll out, and we do it all over again. Now, that's not unusual; that's what people in our business do, but for four lads in a band when your career is exploding, it's reassuring to have all that behind them.

'So the machine just rolled on. And yeah, I was almost deafened every night because the kids screamed so loud. It was just mad. It was mental. It just went off, but the thing is, they're so level-headed they keep their feet on the ground so nobody changed over it. And we just kept going round.'

Snowstorms or no snowstorms. Simon Halfont recalls, 'I'd have Rob [Kahane] on the phone, saying, "Listen, you're not going to believe this. We've got six thousand people queuing up outside in minus fourteen degree weather." In some town I'd never heard of, in some state I'd only vaguely heard of. That was the key to how big it was: they weren't just doing the big cities, they were doing the smaller ones. And selling out huge, huge arenas.'

According to Dale, on that first 1996 tour, 'it was just nuts. There'd be kids in the parking lot at four in the morning when the crew buses would pull in to sleep before starting work for the day. It's the middle of the night, but they're there, lined up. I remember one show in Michigan which sold out in the middle of a blizzard, and so the band decided we'd drop balloons from the ceiling to say thank you, and Gav said thank you to everybody from the stage. That was a cool thing,' he adds. Literally, in fact.

With increased fame, of course, come new situations. Tired, overworked and overwhelmed, it's not always easy to remember your manners. According to those around the band, Bush always rose to the occasion, as strange as the fallout from fame became.

Michael Pagnotta remembers one such occasion.

'It was a show in Hartford, Connecticut on that first tour in 1996. We were doing a meet-and-greet after the show, and I was walking Gavin through the room to see about forty or fifty fans. It was a small room, so it was very confined. The rest of the band were in there, and were beginning to file out, and Gavin was a little bit late as he usually is, chatting to the fans. There was this one girl who couldn't have been more than fifteen years old, leaning against the wall. She may even have had braces, and was intensely shy, almost trembling, by the door. And we're going through the circuit, and Gavin's signing autographs, and as we're about to walk out, she sort of sidesteps in front of us – not in a threatening way, but just so we would have had to walk through her to get out the door.

'And she looked at Gavin and said to him, "I could give you a blow job that would make you see God!" Now, this was a girl who you would never have expected to . . . And Gavin stared at me, I stared back at him, and he looks back at her and says, "Well, I've already got a pretty good relationship with God, thanks!"'

'And then we walked out of the room. It was a brilliant moment. He didn't say it in an insulting way – like, "Fine, but just not with you" – but in a way that said, "Hey, I've got it covered, thank you very much." You know? You can't learn that kind of stuff.'

Bone concurs, 'That's another thing that at the very beginning led me to love these guys. I have never seen, ever – and I've been with them every minute of every day – I have never seen any of them treat anybody with less than one hundred per cent respect. Never once. Not the sleaziest tramp throwing herself at Gavin backstage, not the most refined woman he's talked to, not any young kid with stars in their eyes. It's one of the things I respect about him most. He treats every single person we meet with absolute dignity and respect. I've never seen another artist like that. He has never been rude to one person.' He laughs. 'You know, it's not normal!'

You might not be able to learn that kind of reaction, but somehow Bush already had a pretty good idea of what the seamy side of the rock world entailed, and knew that they didn't want any part of it.

Ross Duncan has spent years on the road with bands and crew – not all of them metal bands, but more than a few. For most, their idea of the perks of rock and roll fame somehow always includes a little 'friendly' exploitation of female fans, ranging from low-level harassment to statutory rape and beyond. He grimaces when the topic is brought up.

'Bush hate that side of things. They hate it and I applaud that. They are not a backstage pass band and I admire them for it, because there's still too much of it. And I've seen it, and I've seen the effect it has on fans, and it's wrong. I've done every heavy metal tour in the world, and those days of cock rock are gone, or should be. I'll tell you what, you'd be out the door before you knew it if you indulged in any of that with these boys. Gavin would have you fucking lynched if you did anything wrong. In fact, I've fired several people for that kind of thing. I'm not a puritanical Bible-basher and I've been around, but I applaud and uphold what the band ask me to uphold. If you're not prepared to be a decent person, then you're not part of our family and that's that. You're not going to besmirch our name through your own lust. I just don't want to know about any of that kind of shit. I've seen it: sleaziness, and crying girls, and all that bollocks. Bush would not have that anywhere near them and neither would I, and that's one thing, amongst others, that we are very, very alike on. I will not have it.

'When I found out that people who worked for us were getting involved in that kind of thing, they were gone, let me tell you. I didn't even ask permission. It was just like, "You're fired. See you." I had one guy on the phone the next month telling me that his wife had left him, and he was begging to come back. And it's like, "Well, tough. You should have thought about it. Don't be phoning and blaming me." '

Asked if Bush are unusually moral in their outlook, Dave Dorrell replies, 'You know what? Guilty as charged. We've dealt with all of those abuses of privilege that one can so often be confronted with. Does that mean the guys are puritans? Are they incapable of having fun? No. But I suppose with great success comes great responsibility as well, and ninety-nine point nine per cent of people that have any success seem to have their heads turned immediately and abuse their luck, their fortune, and everyone around them as well. The diva throwing a phone at her assistant. Any miserly rock guitarist. You know: "Why? Because I can! You're sacked because I *can*!"

'It's pathetic. "I'm now the dictator of this country and I will kill everybody I fancy." Well great, thanks, the music business needs more Hitlers. The band are loyal and, as people, they're somehow still quite human for all of what's happened to them. And you know what? We're incredibly nice to our support bands, too, because you know, we could have *been* that support band. And one day that support band will be us. A good message for all you bastards out there, you know: it is actually quite easy to be all right with other bands. I think the industry fosters an "us and them" approach. It's almost as if it has appropriated some kind of class system. A band that I know were recently on tour with a band that throws TVs out of windows, and they had to vacate the dressing rooms as soon as they finished drying off so that the area was clear for Their Majesties to come through. OK, I can see the fun in doing that *once* maybe. But if you're so absolutely up your own arse where that's how you intend to conduct yourself, get off the planet. There are enough assholes here already.'

More than a year into a tour that seemed as though it would never end, it was perhaps inevitable that someone in the band would run the risk of being let down by his own body. Typically, Robin Goodridge, who began life as a sickly and asthmatic child prone to bouts in a steam tent in hospital, and now at the punishing drum-riser centre of an almost ridiculously punishing schedule, seemed to worry more about letting the band down than what his body had in store for him.

'For a long time, I had just been exhausted. I was probably having a nervous breakdown, if I'm being honest. There wasn't a prescription drug that I hadn't taken or could take that would work. And it felt like that for almost four and a half months.'

On reflection, he says, he probably should have said something sooner. A doctor would probably have said he should be on an airplane home sometime in the middle of the 1996 North American tour.

'But I didn't want to let the band down. Or let myself down. The worst thing in the world is to have your brain blow up in your face and say you can't do it. I didn't have to, thankfully, but I wondered for a bit, Am I going to have to give this up?

'And yeah, the band knew. But they also knew who I am. If I said I'd had it, it would be because I'd had it. But they knew they'd have had to take me home under sedation. I'd have probably been asked to leave. I would have had to have four medical opinions going, "Get this man out of here." Thankfully it never happened.'

Tours, before Bush, were completely different, even for a hard-gigging musician like Robin. 'I'd been for three, four, five weeks around England, and that's not the same; four weeks' hard work and then go home. That was baby food. I could get hammered every night; four pints of beer and playing pool before a gig. Now I don't drink before a show. I realise how much harder I work in this band mentally and physically and it was a thing that Gav did that caught on with me. The fact that I didn't drink before a show was probably my greatest move; before that, if I'd had a third hand, I'd have had a beer in it. I have drunk on stage occasionally, but I'm such a terrible drummer when I'm drunk.

Gavin, aged 6, on family holiday . . .

. . . aged 9, with Aunt Maggie . . .

. . . and aged 12, with first girlfriend Jill Hurley. Note snogging couple in background

One boy and his dog; Nigel with Tinker

David, aged 2, displays early love of touring

Style guru or fashion victim? David aged 14

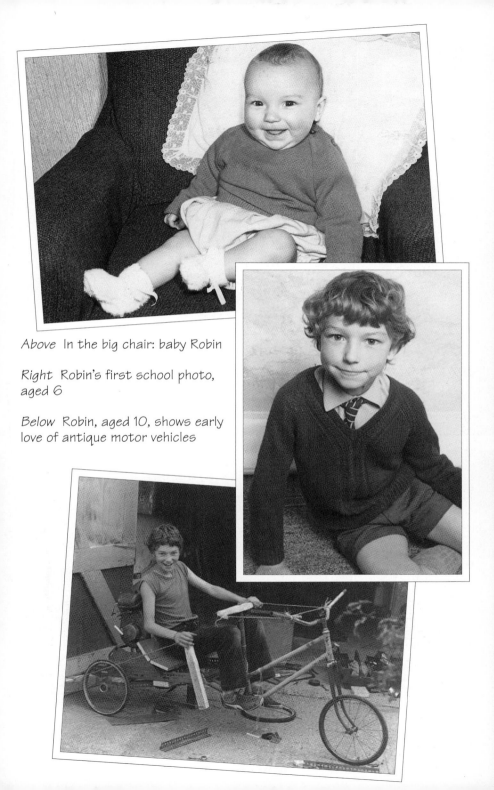

Above In the big chair: baby Robin

Right Robin's first school photo, aged 6

Below Robin, aged 10, shows early love of antique motor vehicles

Left Taming The Outback, the wilds of north London, 1983; Nigel is second from left

Below Midnight, 1986; Gavin is third from left (*Pete Black*)

Above Transvision Vamp, 1988; Dave is third from left (*Joe Dilworth/SIN*)

Below Gavin with Jasmine, basement flat, Montagu Square

Left Bush backstage at Tampa, Florida, March 1995 (*Pete Black*)

Right Nigel with Judith, Los Angeles, 1997 (*Shawn Mortenson*)

Left Another day, another enormodrome; Washington DC, June 1995 (*Pete Black*)

Right Gavin and Gwen Stefani (*Pete Black*)

Above Gavin at
Glastonbury, 1999
(Andy Willsher/SIN)

Left Clockwise from
top; Mez Hughes (band
friend), Sarah Chope,
Glynis Evans, Judith
Rose, backstage at
Reading, 1997

Nigel can play brilliantly when he's drunk; Gavin's really good when he's stoned. Ever seen me? I can't do that. I understand what I can and can't do. Some people can thrive on it and handle that whole side of it; it just doesn't work for me.'

He was, he says, 'very close to being loony. It's everything you've ever wanted and all of a sudden you start reacting against it. I met a guy the other day on a train, can't remember the name of the band, but one of the kids was from Horsham. And the singer's just quit. And they were just really unhappy. He obviously wanted to be in a band, and make music, but they started to get successful and the tour schedule looms, and he said, "I don't want to do this, I don't like it." Honestly, I was the opposite: my mind still wanted to do it, but my body and nervous system were saying, You don't like this anymore. You've got to stop, just for a little while. But you can't; it's about momentum. I'd completely run out of anything. I couldn't go to the gym 'cause I was too tired. Fifteen hours in bed, rest, get up and still feel completely exhausted. Very weird. I didn't have any power. And it gets scary. It started in the summer of 1995, towards the end, when we'd done all the radio festivals, and then another tour. And it got to Christmas, after doing America then Europe; I was absolutely exhausted.

'I've got a handle on it now, there's no mystery anymore. It's just the mechanics of being inside it. It's a hell of a lot easier when you don't have to tour. We used to have to go to radio stations every day before the gig. When you wanted to just have a nap, you'd have to go and talk to a geezer, and twenty minutes later you'd get changed and you're onstage. Every night, and there's no off switch. It all involves a lot of adrenaline, and eventually it just eats you up. You learn to live with it after a while.' He shrugs. 'You manage it.'

Which is a bit of an understatement. According to Bone, who became a sports trainer and massotherapist after a knee injury ended his hockey career, Robin was going through hell. 'We were on the road an awful lot, the demands were incredible, no one was getting home an awful lot and we were huge. Robin's a very strong kid, but he became a little overwhelmed.

'You wouldn't believe the things we had to do for that boy. We sometimes had to feed him straight oxygen all night long because he got such knots and cramps that the muscles in his arms felt like golfballs. He's a trouper, boy, I tell you. A hundred per cent every night. He is the consummate professional.'

'*You* try bashing a pan for two hours,' Dave Dorrell retorts when asked if Robin's job is particularly demanding. 'You're going to go mad within two hours. The measure of Robin is that seventy dates into a tour, he thought he was going a bit wacky. Well, we all do a little bit, because it's like that moment when you discover, wow, you can only go so low with a submarine. Yeah, I think we were probably getting to the point where we were starting to hear creaks as the pressure increased to such a degree that the whole thing was likely to implode. We were fortunate enough that we could come back up for air. And I'm sure if you talk to Robin about it, as unpleasant an experience as it probably was for him at the time – well, that which does not kill us makes us stronger and all of that. And I'm sure he looks back on it as another notch on his gun, another way station on the road of life.'

Ross adds, 'He's a total athlete, but he works like a mother. All four limbs of his work for over two hours, and I'm not taking anything away from anybody else, but basically the man's drumming for two hours and nobody else is. If he had needed to bail then I would have backed him all the way. And he needed that support, and I think when he got the support he rallied. When he was on his own, he was thinking, I can't make this. I can't make this and everybody's gonna hate me for it. But then we talked about it and I said, "Well, you're not on your own, and if you can't make it, you can't make it, mate." There was one time I felt that perhaps we needed to throw in the towel. But, through reassurance, manipulation and basically love, from all of us, it happened. Until you tell somebody, you're always on your own. Once you get it off your chest, it's amazing how much stronger you feel.

'He asked me what would happen if he had to bail. He said, "If we cancel the next three gigs, how much does it cost?" And I said, "Fine. Go and get a massage, go to the gym, go and swim, and within an hour we'll have figures." And that's exactly what happened. And I'll tell you, he soldiered through. He was nearer the end than any of the band will ever know. He's fragile. Strong as fuck but fragile. But so strong, he did it. And it wasn't financial reasons that made Robin carry on. But once it became a real situation where we were looking at numbers and it was a distinct possibility, it became more real, I think, to the point where he was able to deal with it.'

Eventually, of course, even the Tour That Never Ended, ended. Even the band who never stopped touring went home. To make a second album in record time, mind you, but at least they were off the road for a bit. But there was still one more small item of business to take care of: their hometown fans. Selling out London's Astoria on 22 May, the band were more than ready to show London what they were made of. 'I don't think I've ever seen so many people squeezed into that venue,' says Mike Greek. 'The anticipation was electric, and there was just a real, real buzz.' And if it wasn't the amps, it must have been their metabolisms on overdrive.

Dave Dorrell, appropriately, has the final word.

'Bands are as strong or as weak as their temperaments allow for. The bands that choose not to tour or to work hard have it within their rights. And some bands, like Bush, want to do it. Jesus Christ, if you're given a ticket to the Magic Kingdom and you want to go on the Space Ride fifty times, go on it. They had the fucking VIP pass, they could play for as much as they wanted to, and they did, so why stop? As long as you're happy with what you deliver every night, work as hard as you want!'

R

'Recording with Steve Albini? Listen, the choice of producer for *Razorblade Suitcase* was something that was thought about for a long time with great deliberation on the part of the band, and almost certainly in defiance of the wishes of the label. But who's to say that you can't go and do something grittier the second time around? It struck me as a very foolish view that you had to play the game and that the only rules were the ones that were already set. All I can do is applaud Gavin and the rest of the guys for sticking by their guns and making an unpopular choice of producer, though why Steve is supposed to be an unpopular choice of producer is beyond me. Perhaps because he's terrifyingly intelligent, supremely able at his job, human, well-disposed toward bands, loathing of the corporate structure, motivated by love of music, not money, yeah, you're right. What a strange choice for a producer. The guy's great at what he does. And the band were on fire as a unit, having played more gigs than most bands do in a lifetime. Uh, what else was there?'

Bush manager David Dorrell does not mince his words. In fact, give him a topic he is sufficiently passionate about, and he'll direct his words like a blast from a high-pressure water hose. The recording of Bush's second album, *Razorblade Suitcase*, and the supposed controversy surrounding the band's choice of the man to oversee its recording is one of those topics.

An album 'born in the white heat of touring', as Dorrell says,

Razorblade Suitcase was recorded and mixed in a mere three weeks. By the time the band came off the road on 1 May 1996, they had played more than 230 dates in the preceding year and a half, leapfrogging from the tiny CBGBs in New York City all the way to Colorado's massive Red Rocks amphitheatre. The band returned to the UK, rehearsed at the Terminal in Bermondsey for two weeks, played a few festivals and headed to Hook End Studios on 1 June. There, they would meet the man they had chosen to record – Albini doesn't use the word 'produce' – the follow-up to the astonishingly successful *Sixteen Stone*.

And, in so doing, Bush decided that working with the man they wanted was infinitely more important than worrying about what They, whoever *They* are, might have to say about it. Fiercely independent, scornful of the artist-unfriendly attitudes rife in the music business and something of an alternative music icon himself, Chicago-based Albini, who leads the three-piece band Shellac, was also founder member of uncompromisingly intense 80s band Big Black. Perhaps even more importantly, he has recorded so many alternative and independent bands of note that his studio credits read like a who's who of influential noise, from Slint, Smog, Palace and Low to The Jon Spencer Blues Explosion, PJ Harvey, Helmet, The Breeders, Tortoise and The Dirty Three.

Admittedly, for those seeking to follow the line that Bush's debt to Nirvana was somehow more perfidious than any other band's, all of Albini's other credits pale into insignificance next to his credit on the sleeve of Nirvana's *In Utero*.

'Yeah, and you know what?' retorts Dorrell, warming to his subject once again. 'Fuck the journalists, fuck the critics out there that wanted to say, "Oh, you did it because . . ." No. We did it *in spite*. Yeah, like we were so stupid that we didn't know? Of course we knew. But you know what? It wasn't because we knew or didn't know, it was because Steve was a really good person for the fucking job. We went in with our eyes wide open as soon as we said we wanted to work with Steve Albini. We couldn't find another producer that we wanted to work with. We could have listened to our worst fears and thought, Oh my God, we're going to do an album with Steve Albini, we're going to get flak for this. Why would we listen to that voice, the voice of fear? We would have been pandering to people that didn't like us anyway, or to the corporate media. So we were damned if we did and damned if we didn't. And if we'd gone for a more commercial choice, as I'm sure our label would have been happy for us to have done, then we would have ended up with any number of admirable producers out there with multi-platinum band careers. But we wouldn't have been doing what we wanted to do. Fuck everybody,' he concludes, with relish. He shrugs. 'We make what would be called good decisions for other bands, and we're told they're bad decisions for us. The nub of the issue is certainly not about Steve's ability as a recordist. The received wisdom was, don't step on that grave. What, like he's not to work again or something?'

That said, when the idea was first mooted, even the band weren't sure that Albini – one of only two names proposed, along with that of Scott Litt – would be interested in working with them.

Recalls Gavin simply, 'Well, I just called him and asked him to come and meet me.

'He was working in Abbey Road [studios in London] and Dave Dorrell went to see him, asked who he should contact to talk about doing an album. And Steve said, "Well, I don't have a manager, so it's good to speak to me directly." So I did. I had lunch with him and his girlfriend, Heather. I arrived ten minutes early – can you imagine how you'd feel, knowing you're going to meet Steve Albini for lunch? I thought he was going to spit in my face!' he laughs.

'We went to lunch and we didn't talk about music, which was the weirdest thing. And I just said at the end, "I'm in a really weird position because I'm successful and there are lots of people I could ask to make a record with me, but you're my first choice. So I'll have this conversation with you, and if you're not into it, OK, that will be that." And then he sent a fax to Dave Dorrell, which I still have. It's embarrassing, because I can practically quote the whole thing.' Gavin smiles and, better than true to his word, recites the fax from memory:

'Dear Dave,

Gav and I finally got to meet in Chicago. In my line of work I've become so used to the would-be rock stars or drug addicts that I've met that they almost don't make me sick anymore. But Heather, I find, is an excellent bullshit detector and since we both deduced the fact that Gavin is really genuine, I'd be most willing to make a record with him. My schedule works a year in advance tentatively, six to eight months in advance specifically. So please let me know however I may be of assistance to this band. I'm now in Paris and, by the way, the food is excellent and I can recommend it highly.

Yours, Steve F Albini.

'And, what's nice, we survived it,' Gavin concludes with a delighted laugh. 'We made a record with him . . . and did good.'

Nigel, the longest-standing Albini fan in the band, recalls the *Razorblade Suitcase* experience as a wholly pleasurable one. If anything, his high opinion of Albini's working methods and moral principles were reinforced.

'Steve's one of the first people I've ever met who stands by his values,' he insists. 'You can see that by the fact that he doesn't take [royalty] points on the albums he produces, because he doesn't feel it's morally correct to take points when all he does is come in and record you. The irony is that there's so much money to be made, so I almost wish he would, because he lives hand to mouth. He survives, but he works for lots of bands for nothing, or next to nothing, because he believes in them. He's one of the good guys, definitely.

'Of course, we were all really nervous about meeting him. Everyone was scared to death of Steve, because of who he was and because of his reputation. If you read anything he's written, you get the impression he won't suffer fools lightly. But in a way, you know, his PR is completely wrong. He's not at all like that. He's very mild mannered, very polite, very easy to get on with. Although I think when he was younger perhaps he wasn't, which is where his reputation comes from.

'I remember arriving at Hook End studios the first day. We saw a very quiet guy going around the room setting the drums up . . . and it was him. We were standing in the other room whispering amongst ourselves, kind of nervously, like, "When should we go and say hello to him?" But he was fine, he was really easy after that. And I think because everyone was a little in awe of him, we all behaved ourselves; none of us got pretentious or control freak-like in the studio, so he was a really good influence on the band. And the record sounds really good. Apart from a few songs, I think it's the best stuff we've done.'

What helped, he says, is that 'we knew the songs when we went in'. Tracks like 'Greedy Fly', 'Swallowed', 'Insect Kin', 'Mouth' and 'Cold Contagious' had all been either played on the road or rehearsed prior to recording. 'It was like a performance. It was a different approach, and a good one. We simply played the songs as they were and we did our best as a band.'

The only hitch in the recording process, in fact, had nothing to do with the band or Albini, Nigel recalls, but with the long arm of the law. 'Steve got deported, basically,' he laughs. 'Halfway through recording, they decided that his visa wasn't adequate for what he was doing, because the regulations had just been changed. We thought we were going to finish on schedule: we'd done thirteen songs in eight days or something ridiculous like that, so in fact we were more than working to schedule to complete recording and mix as well. But then Steve got threatened with deportation and our management had to work on getting him his visa back. I think he might have gone to France, got to the airport, got his papers sorted and turned around and come back. So that sort of fucked it up a bit, and we had an enforced break. When he returned, we went to Abbey Road, where we were meant to mix; but, because Abbey Road sounded so brilliant, we re-recorded a couple of songs. It just sounded so much better there – imagine being in [Abbey Road's] Studio Two, where the Beatles recorded! We did the strings for "Bonedriven" and "Straight No Chaser" there, and mixed for a couple of weeks. All in all, making the album was, like, twenty-five days in total.'

Working with Steve, Nigel says, 'was very much what I'd expected. He works really quickly, because it doesn't take him hours to get a drum sound – he just brings his microphones and does it all, boom boom boom, it's done. So it was a really healthy way to record, and nearly all of it was live except for the vocals. There are maybe three or four overdubs on the whole thing. He's not into too much embellishment or candy-flossing. He wasn't into overdubbing, but he was into editing takes together; he was really good with a razorblade and a bit of tape. Which is good, because most of it was done without a click track, and Robin kept the old tempos fairly even, and you wouldn't hear the join. Steve doesn't like filling tracks up artificially, so if the guitars are loud it's because they're fucking *loud*! It's because they're played loud as opposed to being hoiked up. Steve really likes to leave the faders where they are, that's why you hear the anticipation noises with guitars being turned up before big choruses.'

'Bush hadn't really recorded like that before,' Nigel notes. 'On the first album, we did virtually everything except the drums with the view that we'd replace them with the proper thing after, because the sounds weren't right when we recorded them. But this time we were, I suppose, really played in from touring so much, so we just kept going until we had a good take. If we hadn't quite got the arrangement together, Steve would say, "Maybe you guys should go away and work on this one, I'll come back in two days," when we were arguing about arrangements. But he got it as it was.'

'I love his form of production,' Gavin exclaims. 'This is Steve producing: "OK, ready everyone? Rolling . . ." And then he just reads a magazine! You look into the control room and he's not even looking!

'In twenty songs, I did three overdubs. All that album is live, nothing else; it's exactly how we recorded and played it. I sang a lot of stuff again simply because you get so much spill. And when we did the strings, I had to rehearse with the string section. I had thought it would be a case of having a click track in your ear, putting the guitar down, and then singing it. But Steve was like, "No, man, you've got to rehearse with them." The way I knew he was right was when he would argue with us, because he was uncanny about knowing when we'd got the right recording. He would look like he wasn't paying attention, but *nothing* would go past him.'

Not even the opportunity to editorialise, in fact. Famously, he didn't think 'Swallowed', which would go on to be the band's biggest hit in the UK and many other territories, was up to much. 'It was the only song he didn't really like on *Razorblade Suitcase*. But he was like, "Come on, don't worry, at least there's only one turkey. Out of twenty songs, that's not bad. Most bands have *two* turkeys"!' What's more, he didn't shy away from making his own little comments about what was going on in the booth. 'One time,' Gavin continues, 'Dave looked down on the sheet of his track listing, and it had the words "pointless harmony" [in Steve's handwriting] written next to a song I was working on the vocals for. So as you can imagine, I was really ready to call the entire record *Pointless Harmony*! But I couldn't work out how to get a front cover image for that, and besides, I was trying not to be grunge.' He laughs. 'The record was guitary enough; I didn't want any more potentially self-pitying things associated with it, and 'pointless' is such a strong dark word.

'The way I actually found out Steve liked us was reading it in quotes from the press. What I read he'd said about us was that of course he understands what the fuss was about, but that recording with us was no different to any other band he's worked with in terms of music that he likes and bands he'd liked. And he said that in his opinion, of our time and style, we're easily the most textured band. And there's other stuff, which Nigel has read, in which he's said that Nigel was one of his favourites of all the guitarists he has worked with.' Gavin laughs. 'Nigel's got that quote tattooed on his back, now, of course.'

Nigel adds, 'He was one of the most charming people we ever worked with, which is great, because no one ever believes he's like that. They all think he's a horrible, scary person who's going to shout at you all the time. He was just a laugh. He likes to take money off people at pool. Doesn't drink – he had half a cider with us one night and got a bit pissed. Didn't even drink all of it. And while we were recording, I think I even managed to start him smoking again.'

Albini himself recalls his initial contact with the band.

'Over the course of a few weeks [on the spring 1996 US tour] as Bush were doing pre-concert interviews Gavin was dropping names of his favourite bands, he mentioned me a few times and, sure, I was flattered.' When he, Heather and Gavin had lunch, Albini recalls, a friendship began easily. 'My girlfriend has a real razor-sharp ability to spot a bullshitter, and we both got that he was a genuine music fan who had ended up in the circumstances of being in a popular working guitar band. And basically after that, I took everything he said at face value.

'It's pretty easy to tell when someone has an agenda,' says Albini of the theory that a commercially successful band like Bush might have sought out his services purely for second-hand credibility. 'Normally, if someone is sympathetic to the same things that you are, that makes itself transparently obvious. And if someone isn't, but is pretending to be, that's also extremely obvious. There's an old expression in pool circles: "game knows game". That is, if I play a certain game in a pool room, and if I'm a specialist in a certain game and I'm talking to somebody, I can tell whether or not he's versed in this game. And that's exactly how I approach people I meet in the music business. I can tell by what records he thinks are important whether this person comes from the band end or the business end. Generally, the business end types have an ulterior motive, and people from the band end speak from their hearts.

'With a lot of people I deal with in the music business, there's a threshold of bullshit that your conversation may or may not rise above. Everyone who works in the music business has a side. The only exception to that are people who are in bands who don't have any axes to grind and still feel free to speak their minds. And Gavin's in that situation: a guy in a band trying to make a decent record. I have very little time and patience with people who are "professionals" in the music business. Not just because they constantly lie to you, but because their sympathies are not mine. I tend to communicate better with people who are in working bands, because we come from the same background.

'From the moment we started working together, it never seemed like a bad match to me. Listening to their one album prior to going to work with them, it didn't sound that far afield from the sort of stuff I was working on with a lot of other bands. It was just a lot more popular. And I don't really take things like that into consideration. I don't actually know if I'd associated that music [from *Sixteen Stone*] with the name Bush before, because I don't listen to the radio and I don't take notice of what you might call the greater culture, so, you know . . . Bush could have been utterly unknown and I would have responded in the same way.

'I talked to David [Dorrell] at length and I tried to make it clear that I didn't think I'd make a better record than other people who'd tell them what to do, and that my experience has been that if the band try to please anyone but themselves, they ultimately end up dissatisfied with their record, and they won't end up pleasing anybody anyway.'

Asked if he thought the band were surprised that he agreed to work with him, he shrugs. 'I don't know. By the time they spoke to me, they had quite a bit of momentum behind them, and by then they were probably used to people saying yes. And when we started, there was a lot of sort of – I don't know how to describe it, non-productive joshing around. You know, talking about bands they liked and stuff. Like I say, my first impression of the band was that they love music, and that they like *good* records, not popular stuff. But I also got the impression that everyone was into the job.

'There's nothing that strikes me as significantly different,' Albini adds of the recording process of *Razorblade Suitcase*. 'The only thing that was odd was that in the majority of the bands I work with, there's at least the impression of a democratic songwriting process; in Bush, Gavin pretty much writes the song and lets everyone know when it's going as it should. There would be times we'd be working on something and I'd say, "Shall we finish that?" And the answer would be, "Oh, I think so, but let's run it by Gavin." That was the only thing that was out of the ordinary for me.'

Albini never thought that the band, as respectful as they were, deferred to him. 'I got the impression straight away that they were comfortable producing their album. That's the only way I've ever worked, with the band pretty much calling all the shots. I think they were waiting to see if I was going to start reining them in but, after the first day or so when it became obvious that I was asking them what they wanted to do, Gavin particularly seemed to appreciate it. I got the impression on their first album – and maybe it's a mistaken impression – that a lot of the decisions were handed to them. "Oh, you'll be playing through this amplifier," and that sort of thing.'

Asked if he had had preconceptions about UK bands' approach to hard work, or lack thereof, Albini draws a firm distinction between Bush and other acts.

'There's a dole culture in England which has always somewhat offended me. There seems to be a very explicit attitude amongst young people in rock bands that holding down a job is for suckers or stiffs and it's not something to contemplate if you're trying to be a rock musician, and that shows itself in a characteristically lazy approach. People don't want to do things for themselves: they want to find someone to do it for them so they can carry on drinking. That's about the only common thread that I've seen amongst British rock bands, and I attribute it directly to the dole culture. They don't think they're expected to pay their rent and stuff, and if you substitute the words "music business" for "government", that's how a lot of British bands behave. But I certainly don't mean Bush here,' he adds firmly.

'I think they've all gone through the process of playing in other bands, so they don't have a romantic notion of it. Robin and Gavin were both sort of similar, although they come from different social backgrounds. Robin wasn't frightened of working for a living, and Gavin had travelled and had this English youth version of the same thing. They have much more attitude. For example, the first session we did, they had the technicians basically doing everything for them, changing strings and so on. And then they got the idea from me that that was an inefficient way to do things, so they started to set themselves up, and things did work more efficiently. Once they made the conscious decision to take responsibility for their equipment rather than wait for someone to come and fix up the amplifier, they'd do it themselves.

'Robin is one of the most efficient drummers I've worked with,' he notes. 'His drums always sounded good. His technique is astounding. His delivery is consistent, and he worked very well at taking direction from Gavin. Gavin would give him a structure or an idea of a song, and Robin interpreted it really efficiently. They're all astounding musicians. Nigel's got a real personal take on his guitar; he uses a lot of funny sounds, but they're clearly used for effect, and he's not just screwing around. He's got an approach, which he's developing, and he's using those sounds to develop it.'

Ultimately, Albini says, he remembers *Razorblade Suitcase* as being 'really good. When I got a [finished] copy after it was fiddled around with, the remixed stuff didn't really do it for me and I lost interest in the record as a product, but I still think fondly of having made the record. I think they did a good job and I did a good job.'

And yes, he still thinks 'Swallowed' wasn't up to much. 'Yes. That was the only stinker. There were quite a few others that were head and shoulders above that.'

Almost three years later, Gavin is still full of enthusiasm about the experience of working with Albini. 'And I'm still friends with him!' he laughs. 'I know, I'm the last of a dying breed, because all the big bands that he's worked with have fallen out with him. Obviously, he fell out with Nirvana really heavily,' he adds with emphasis. 'And if we wanted to make another record like that, we'd do it with him. People always think of Steve that if something wasn't heavy and punk, he'd hate it, but I love all the slow stuff he's done, for Palace and Low and Smog.'

'I remember when I met the guys in Bush,' recalls David Yow of The Jesus Lizard, another fast friend. 'They were in the middle of recording with Steve. And I've known Steve for such a long time – we used to be best friends, in fact. And so it was funny to meet Gavin and hear him saying about Albini, "He's so pure, so totally pure".' Yow laughs. 'And I mean, Steve's a great guy but . . .'

Yow isn't surprised the band and Albini got on well. 'Steve's a swell guy, and in some ways very Gavinesque. Very intelligent, extremely generous, in fact the most generous person I've ever known. And they both know a tremendous amount about music.

'You know,' adds Yow, putting paid to any remaining claims that Albini's decision to work with Bush didn't constitute a vote of confidence, 'Steve claims he'll record anybody, but I know that's not true. After he did the Nirvana record, U2 wanted to record with him. And he said no.'

S

'So maybe it is true that all writers have a sliver of ice in their hearts. It's not just detachment; I think it starts out as the survival instinct,' Gavin Rossdale says.

'And maybe you modify it and it becomes ... professional detachment. Because if you use words in your life – well, every time anyone's ever left me, it's just been great for songwriting. The bleakest things provide the drama to write things about. When I think of being able to write simple, perfect, clear, beautiful songs like, say, Stevie Wonder does ... well, I haven't really found that yet. I've still found that everything that is good is also tempered by things that aren't so good. And yet it's really wonderful when words fall together, and it's great to have that detachment so that even while it's totally painful, there's a point where you can go, "There, that lyric's done, great!" When I think of writing the line *"war on all sides"*, I remember being totally crumpled inside; but still, when I got those words down, thinking, Yeah, I've never heard *that* in a song before!'

If *Razorblade Suitcase* was recorded quickly in pleasurable circumstances, the bulk of the lyrics themselves were written even more quickly. And, as Gavin says, in distinctly unhappy circumstances.

For a start, there was the physical side: Gavin had spent much of the first half of 1996 touring in constant stomach pain as the result of a chronic gastric infection.

'It got to the point where I was coughing blood. It was really bad. And because we were only ever in one town for a day, I'd see doctors, everywhere we'd play, and they'd all say, you've got an ulcer, and give me all sorts of things that didn't help. I got all the strongest antacids in the world, painkillers, everything. So I just had an infection for three and a half months which hadn't been treated properly because everyone was doing it the wrong way. Had anyone had the time to look properly they would have seen it. But it had all the same symptoms as an ulcer, so around that time it was just bad, bad, bad.' He shakes his head. 'And the only thing that could help me, really, was smoking weed, to help control the nausea. It was just horrible, because I couldn't really eat, and then when I had to eat, you know . . . it's not good . . .' He makes a face.

'And when I came back off the tour, the doctors were finally able to tell me that in fact I had had a stomach infection. I went into hospital and had all that tube stuck down my throat thing. *And* had to do a show the next day, a live performance on the Internet. We were meant to be rehearsing the day I had the operation, and I said I'd do it.' He shrugs. 'I thought if I could have the operation in the morning, then I could go and rehearse. So when I came back from the hospital, I called everyone and I told them I was fine to rehearse, not a problem. And the only way that they realised that I wasn't fine,' he laughs, 'was that I had five calls to make, to the band and to Dave Dorrell, and I had just started to come back round the list and was on my *seventh* conversation with someone I'd already had the same conversation with. It was really funny.

'It wasn't a general anaesthetic; I wasn't under but out, still awake, but I can't remember a thing. And apparently I just sat up on the bed and refused to lie down, and sat waiting for my dad like a five year old on the edge of the bed, fully clothed, refusing to lie down and recuperate. I remember the last thing the doctor said to me was, "I'll give you some of this for later, but *this* here, this is the best stuff, and unfortunately I can't give you any more of this." That was the last thing I remember, and suddenly I was sat in my dad's car and he was taking me home.

'And then the next day all I could do was croak – *aaaack* – like that. And I remember going and trying to sing for this Internet live show, and when I first opened my mouth it was the scariest thing, because *nothing* came out.'

The second challenge, in the writing of the album, was emotional.

'It was a lot of pressure to get the lyrics ready for recording. Ten days – I knew I had ten days before I'd see Albini. So it was ten days of writing. I was so tired by the seventh day. Me and Jasmine were breaking up, she was leaving. She was literally packing her bags in one room when I was in another writing songs. It was horrible. And that's probably why lyrically it was our best record so far. It really was a terrible time. And maybe all that turmoil going on just gave me some kind of awful burst of . . . I guess I have a large slice of cold heart. The fact that I could do it, because I knew I had to do it. I had to get on with it. It betrays a side of me that's not that good, I suppose.'

It's perhaps not surprising, then, that the album begins with the lyrically outstanding 'Personal Holloway', its title an unforgettable metaphor for emotional imprisonment and its musical and lyrical landscape painting a tableau of darkness, winter and containment.

'It's about finding someone pretty close to me who tried to commit suicide – hence the reference to paracetamol. I remember going to see her, drove there really fast at night, and the ambulance was there and all she was saying over and over was, "Don't tell Gavin" – even though it was only me with her and the ambulance people. So a personal Holloway would be a personal prison, and because it was female, I thought that Holloway [a women's prison in London] was appropriate.

'One of my favourite bits in this song is *"married by signs, deaf and dumb"*. Some time before, I had gone away to an old country house and, in the toilet there, they had a list of all the people who'd lived there for the last 300 years, listing "so and so, married this year to that person". And for one couple about two hundred years ago, they had written "deaf and dumb, married by signs". Often when people try to commit suicide it's from the feeling of being misunderstood, and a cry for help, and I was thinking of the struggle that people must have had 200 years ago to live with being deaf and dumb. Though of course it's not dumb, it's just deaf. And being *"deaf and dumb with the lights on"*, it's like being trapped in a world where you can't speak or you can't hear, but it doesn't mean that your brain isn't fully functioning, as we obviously know now. So I suppose the song is about female struggle; my female song.' But the important thing, he stresses, is the optimism in its conclusion: '*Move a little way forward, breathe life, could be a better plan.*' 'In other words, it's getting better. I was looking for something like an anti-grunge sentiment, totally the opposite of the bleakness before it. Something hopeful.' He pauses. 'I love that song.'

Not that bleakness doesn't have its power. 'Like Joy Division. But with them, of course, there was no chance for resolution, to move forward, because Ian Curtis hung himself and we'll never know what he would have written after. But for what you write to have some worth, it can't be a bleak run every song. It's about having to deal with a really terrible, terrible situation and watching someone nearly die twice and sitting in a hospital. But if I just left it as *"drinking kitchen paint"*, it doesn't have any resolution. And not that things should be resolved perfectly, but there have to be dips and dimensions to it; I couldn't just write the bleakness of that event straight through. Because it's all worked out now. It just was bleak then. I was just a kid when that suicide attempt happened. I was at school; I was sixteen. It's a bad scene. But those are things you deal with and those are the kind of things that make you strong. It's very dramatic now that I think about it, but so valuable. It teaches you more about life in one ambulance ride than you'll get through any university.'

'Cold Contagious' is a song Gavin has more than once introduced in concert as being about revenge, as the terrifyingly emphatic cry of '*You will get yours*' underlines. But it's more than that, he insists.

'It's such a sad song,' he says softly. 'As usual, it's about four different things. It comes from that period when I was writing, of course, and of seeing how when relationships break up, how lovely happy homes just get destroyed. It's funny, isn't it, when a physical place has symbolised really great happiness and security and warmth but, as soon as that goes, the place becomes alien and barren and it's so full of memories that it's just too painful to be around. So there's bits of that, and there's bits of the desire for revenge, yeah. And it's as much to do with my own belief in myself as other people's belief in me. And it's to do with family stuff and it's to do with people around me, to do with that fear that success will twist things, and with bitterness, in *"You were never that around"*. Things always seem much more acute in moments of panic. But once there's a little bit of distance and perspective about a problem or disagreement, you can use it lyrically and it can still be sharp.'

When writing about one's own life, of course, the need to be ruthlessly truthful can be a difficult razor to use when other people's feelings are taken into account.

Bush – 27th Letter

'Of course lots of times, as a writer, I back off of subject matter, because I just don't think it's fair to hurt other people. It's bad enough that those times and those people can sustain parts of your lyrical adventure, let alone actually naming them. Even if a lot of it, the truth of it and the simplicity of it, still holds true. It's probably one of the things that makes me most happy about the line "*Wherever you are, you will carry always/Truth of the scars and the darkness of your faith*". It's about all of us who have doubt and are wary, a bit hung up. Looking at this now, I think it's a pretty good song for someone who's hung up about a bunch of things. If I read that from someone objectively, I would get a lot of bitterness from it – "*reality daytrips*" – and I think I am bitter in some ways. But it's almost like, to recognise it and to understand it will diminish it. Give it a chance to breathe. It's that English thing of being so repressed and so wrapped up, you end up covering up so much of yourself that by the end of the day, it would be really hard to penetrate or to understand yourself in any way. Because it's just walls and bridges. It gets so removed from who you are and the truth of it. That's why I'm always oversensitive and over-analytical of things, because – it's just allowed me to have a sense of being grounded in some ways. That "*deeply grounded*" line comes from being right in the eye of everything there. Everything was going crazy. I had fucked up. Jasmine had left me. But I still felt like people expect you to change and to become something else and it was a point of defiance that I hadn't. It was enjoyable to me that I hadn't. Perversely. Often I find songs to me are prophetic – as if they're warnings. And part of the song, a lot of it is that whole maleness thing – "*the mighty mighty men*". So it's just kind of a personal wariness. It's funny, it's really revealing for me revisiting the old mindsets that fuelled these songs.'

And it's about communication as well, which is why, Gavin points out, longtime friend, photographer and multimedia artist Mark Lebon, who directed the video, chose to have Gavin speaking into a phone, in a surreally anonymous hotel room. A cliché, perhaps – the telephone as communication tool and as distancing mechanism – 'but Mark was very much into getting the truth of things, literally', Gavin insists.

And that motel telephone wasn't nearly as silly, he laughs, 'as that dumb fucking dog collar I had to wear in the video for "Greedy Fly".' A huge, adventurously dark and more than a little shocking big-budget video directed by Marcus Nispel, it was shot

172

in the same location as the film *Seven*, with many of the same creative team. ('I had already seen *Seven* before we shot it,' Gavin recalls. 'But seeing it again after the video, I have to say I was a little embarrassed, thinking I wish they'd had a few more new ideas.') Considered un-televisable in some countries because of its (mostly implied) violence, it was probably the first and last promotional video to feature Bush dressed as giant insects, crime suspects and – in lucky Gavin's case – a psycho in a funnel-shaped neck restraint.

Gavin laughs. 'I said, "It's gonna look really dumb! I'm not going to bite anyone! I'm going to leave my ankles alone, I swear! I'm not going to touch a thing!" It was just one of those video moments where you're thinking to yourself, "Mmm, I've got to live with this!" It's a very big collar.'

The euphorically catchy, unabashedly Pixies-tinged 'Swallowed', the only song on *Razorblade Suitcase* that Steve Albini considered a turkey, would also be the band's biggest hit in many countries, including a Top Five success in the UK that brought the band its first performance on the long-running UK TV institution *Top Of The Pops*, the benchmark for any British band of having 'made it' in the public eye. (And with other artists: Nigel recalls a heavily shaded and minder-surrounded Artist Formerly Known As Prince, also appearing on that day's programme, affording Gavin a tiny, imperious wave of recognition.)

When he looks at the lyrics, Gavin smiles mischievously. ' "*Piss on self esteem*"; that's not a bad set of lyrics to manage to get on the radio!' As for the whispered, heart-rending line '*simple, selfish son*', he owns up immediately, 'Oh, yeah, I'm very selfish.'

Evidence might prove otherwise: Barbara Stephan, for example, recalls Gavin's support when her second husband, Peter, died.

'Gavin organised everything. He took over completely: registered the death, organised the crematorium, the church, the flowers. He arranged to have booklets of the service made and went up to the church so the booklets were in the pews when people came in. He arranged the music and he stayed with me for the entire week, and he cooked for everybody coming to my house. He was absolutely together, because I was completely at a loss, and he was brilliant. He was so, so sensitive to everything.'

Pete Black, family in all but name, also recalls that when his own father died, Gavin appeared at the hospital within half an hour.

Reminded of these stories, Gavin concedes the point that perhaps he's not as selfish as he claims. 'I'll tell you what that is, though: I am wicked in a crisis. If there's a crisis, when someone dies or people are severely injured . . . well, I don't like blood, I hate all that stuff, but for some reason in tragedies I can always strike through to what's needed. When it really counts, I'm there, yeah. But there are other times when I *am* selfish. I don't share enough of what I do with my family, for instance; I don't think I've ever shown them any of my videos. And I am selfish with my time, because I don't have much of it.'

Returning to 'Swallowed', he adds, 'I've always said that this song is my version of the Beatles' "Help", which was written at the height of Beatlemania, even if "Swallowed" is really about as far away from sounding like "Help" as you're going to get.'

Hence, perhaps, the elegantly concise way of expressing that sense of loneliness in the eye of the storm, *'I'm with everyone and yet not'*, as the video for the song underscores. 'I wouldn't admit it to myself, because I thought that it would be a kind of self-aggrandising move to say that I felt isolated. You know, the more people build you up, and the more you say you're feeling pain, the more fake it seems, so the way I was trying to deal with it was to be as stoic as possible. But I wasn't – things were taking their toll physically on me, and on all of the band, because of the workload and pressure load. I remember talking to Michael Stipe after a fan club gig he played in London and, as I listened to him, I was remembering what that was like, being exhausted at the end of a really heavy week on a tour. That inescapable cycle of being a performer, because that's what you are, and often feeling that it hadn't gone very well.

'And you know,' he adds, 'it doesn't help if everyone in the audience loves it. In fact, it makes it worse. Because then you feel like a fake, a fraud, like you've kind of got away with something. Those nights where things just don't gel, and no one else even notices it, maybe not even the rest of the band. But if you're in it, it's just really, painfully acute. It's a weird thing for me: when I play a set, I'm fine, as long as I make no mistakes. As soon as I make one mistake, it just pisses me off, and then I spend the time thinking about that instead of anything else.'

'Insect Kin', one of Gavin's three favourites on the album along with 'Personal Holloway' and 'Cold Contagious', 'is Beat-like, totally riffing and unconscious-driven, in which you can pull out lines and isolate them. But overall it's all to do with tone and how you present it,' says Gavin, longtime fan of Allen Ginsberg and other Beat poets. It starts with a nod to '*Red Stripe and Vicodin*', the former a lager, the latter a stomach medicine. 'They're pretty much what I lived on when my stomach was really bad.'

Intense, yearning, with one hell of a shift halfway through, 'Insect Kin' is 'just mood to me, pure mood, all struggle and trying to fit in. "*You'll never people me*": you'll never make me into who you'd think I should be. Maybe it would be easier if I was more standard, more expected,' he adds, referring to surprise and even hostility from some quarters that someone who might appear on the surface to be one of life's winners ('he looks like the popular, good-looking high school team captain', as the Toronto *Sun* put it) might wish to align himself with outsiders, or express insecurity, pain or self-doubt.

'Insect Kin' also contains references to Rossdale's friend, Hole frontwoman Courtney Love, in simple, moving lines like '*All the pain in the way she walks/All the pain in her wave goodbye*'.

'That stuff is totally about Courtney; I don't mind saying that at all. It comes from when I was first friendly with her. I met her in Washington, where we both played a big radio show, and then when we went to Seattle to record a song for a film, we got apartments there and stayed for a few weeks. I rang up someone, a mutual friend, to get her number. I just wanted to talk to her, and used my coming to Seattle as an excuse. We spent a lot of time talking, at one point every night we'd spend hours and hours on the phone. I think we were a lot of comfort for each other; had a lot in common, as people and in what we were going through individually. So it just worked out like that.

'She's just full on; when she's there, she's really there.' He laughs. 'People were so nervous when I first got friendly with Courtney. She'd just find me everywhere. Literally. I'd be doing an interview, I'd be in a restaurant, or out doing things, and she'd find me. What did I learn from her? That it's really good to soak up knowledge; that it's good to strive to be erudite and articulate and culturally involved. It's just like kindred spirits; I've always felt that with her. Which is what this song originally was called, "Insect Kindred". People of the same ilk. I think that anybody you connect with who becomes a good friend, is always a good friend. You learn stuff about the contradictions of life, and that it's really rewarding and satisfying to find people you can identify with. And there's many things in her past that's really similar to mine, in a weird sort of removed way, and the different places we've come through. Whenever we see each other, it's a lot of fun. It can be so grim doing festivals and sitting in Portakabins when it's raining and you're somewhere in Germany. You could fucking go mad. I mean, you do. You're away from home for months and months and months, and it's nice that there are people you want to talk to and you want to hang out with, as opposed to people that you don't, as invariably happens.'

The difficulty, of course, is that when a hugely successful, much admired and much speculated-on male frontman becomes friends with a musical peer who happens to be a hugely successful, much obsessed-over and much speculated-on female artist whose late husband was Kurt Cobain, tongues are bound to wag and tabloids spring into action much more furiously than they did when Gavin became friends with, say, David Yow of The Jesus Lizard.

'Yeah,' Gavin nods, 'that's true. But also, you know, I mean obviously it was more than just friends. And that's what makes it difficult.'

In fact, when Hole's most recent album *Celebrity Skin* was released in 1998, Love herself indicated in interviews that at least one track, 'Awful', contained references to Rossdale in the lines '*he's drunk/He tastes like candy/He's so awful/He's deep/As muddy water*'. At a surprise gig in London at the Forum in October of 1998, Love jokingly protested to the audience that Rossdale, who was present at the show, had misinterpreted her words and that they were intended as a compliment.

Gavin recalls the event. 'Oh, yeah. I just went . . .' He mimes a sharp, alarmed intake of breath. 'I'd never do that to somebody. How embarrassing would that be – Hey, yo, you out there, what's up? All I could think was No, no, don't do it.

'But I don't look into her precise words too much. Still, there are some really great songs on the [latest] Hole album. I love "Malibu", and I think my version of something like that is "Warm Machine" [on *The Science Of Things*]. Her escape is to go to Malibu; mine is to get inside or on top of some warm machine that will take you away to a place of solace.

'I would imagine that it would probably change by the hour, who her lyrics are about,' Gavin says when he is asked if the line '*he rages to be true*' on the same album might be about him. 'And, knowing Courtney, I won't claim anything of that.'

To the author's disappointment, Courtney Love was not available to be interviewed for this book.

'If you're offended on my behalf, that's very sweet of you,' Gavin replies. 'It's a shame you didn't speak to her, really, because she's always good for a good quote. But I don't know, maybe she's just too uninterested in it. I've done stuff for her. I've been interviewed for her. When people are doing stuff on her and she's asked me to speak about her, I have. So it's not as if we haven't done it before. But that's okay, you know what I mean?

'What's so amazing about her is that she's the most incredible, talented, interesting sponge. She has such an ability to learn from other people; she just knows how to get the best out of people, to find out whatever is interesting about them and make sure it goes safely into her net. Courtney's really good with insight. I think she knows stuff about me and has insights into me that no one has, because no one's been there through the hours and hours and hours of time that we spent together. So it's just strange. When I think of the people that have spoken to you for the book, and I think of my relationship with her and how she knows me, and we're such peers. Now more than ever, which I love. It's a shame, because she has relevance in it.'

'History', as Rossdale has mentioned in numerous interviews, is the obliquely-imaged story of an abortion, told from a woman's point of view. A difficult subject for any lyricist to tackle, let alone someone who, being male, couldn't have experienced it first-hand. 'Yes, of course,' he agrees. 'It would have to be second-hand for me, but it has happened to me, and partners at the time, in my life. It's very strange to think that you might, if things were different, have children. I always remember Sinead O'Connor's song "Three Babies", which is one of the most beautiful songs in the world; all about how you learn from that experience, take things forward.

'It's so odd singing *"mouth of our father"*, *"mouth of my father"*,' he adds. 'Singing "father" in a song is so weird, because it's such a really stern word; frozen, stand-offish. *"Piss on me, piss on the underlay"* – there are so many weird things in here. This flat that I lived in, in Montagu Square, didn't have carpets there for two years. And then we found this grey carpet underlay, so we had it running down the centre of the cement floor, and the rest of the floor was all painted and graffitied.'

'Bonedriven', with strings arranged by the estimable Nigel Pulsford, not only drips with yearning and regret – *'heaven knows who walks away'* – it also packs a lot into the first three lines. The '*twenty-seventh letter*' which gives this book its name is, as Gavin has said, about wanting to communicate; about wanting more.

As for the words '*much maligned/beat me clever*', they are a direct reference, Gavin concedes, to the sometimes startling degree of enmity that has greeted Bush in certain media quarters. Not least of all because those suspicious of their success, seeking to suggest that the band had copped Nirvana's action after Kurt Cobain's suicide, presumed that the band was unaware of that fact. And in using the word 'Nevermind', the indication is that the band not only knew, but the songwriter wasn't afraid to acknowledge it. 'When I sang that line, I remember Steve Albini laughing and laughing, and going, "Hah! That's great. That's great! I like that." I like pissing in the face of danger, in the face of everything.

'It's a wistful song,' he admits. Even if it comes with a joke, given that the band's longtime crew member, assistant tour manager and Gavin's personal assistant Guy 'Bone' Johnson began as the band's bus driver on their first US tour in 1995. 'So we literally were Bone-driven!' he laughs. 'But also, bone driven, to me, means that power that comes from the deepest part of you, from the bottom of you; your bones are as deep as you get, and what holds you together. It's the most powerful image of yourself, your bones. If you're scared to your bones, or if something gets to your bones, it's beyond the realm of the superficial. "Bonedriven" was really like that sense of walking in a hailstorm, just making it up to the top of that hill where there was a warm place to be. It was about us, about Bush, and about this whole thing we're doing: "*We're all confusion, we're all the rage*", which was perfect. Which means, it's all right to be all confusion. "Wow. Such a depressing writer," people will say. And maybe we are the misunderstood lot, and that's why people relate to us. And so many people relate to us, and so many people like the words, that you just know you must be doing something right.'

And words, even if they are not prosaic and clear, have talismanic value. 'That's what it is,' he agrees. 'That's why it's important that you have those phrases that you pull out.'

And as for the album title *Razorblade Suitcase*, which appears in 'Synapse', Gavin recalls, 'Everyone was trying to look for a title that came from a lyric. I've said in interviews from day one what a "razorblade suitcase" is . . . And then of course,' he laughs, 'I said it was a lie and changed it because I got bored. But going back to the original idea, in the song itself, is probably easier to work out.

It's about emotional baggage. And the amount of emotional baggage that people have is just stunning, isn't it? And especially in your late twenties, going into your thirties, for you to meet someone new on any level brings all that baggage in. I mean, you end up feeling you have to say, "Do you mind if I just bring this big bag of emotional shit along with me into this?" '

Lyrically, *Sixteen Stone* and *Razorblade Suitcase* are 'absolutely very different albums in many, many ways', Dave Dorrell suggests when he is asked. 'I think there's a consciousness about *Razorblade Suitcase* that isn't as upfront and obvious on the first album. And I think there's a conscious desire to exorcise some demons, perhaps to respond to things that on the first album Gavin hadn't had to respond to, and to answer questions that hadn't previously been asked. I think the first album is representative of a certain kind of openness. Not that it isn't cynical, lyrically, sometimes, or knowing; I don' t think Gavin wrote it from some naive standpoint, because he'd had enough experience of the world to add experience to his ink. Yet across the two years that *Sixteen Stone* ran its course, I think he dealt with a lot of issues. First off, along with great success came criticism, which I suppose was to be expected. That said, however, you don't release a record, your first record certainly, and have your first thought be, OK, now, let's see what the critics are going to think. You think, Is it going to be successful? Are people going to like this record?'

In the event, people – if by people we mean millions of record-buyers rather than a handful of critics – came to like the darker *Razorblade Suitcase* as much as they liked *Sixteen Stone*. Rather faster, as it happens.

Razorblade Suitcase would be released in November 1996, two months after the band claimed the coveted Viewers' Choice honour at the MTV Video Music Awards in New York. Entering the UK charts at number four (a record buyer-driven retort to claims that the band were unsuccessful in their home country), *Razorblade* made its US chart debut at number one in the Billboard Top 200 Album chart, and went on to sell two million copies before Christmas.

Not bad for a bleak collection of emotional baggage, then. 'I remember I recently saw a picture of me with a journalist I know called Fritz from Berlin,' Gavin recalls. 'He's the most serious interviewer ever. He'd done two interviews with me on the first album, both times we were in Berlin on those tours. And when

Razorblade Suitcase came out and we went back, we met him again and he said, "So, Gavin, congratulations for getting the most depressing record ever to number one in America." '

The writer in question laughs. 'And of course I find myself saying, "Aww, come on, Fritz, it's not depressing! Well, okay, maybe it's a *bit* depressing . . ." '

I'd die in your arms if you were dead too
Here comes a lie
We will always be true

'I suppose, if I'm honest, I was frightened of Gavin's success, because I knew it would take him away from me. I couldn't help thinking, He's mine, and no, you can't have him.' Jasmine Lewis pauses. 'And then he made a record, and America got him. The Americans got him. The Americans stole him away from me.'

Succeeding at the only thing you have ever wanted to do is all you could ask for. When *Sixteen Stone* became a success story of runaway proportions for his band, Gavin Rossdale got everything he had ever dreamed of and more. But behind success stories there is often another, sadder story, and this one belongs to Jasmine Lewis, Gavin's girlfriend for five years.

'I met him through a friend of ours called Sam when I moved into Sam's house. Gavin used to call up and I'd speak to him on the phone. Sam had told him about me: "Look, there's this little Irish girl" – I think I was nineteen at the time – "who's a model, and she's just moved in, and she just sits in and watches videos all the time. She doesn't go out at all."

'So I remember him coming over one day. He used to wear these leather trousers, used to live in them. I remember I used to say, if he took them off, they'd stand up on their own. His hair was really long and he used to wear all this silver jewellery and boots; and I always remember the sound of them on the wooden floor. Gavin had this ability to make me really shy. I'd suddenly become really girly. And for years, that happened; every time I'd see him, I had nothing to say. But he used to come round to the flat and I thought he was so cute. I wasn't really interested but he was just so sexy. I remember one night he was playing this song to me down the phone, singing along, strumming his guitar. And then one day he asked me to meet him with a lot of other people to go out, but I didn't turn up. I can't remember; I went somewhere else. Anyway, he ended up going to LA, and we lost contact. Then he came back from LA and he was seeing this girl Suze off and on, and he kept asking me to go on a date, just one on one, and I kept saying no, 'cause I'd just get really embarrassed. I knew something was going to happen.

'In the end I decided I would go, and I was so nervous. And I met him outside this club and I was late, so I was even more nervous. And then we went for a drink and I just drank myself silly. We were drinking these Brazilian drinks, caipirinhas, and I was really drunk. I was hammered. They're supposed to be aphrodisiacs, and I think he knew. And we chatted all night; we stayed in this bar. I think I told him my whole life story; bored him silly. And I remember it was so romantic, walking back to his flat. And he stopped me outside John Lewis [department store] in Oxford Street, and he took me in his arms and kissed me. And my knees just went. I was in love. I was completely hooked.

'But then I went away; I went to Jamaica for a modelling job. And it was really weird, because I was a lot younger than him, but I was trying to be really cool about it. You know, thinking, He's still seeing Suze; that's fine, it's cool. I came back for Christmas and he and Suze were still together, so I tried to cool it down. And because he was still seeing her, I thought I should see people too. So one week he was off seeing Suze and I thought, All right, fuck it. So I ended up seeing someone. And the night after it, I told Gav, "Look, I'm seeing someone, too. I can do it too. And look, it's not going to work out, is it?" And I went out that night to a club and I wore a black wig, as though I was in disguise. And the guy I was meeting didn't turn up.

'But Gav did, and he kept walking past me until he realised it was me. I used to wear this locket and so finally he came up to me and said, "So, who's in your heart?" and I showed him. And there was nothing in it. He didn't like that. So then we went back to his

flat and we talked about who he was seeing and who I was seeing.
And then he called Suze and finished with her while I was there. I
went to Italy for a while, on a job, and when I got back he'd moved
all my stuff to Montagu Square and then Alex [Tate] moved in.
Mind you,' she laughs, 'he was only supposed to be there for a
month. But he was a great flatmate.'

And it was, despite Gavin's and Alex's relative poverty, a great
time for all three.

'We'd stay in bed like John and Yoko, and smoke all day and
watch videos and get so much crap food in it was unbelievable. But
Alex was the one who'd come in with trays of really wonderful
food. He was like our private chef, he was such a sweetheart. "Shall
I get another video? Do you want another Pils?"'

'Gavin would have parties and he'd sit in the kitchen and hand
out songsheets. I bought him his first electric guitar, a blue one,
when I came back from working in Japan. He learned how to play
on his own. He'd sit around and listen to songs, that's how he
learned. Gav can play amazing guitar now, of course. He used to
go, "Oh I've got this riff" and then he'd go, "Oh, I've got this other
riff." And I could never tell the difference and so I'd just say,
"That's great!" I remember one time at Montagu Square he was
playing something that ended up on the first album. There were so
many people in the kitchen and he passed out the songsheets and
they were all strumming. And I remember two of my photographer
friends were there, and later after *Sixteen Stone* had come out, they
said to me, "Gosh, do you remember when Gavin used to play that
in the kitchen?" Nobody thought he was going to do well. I guess
because it was Gavin, and he was wonderful, but he'd already been
in a band and nothing had happened. But he never gave up.

'And of course people did say, "You'll have to give up." I think
his mum said that a lot. But he just had so much heart for it. He
painted and decorated; he did any job he could do to get money,
but he always came home and wrote. And he'd do the weirdest
little jobs. I remember this job he had with Alex one Christmas
to get some money. They went all round the pubs to check out if
they were selling certain beers. Poor little things, freezing their bits
off.

'He taught me so much about femininity, because he loves a girl
to be a girl. He's such a woman's man. And he taught me about
how not to be jealous. He's got a lot of women friends; he and his
friend Zoe are like an old married couple together, walking along

the street holding hands. It's so funny. Even now, people say to me, "You're so touchy-feely, Jasmine!" So it's rubbed off.

'I think anybody's life he enters, he'll play a strong part. He's got mostly women friends. Maybe it's easier than having men friends, because men get jealous of him. Though he's got David Yow now. I've never met him, because I wasn't with him at the time, but I remember Gavin going, "Jas, guess what – I've got a male friend and he's a really cool guy!" And I was like, "What, you've got a *male* friend?" And David takes so much stick for being Gavin's friend. He's in the world of cool, independent bands where people think if you sell lots of records you have to be crap. But that's what's so endearing about Gavin – he got so excited about it. A new friend – and it's a male!

'Back on the femininity thing: he really did teach me stuff. He's very good at buying girls' clothes. He likes things that aren't your typical high street stuff. One year he bought me this woollen dress in scarlet and black stripes – and I looked like a bumblebee! But it was a great dress, because it was quirky. And one Christmas he had hardly any money at all, but he bought me a necklace that was so brilliant and so special, and he spent all his money on it. It's great that he has money now, but I think everyone wants a piece of it. When he started to get successful, that phone rang and rang and rang, and it would be people I'd never heard of, and I'd known Gavin for five years. All I could think of to say was, "Don't let them get to you this way."

'We had some wonderful times. I remember when Future Primitive had their first really good gig offer and it was going to be at the Mean Fiddler. And I'd done this show in Paris, and this woman came up to me and she said, "I've got a job, but I need a male and female model to do it." Now, Gavin hated anything to do with modelling. But I went home and said, "We've got to do this; it's a big job, we're both going to get paid really well . . . And it's a fashion commercial with a couple kissing in it, and it's in Tahiti!" And he said, "I don't want to do it. I'm in a band." So I said, "Well, if you're not going to do it with me, I'm going to do it anyway." '

She grins. 'So Gavin agreed. Nigel went mental, 'cause they lost this gig at the Mean Fiddler. But it was amazing. We spent four days in Papeete and the rest on Marlon Brando's island. It was so romantic; all the lights went off at seven o'clock at night and you had to walk along the beach with a little lamp. The first day we did the job, they asked me if I could dive and I said yes, but I thought they meant in a swimming pool, not the middle of the ocean. And I kept having these panic attacks; I couldn't stay down, and I kept floating back up. Gavin was like, "Come on, you've dragged me all the way out here." And I remember hanging onto the side of the boat and Gavin going, "I'm so embarrassed." And the photographer saying, "Oh you know, it's OK, we'll do shallow shots." And I'm saying to Gavin, "I hate you! I hate you!"

'I remember reading *Men Are From Mars, Women Are From Venus* – I used to read it in the bath – and one night we went out to a gig at the Astoria. And I remember being really tired after the gig and saying, "Gav, I want to go, I'm really bored with this." And he looked at me and said, "You don't want to go, you want me to put my arms around you and tell you it's all right." I said, "What?" And he said, "Well, I've been reading your book!" ' She laughs. 'And I was like, "No, I actually *am* really tired, and I want to go home!"

'We had some great times. Even though we had no money, we'd go off somewhere whenever we could: I remember going to the Lake District and, of course, we always had to go with the dog. We stayed in a pub, I think, and we had an argument that night and I stormed off. Couldn't see a thing; it was all heavy forest, and there was Gavin storming off, himself, ahead of me – and he stormed off right into a swamp, and he had these suede boots on that got completely ruined. I couldn't stop laughing: "It serves you right!"

'We used to go to this place on the edge of Scotland, walking with the dog. I remember once the both of us deciding to climb up a hill because it didn't look steep. And then it got so steep that Winston couldn't get up the mountain, he started sliding down. And I've never seen Gavin look so worried in all his life: he had me and Winston just about to go right down, and he ended up with me in one arm and Winston in the other.

'He taught me so much about music; he'd always be like, "Listen to this, Jasmine," and all I could think was "Noise! Noise! Noise!" I remember having a real fight with him in HMV because I wanted to buy a Jamiroquai album. And he said, "You're not playing Jamiroquai in *my* house!" So I said, "Well, it's my house too." So when I left,' she laughs, remembering all the false bravado of the statement, 'I said, "Now I can play music I like . . . *forever*."

'Every now and again, he'd get these really down periods. You know how they say women get down during their period? Well, he would, too. And he'd sit there and me and Alex would tiptoe around him. And all this time, Future Primitive were doing their thing, and basically record companies came and went. This sounds really awful, but I didn't want it to happen. 'Cause I knew if it happened, he'd go away a lot. I travelled, because I was modelling, but the longest I went away for was two months and that was Japan.

'And then, of course, it did happen for him. The Americans came and that was it and it was so weird. I remember when they got signed. I remember them going on their first tour. I just didn't want him to go. He went off for ages the first time. And I remember going over, me and all the girlfriends, Judith and Glynis, and we were picked up in this limo, and we just couldn't believe how big they'd got. And going to the first gig and it'd sold out. I remember just standing there, thinking, Oh my God. Thinking how different it was compared to London; now there were thousands of people crammed into this tiny space.

'And then,' she says, 'they got massive, massive, massive, massive.' She shakes her head, and says, 'I can't listen to the first album. It still makes me weep.

'It's all really weird, thinking back. When you go out with someone and they go away for two or three months at a time and everything changes. He'd be so manic from coming back off tour, it would take a while for both of us to get used to each other again. And then he went away for ages and he came back one Christmas, and this was when we had a bit of a falling out because he got friendly with Courtney Love. I'd always admired her; to me she was just amazing, stunning. But also I knew how powerful she was. I used to get the telephone calls where she'd hang up on me. And I remember saying to him, "Gav, you know that she likes you, don't you? I know that it's good, because you love her and you love Kurt, but it's hurting me." I was thinking, I don't like this and I don't like this calling. And I said, "Well, if you were in the same room as her, don't you think she'd try it on with you?"

'And it was the weirdest thing when she rang. She called him and had a go at him about something. And he was like, "Look, it's Christmas," basically saying she should calm down. He put the phone down – not *on* her, but she thought it was. And then in the end she ended up swearing and screaming and throwing the filing cabinet down the stairs. I think she got her assistant to call for her, and say, "Look, you've got to talk to her, cos she's losing it." And when I was in Japan I had a picture of Gav in the back of my book and someone said, "Oh my God, that's the guy who's going out with Courtney Love." It was in the *New York Post*. And when I spoke to him I said, "Gavin, you fuckin' arsehole." And he said, "I didn't want to tell you, 'cause I thought you'd never find out about that bit of press." And I said to him, "It would be better if you had told me about it." I know it's hard. Especially when you're suddenly famous, hanging out with all these famous people.

'I still like Courtney's music,' Jasmine adds evenly. 'I just think she latches on to every new pop star. And then when she's taken everything out, she dumps them and goes on to someone else. She doesn't seem to have any friends. She uses them all up.

'And then Gavin came back and I thought, Right, well, I can go away too. And he was like, "No, please stay, please stay, because if you go it might end," and I was like, "Fuck it, I'm going anyway." And I was thinking, This is how my life is going to be. He's away so much and I go away too, so one drunken night I phoned up and ended it. "No: you're away, I'm away. I've put so much on hold for you and you can't do the same for me."

'Even so, we lived together for six months after we'd split up. Even though he was seeing Gwen. I told myself, that's his life; he's a rock star. I just hope he's happy. Sometimes I just wanted to hold him and say "Gav . . ." It all backfired, me trying to be more hard, but I don't think I would have been able to deal with it. I don't want to be just somebody's girlfriend; I want to be Jasmine.

'I remember when he came back off tour, and he'd done the stupid thing of sending his luggage ahead of him, so of course I'm afraid I did that fatal thing of looking in his suitcase. And that's when I found all Gwen's stuff. I found all these love letters and I burned them in the sink. You see, when I'd ended it, he was feeling low and he met Gwen and fell in love.

'Alex has always said to me, "You two, you're meant to be together." But I'm very demanding. He's very demanding. And if he went away I'd have to give up my life and be part of his life. Modelling is hard; sometimes it's fun to do but it's a lot of work. I'd be on a shoot, freezing cold outside in this summer dress, and Gavin would say, "Why do you do it?" And I'd say, "Because I'm not ready to give it up yet." It's still what I want to do. And the older I get, the more money I get. So I don't mind really. It'd be like saying to Gav, "Why don't *you* become something else?"

'He's so talented. And he did it all because he loves music. He just wants credit for it. The thing is, he is so intelligent he could do anything he wanted if he put his heart to it. Yeah, it fucked up a lot of things, but it got him what he wanted.

'But when we split up I felt half of me had gone. It's like my arm had been chopped off. He was in my conversation the whole time. He was still part of me. That's why I couldn't see him. He was getting on with his life and I had to get on with mine. As soon as I start seeing someone, and they meet Gavin, they say, "You're still in love with him, I don't want you seeing him." And then I have to say, "Well, you'll have to get out of my life then."

'I've got nothing bad to say about him. He's the loveliest human being, the most considerate, talented, beautiful person. And beautiful all round, you know. I've never heard him slag anybody off that badly. Which is why I hate it when people slag him off; I think, Some day they are going to get to him. Someone's going to slag him off really badly, and he's going to break. I think criticism affects him a lot.

'Some things have to be sacrificed, I suppose. I wanted to let him go, knowing that that's what he wanted to do. Because I couldn't cope with it as it was. When I went to Japan, I wouldn't speak to him on the phone. It was like, "No, fuck it, I want *him* to be hurt now." But if I was still with him and we were back together, I don't think it would have lasted. Not unless I gave up what I was doing. Not unless I was going away with him.

'I've heard the new album, been to the studio. I'm so proud of him; it's come on so much. Last summer he played me the demos and I just sat there and cried. And I said, "Don't put this stuff on. You know I can't listen to it." It's funny, because even though I get upset, he gets upset too. He says, "You know, you always think it's easy for me, but it isn't easy for me either." You know. Still knowing that you love each other, but not being in love happily.

'If anybody asked me, should I go out with somebody in a band, I'd say no. Never be there at the beginning. At least wait until they finish. Because it's not your success; you always have to be in the background.

'I remember once he was on the phone saying, "Please, get a ticket and come and see me in LA, now." And all I could say was no. And I should have gone, but then really, I know it was better that I didn't. The whole success thing, he needed to do it on his own. And he did.'

Alex Tate, musing on the personal tragedy he saw unfolding for his two friends, will say, 'The worst thing is, it wasn't one person that took Gavin away from her. She was fighting thousands of people, millions of people. She couldn't get him back, and he couldn't leave. He was committed to three other guys and a record company. She was saying, "Rescue me." "Fly to America," he'd say. "But I can't fly to America, I've got a job, I've got to be in Marrakesh next week. I've been paying my bills all my life." And he'd say, "I've got three guys expecting me to get onstage tonight." The thing was he was lonely, travelling in a country he didn't know very well, and the one person he needed, his intimate lover, was struggling to give him any kind of support at all. Are chart positions and front covers ever going to be enough to replace it?' He shakes his head.

'I don't know if I'm being unselfish,' Jasmine Lewis says quietly. 'All I know is that Gavin was the biggest thing in my life and the one thing that hurt me the most. He taught me a hell of a lot and I really appreciate that. He said to me, "Jasmine, I'm as hard as nails now." And I'd say, "Gavin, listen, I'm a *bed* of nails." It helps to know that he loves me and I love him; that's a beautiful thing. I had the best five years of my life. Lots of fun, lots of love.' She closes her eyes for a long moment. 'Why be bitter about that?'

'Ugh. I hate that accolade of hard work. It's so awful. It's like being famous for being "Britain's loudest band" or something. Like, yeah, they sound like shit, but at least they play every night! I hate that. I hate that accolade.' – Gavin Rossdale

26 OCTOBER 26 TO 14 NOVEMBER 1996

Auckland, Brisbane, Sydney, Newcastle, Canberra, Melbourne, Adelaide, Perth, Osaka, Nagoya, Tokyo

Before they knew it, the already legendarily hard-touring Bush were back on the road again, with a second album under their belts. As an artist, Gavin Rossdale might not like being praised for his band's stamina, but there was no denying that they had that quality in spades. And, as agent John Marks observes, even with a brief pause to make a second record, they hadn't let any grass grow under their feet.

'The whole intent [with recording *Razorblade Suitcase* and releasing it quickly] was to try and get it out for the holiday season. It was probably one of the quickest I've ever seen, in terms of them delivering the finished product and getting it out in a year.'

Even the normally unflappable Marks was surprised. 'Usually, with any band that rises that quickly in the first record, there's usually a big turn off [on the second] because what was once cool is now accepted by the masses, so subsequently it sort of loses the edge it had in its earlier incarnations. We didn't really have that with Bush, even though the second record didn't sell as well as the first,' he adds. (In the event, the harder-edged *Razorblade Suitcase* would go on to almost match the sales of *Sixteen Stone*, and significantly outperform its predecessor in many markets, including the UK where it is now platinum-plus.) 'Even so, on the second record,' Marks points out, 'the band would out-tour anything they'd done before.' In fact, Bush would become one of the Top 10 grossing touring acts – a list that includes everything from country to R&B to the alternative rock field Bush inhabits – in the United States in 1997.

In industry terms, which are the terms in which Marks inevitably speaks, *Razorblade Suitcase* and the 148 dates that followed it were a roaring success. And in creative terms, which are those the band speaks in, it was an even greater success. In personal terms, however, when you ask Gavin Rossdale how he celebrated the number one US chart debut of *Razorblade Suitcase* in November 1996, the story he tells doesn't include either of those perspectives.

Ask him if there was a party, and he sighs heavily and says nothing for almost a minute.

'No. No. I just wish . . .' He pauses. 'I was with Gwen,' he begins. By now, Gwen Stefani and Gavin, who had spent so much time together on previous US dates when her band No Doubt had supported Bush, were a couple. 'We were there on the road with everyone, and it was good. But I mainly remember that time . . .' He sighs again. 'I did something really awful. I said something really awful about someone, probably because I was just exhausted and out of it and stoned and lost in my own world, and I just made a big mistake that I've given myself a sentence of four years of feeling bad about it.'

As it happens, the friend about whom Gavin made an offhandedly unkind comment overheard him. 'It was one of the worst things I've ever done. I didn't say anything particularly rude, I just spoke my mind. And he was right behind me when I said it. And it was very uncomfortable. I mean, I've done bad things, but this was a different kind of a bad thing. And I made someone feel bad.

'Of course, when I realised what I'd done, I just apologised to him. I said I just made a mistake and I just felt really bad about it. So our celebrations were really tempered. And then I wrote him a letter, apologising. My note just said that I apologised for saying this stuff about him and how ironic, there I was going to number one and I was supposed to feel happy, but instead I was just feeling really shitty about this.

'I don't often fuck up with my mouth, you know, and say stuff about people that I truly regret. But this was a major fuckup. We've all had our major social *faux pas*, where you don't know how that happened or you just wish you had just had a big fucking sandwich in your mouth at the time and shut the fuck up.'

He pauses to count the months since the event occurred. 'So I've got two years left,' he smiles ruefully. 'But even now, I get a lurch in my stomach when I think of it.

'Still, because of that, something good came of it. One of the sweetest things Gwen ever said to me, she said to me then. We were in the hotel room at four in the morning that night after I said it, or the day after. And Gwen was saying to me, "You know what? You apologised to him, and he totally took the apology and he was fine about it." She said, "You know, if he knew how upset you were about this right now, he would feel really bad and he wouldn't want you to feel like that."

Gavin smiles. 'That was one of my favourite things of everything she's ever said to me. It was really just . . . pure female comfort. And that's when I thought, *That's* the kind of person I'd want to spend all my time with, because it's such a brilliant insight. And it saved me. It was the only thing that could save me because I was so disgusted at myself.'

He looks up and laughs. 'So, when you ask me about the album going to number one, you were probably expecting, Yeah, we had champagne! Yeah! A party!' He shakes his head. 'Of course, the funniest thing was then having the album knocked off the top of the US charts by No Doubt.'

Gavin shrugs at the incongruity, and adds cheekily. 'Only *I* could go out with someone who would remove me from the number one spot.' He adds hastily, 'Of course, I was really happy for her. Though to be honest, I probably wouldn't have minded if their number one had come at a slightly different time. But I suppose that if it was going to be someone, it was good that it was her. But it was funny. "Gee, Gwen! Thanks a lot!" '

In the meantime, another member of Bush had more to celebrate than just a number one album. Robin and Glynis had a number one daughter, Ruby Rose, to cheer about, too. Rather improbably, and due in no small part to Robin's determination, the proud father actually made it home for the birth, despite having to film a video for 'Swallowed' in London prior to the south-east Asian tour, worrying the whole time that he might be called away.

Glynis remembers, 'Robin was around for a few weeks before she was born, and when he went off to do the video, I know when he left I thought I was going to have her. I rang him, and he was halfway to London. He decided to carry on, and I said I'd call him if there was any change. It didn't happen then – in fact, she was two weeks late, which was really annoying!' She laughs. 'I know I had her on a Tuesday and I came out of hospital on the Saturday, and on the Monday he went away and stayed away for a couple of months.'

Still, she confirms, 'He was definitely there for the birth.' As for family resemblance, she laughs, 'Oh, Ruby came out of me looking like Robin' although much prettier, of course! My mother came into my room and said, "My God, it's Robin!" Occasionally, somebody says she's got my eyes,' she adds. 'But she has got very, very curly hair. She's like him. And he's a lovely daddy. He's totally besotted by her. And if you ask her now what Daddy does, she says he's a drummer, and she does it with her hands. I don't think she can understand the concept of a band, but she does understand Robin plays the drums and she can pick him out in the weirdest photos or videos.

'I have really nice memories of the birth,' Glynis adds. 'Robin still has a pair of trainers that he was wearing when she was born that have blood on them, and he loves to show those trainers to people. I know he had a list of people to phone as soon as she was born, and he had people coming out of other hospital rooms telling him to be quiet! He's got quite a boomy voice.'

In the meantime, there were shows to play, even for new fathers. With *Razorblade Suitcase* completed, a video shot and the second Bush baby in existence – David and Claudia Dorrell being the first Bush parents some months earlier – the band made their first foray into south-east Asia with a number of club dates in Japan. It may be the only country left where the band have to play venues that size, in fact. But according to agent Mike Greek, however, 'from the band's perspective, they view it as a case of knowing that wherever they play, they convert more and more people to what they're doing. They are a very, very well-informed group of musicians, and are very much aware that, by going and playing to real fans, you can make them into lifetime fans.'

31 JANUARY TO 1 MARCH, 1997
Portsmouth, Manchester, Glasgow, Wolverhampton,
Nottingham, Cambridge, London, Frankfurt, Hamburg,
Copenhagen, Stockholm, Oslo, Berlin, Cologne, Stuttgart,
Munich, Vienna, Zurich, Milan, Paris, Ghent, Utrecht,
Groeningen, London

After Christmas, the band returned to Europe, and saw UK
audiences expand once again on the British first leg. Mike Greek
recalls, 'We upgraded just about every venue on that UK tour. We'd
taken a very conservative stance just to see how things developed.
And in Manchester and Wolverhampton, we moved from venues
with eight hundred capacity to two thousand capacity and sold
them out. The Bush train had definitely come to town. Things
basically went from strength to strength.'

As ever, of course, the UK media found opportunities to express
scepticism about a band who had become successful both without
their permission, and in countries far outside of their sphere of
influence.

Heather Redmond, the band's UK press officer at the time, says,
'I remember a news piece that ran on ITV, when the band were
doing their first tour in 1997, just before the London show at the
Forum in Kentish Town, which was sold out. Anyway, they sent a
news team to Shepherd's Bush, and they were stopping people on
the street. You know, people like your mum or your aunt who
wouldn't know anything about rock bands anyway, and they were
asking, "So, have you heard of Bush?" Naturally, people were
saying things like, "What, Bush the electronic firm?" It was just the
most ridiculous thing you've ever seen. Of course they're not going
to know, and it just seemed spiteful and stupid. It was the case for
so long here – just lazy, lazy journalism – and the thing we had to
fight all through that campaign was everyone in the press saying,
"Oh, they're big in America, but they're not big here." It's fair
enough to begin with, I suppose as a way of drawing people in, but
it gets to the point when people want to read something else.' Not
least of which the people who put *Razorblade Suitcase* into the top
five of the UK album charts the week it was released, of course.

In the meantime, the band were unstoppable. Even, occasionally,
with no electricity. Guitar technician Dale Meekins recalls, 'When
we were in Oslo on that tour, the power went out every other song.
We had a guy stand there by the breaker, turn everything off when

it happened, and turn it back on again. You just get through it, though,' he says philosophically. Did the band throw a strop? He laughs. 'The band? Oh, they just go, well, whatever, and keep at it. They know we're not there to create problems, we're there to fix them.'

And no matter how many dates the band play, Gavin insists, there's always something new to see from the stage regardless of whether you're in Grand Rapids or Groeningen. 'I just love seeing who the people out there are. Sometimes you look out and see the crowd and you get off on thinking how mad it is, and who they all are. Sometimes if you've got to do an interview somewhere, you have to walk through a part of the crowd, and I love to see all the people hanging out, buying drinks, talking, waiting for the show.'

He laughs. 'Not that I don't still find it all really weird. On some level, I've always been half convinced that one night, the place will be completely empty. That everyone will decide that they didn't want to come, just that night – like, every single person would end up saying, "Oh, I had to see my cousin that day." And suddenly there's no one there. What happened? Sorry, no show. "Gee, if you'd just done it on a Saturday like we said . . . This Wednesday shit just isn't working . . ." ' He laughs again. For the record, this empty-house scenario Gavin Rossdale has been carrying around with him did not occur at any point on this tour, or any other so far.

20 MARCH TO 24 AUGUST, 1997

Miami, Tampa, Orlando, Pensacola, New Orleans, Little Rock, Memphis, Nashville, Birmingham, Atlanta, Columbia, Winston-Salem, Charlotte, Landover, Roanoke, Philadelphia, Pittsburgh, New Haven, Boston, East Rutherford, New York, Buffalo, Toronto, Detroit, Grand Rapids, Cleveland, Dayton, Chicago, Moline, Ames, Minneapolis, Madison, Indianapolis, Louisville, St Louis, Kansas City, Oklahoma City, Shreveport, Lafayette, San Antonio, Houston, Rock Am Ring, Rock Im Park, Pinkpop, Denver, Albuquerque, El Paso, Phoenix, Las Vegas, San Diego, Hollywood, Mountainview, Inglewood, Sacramento, Concord, Reno, Portland, Seattle, Spokane, Vancouver, Dallas, Edmonton, Calgary, Saskatoon, Winnipeg, Milwaukee, Clarkson, Columbus, New York, Candiagua, Hershey, Saratoga, Boston, Ottawa, Montreal, Toronto, Glasgow, Bizarre Festival, Hamburg, Berlin, Vienna, Stuttgart, Reading

The audience didn't suddenly decide to stay home on the next tour, either, which would be the band's biggest and longest to date, and which would see them headlining consistently huge venues in North America. What's more, it would see them take in a sold-out show at Madison Square Garden in New York; the largest ticketed event in the history of rock'n'roll in Dallas, which the band headlined; and the emotional high-point of a rapturously received performance to some 100,000 people at Reading, England's most prestigious rock festival.

In fact, says Bone, 'The only time I've really ever seen Gavin nervous was at Reading. He was *tight*. He and Gwen had to walk and walk and walk before he could loosen up before they went on. You know, playing there was probably the equivalent of playing the Super Bowl in his home town. I think it had bothered him for a while, that feeling of not being as successful in England as elsewhere. But Reading pretty much put an end to that and, on that tour, we sold out at the Brixton Academy [in London], and we sold out in Manchester. We could have done ten thousand people there, easy.'

Another high point, for Gavin in particular, was that, on this tour, Bush were able to bring longtime alternative cult heroes The Jesus Lizard out as a support band for several North American dates. David Yow, the band's frontman and now a close friend of Gavin's, recalls, 'I first met them at the Roskilde Festival [in Denmark]. Their tour manager came and found me and said, "I'm so glad you're still here – the guys really want to meet you." So we sat and had lunch together. Later we were asked to tour with them in Canada and the Northeast [of the US], so somehow or other, that's where we ended up.'

For a band whose uncompromising music has earned them truckloads of critical and fan acclaim, but very few shows at the sort of venues Bush were now playing, the experience was, laughs Yow, 'a trip. It was a blast. There's one time when we were in Hershey in Pennsylvania, at a football arena, where they've got the portable trailers as backstage areas. And you'd look out the window and the street was ten feet away, and there would be thirty adorable little girls and several of their mothers [who] kept trying to see the band in the dressing room. And I remember Gav said, "Would you do me a tremendous favour and wave to these people, *hard*?" I was laughing so hard I fell down!

'We talked about what they go through. I said "Man, I just can't imagine the attention you get." If it was me, I'd love it for about a week and then I couldn't take it. I think Gavin handles it incredibly well. It would be so hard not to believe in all that, though, and think, I *am* God! The first show we ever played with them was in Milwaukee. We went into the dressing room, and all of a sudden this crazy noise goes up – honestly, it was like a hundred million screaming mice – because Gavin and Gwen had just got out of the car. There were probably a thousand girls and a few boys and their mums, and as soon as they saw Gavin and Gwen they were screaming.

'It's like that every day,' he grins. ' Every day. It's just incredible.'

After the tour, Gavin's friendship with David, in particular, grew and grew. In fact, Gavin recalls with some pride that David's e-mails to him always end with 'your best friend, David Yow'. Of course, with the schedules of both bands to consider, actually hanging out isn't always easy. 'We don't actually see each other a lot. This past April we were playing London, Paris and Amsterdam, and Gav came to Amsterdam, but it was really a drag. He was really looking forward to it and so were we, but we were all completely jet-lagged and tired, so we ended up sitting backstage not saying anything much. Apart from talking on the phone, we never get to hang out. Considering what friends we are, the amount of time we've actually been in each other's company is very small. In total, probably about three weeks.'

Thank heaven for the phone, then. Well, kind of. David laughs when he says that the two spend hours talking. 'But it's always long-distance, and when the bill comes, my wife says, "Darling, you *really* can't talk to Gavin for an hour next time!" '

On the subject of bands Bush may or may not sound like, David Yow – whose band shared a seven-inch single and plenty of hours with Kurt Cobain and his band – is refreshingly to the point. 'I don't think it's fair they get this Nirvana shit all the time. There are so many other bands who are so much closer. I don't get it. To me it's simply late 80s, early 90s, mid-90s rock/pop music. Sure, there's a Nirvana influence. But God, there's Nirvana influence on every band that's alive nowadays. I don't really hear it in them more than I do in anyone else.' As for Bush sounding American, Yow's assessment is that 'I can hear a very clear English accent when Gavin sings. The guitars sound an awful lot like guitars,' he adds with a grin. 'And the drums sound like drums. I think that's an international thing.

'Of course those accusations must hurt,' he acknowledges. 'Gavin's pretty sensitive. I don't think I've had specific conversations with him about it, but when you're famous, there's always going to be a lot of people who love you and a tremendous lot of people who hate you. Even my friends. I mean, people I ran into in the States would say, "What's the deal with you and Bush?" And the other day in Germany somewhere, we got to the venue and there was a big cardboard box in the refrigerator, and it said, "David Yow, please please *please* stop having anything to do with Bush. Please stop."' He laughs and shakes his head. 'And I have no idea who wrote that. I mean . . . what the fuck. Do people who like The Jesus Lizard think I'm going to be somehow tainted by hanging out with people who happen to be English pop stars? That's ridiculous!'

That said, his real friends know the score, he underlines. 'I have to say that no real friends of mine would criticise me for being friends with Bush, because those kind of people I just wouldn't be hanging out with, but a lot of them do think it's really odd. But they're generally willing and eager to hear why it is OK. I mean, what's the big deal? They're great guys. They're tremendously nice people.'

On the road, Yow says, The Jesus Lizard were treated every bit as well as Dorrell emphasises that Bush strive to do with every support band.

'Were we looked after? Absolutely. Anything we wanted that we didn't have, we'd just say it and it would be there. That's one part of that rock star thing that did sometimes really blow my mind. Sometimes Gavin would not even be saying he wanted it, he'd just mention it in passing, and five minutes later it would be there. It's weird. Incredible. And they're completely generous.

'It's amazing when you think of it,' he says of Bush's level of fame. 'I mean, can Gavin really blank out all that stuff which is in his face all of the time? If he lived in the States, he'd have no personal life whatsoever. I guess it's good he lives in England.

'It's so funny that on tour sometimes you can't even hear the band, the audience is so loud. There were a few times that Gavin and I would go out, and they'd make him put on this cap to cover up his hair. And you know, you can still sort of see that it's him. And it ends up being like *Invasion Of The Body Snatchers* when people work out who he is.' A crowd would descend, Yow recalls, 'and all of a sudden, he gets scurried away by security'.

Asked if he ever coveted Bush's level of fame, Yow replies without hesitation, 'I've got to admit that I really would love to have the amount of cash he's got!' He laughs loudly. 'But the fame sure does not appeal to me. But the financial liquidity that he's got? Sure. Like, I know he just dropped off to Milan for the day. Jesus. Sure, I'd love to be able to say, "I'd like some Indian food; think I'll go to Bangladesh." I know this great Thai restaurant in Bangkok . . .'

The fame, on the other hand, makes it difficult to live a normal life. Gavin insists that he tries to retain some semblance of normality on tour. Sometimes, it transpires, at the expense of his own safety.

'As soon as people take away a few responsibilities, and everything's arranged, like it is on tour, you become absolute babies. And then I cope with that by just going off. I think it was in Chicago that I decided to walk to the venue one day. And on the way, I stopped in at a bookseller's to buy something.' People en route to the venue, naturally, spotted him. First a few, then a few more, and then an embarrassing – and potentially dangerously large – crowd. 'The way it happens is that you get a few people, and then ten or twelve, and then there's a whole crowd, and then they're stampeding. I don't know what I was thinking,' he laughs. 'It was so dumb. And I couldn't get hold of anyone on the crew, and so no one could help me, because no one knew where I was. So I'm in this bookstore buying a book, and it got really jammed full of people, and I had to get away from them. It ended up like a Benny Hill chase. That was a bit weird – I had to get helped by the police in the end. Can you imagine it?' He laughs. ' "Uh, excuse me officer . . . I'm in a band and we're playing tonight and I think it might be my fault but I'm a little bit worried about the size of the crowd here . . ." '

Comments tour manager Ross Duncan, crisply: 'Yeah, I fucking loved him for that. I was over the moon about that . . .'

Sometimes, of course, it's the audience that needs a bit of sorting out.

'I remember playing a festival in Portland,' Gavin relates. 'There was a huge fight in the pit; it was really rough in there. So I stopped the song – I think we were playing "Zen" – which is really weird, stopping a song in full flow. And I said, "Right, both of you come up on stage and you have to explain what is going on." So this guy jumps up – a really big guy, like a Reading stagehand – and he's huge, massive. I was like, "Ohhh, fuck." And he takes the microphone and says, "This guy's been an asshole all day; he's been knocking people around, fucking up." And then I gave the microphone to the other guy and he went . . . Well, actually, he just grunted. So I said, "Right, him – out – and you, the other guy, can go back in there." It was pretty scary though,' he laughs, "Cause they were pretty massive!

'The violent ones, you know . . . I think it's just to do with the audience you get being in a rock band. Any rock band that comes to town gets their alotted number of jock thug looser fuck-faces that will destroy everything if they can, but you just try to have them monitored. Even so, you have to be careful with *that* in some ways, too. It's a thin line between crowd control and elitism. You don't want to be too elitist, although that in itself is quite punk. Punk rock, originally, was very elitist and very separated, and you know, very conscious of not being allowed to listen to any other kind of music, except maybe reggae. Back then, that was a no-no.

'And I can understand why. I think it totally makes sense. Obviously when you play to five hundred thousand people at Dallas Raceway, you're not gonna have five hundred thousand like-minded people, but I would say that it's still worth believing that, with the power of music, you can unite a lot of people, and a lot of people can identify with some of the sentiments in the music. And for that reason you don't want to exclude anyone. I mean, violence is out there, it exists, it's inevitable. The only way to totally safeguard against that is to only play clubs. But are the first three hundred people that make it in also the sort of people you want to hang out with? You can't be sure. It's a weird one. But I totally understand that idea of worrying that some of your audience will be assholes.'

On the other hand, Heather Redmond recalls, Bush often go out of their way to treat their audiences well. Attending the Orlando show on this tour, she recalls seeing the band come to the assistance of two stranded girls from out of town. Quite far out of town, as it happens.

'When we turned up for the gig, there were two Japanese girls there, sat outside the venue. They'd flown in from Tokyo and not only did they not have any tickets for the show, they had nowhere to stay, they had very little money, and they had just travelled there because they were desperate to see the band. And Gavin was just brilliant. He got them sorted out with tickets; they got laminates, they got taken to the dressing room, and they were told to feel at home and have whatever food and drink they wanted. And after the show, the band put them up in a hotel as well. Can you believe it? Just like that. They're amazing.' After years in the music business, she says, this was a first. 'I've never known any other band to do that.'

'What I like about our audience,' Gavin says, 'is that it's really mixed and really balanced. Obviously at the front you get the younger ones, but you know, it's just so varied. And everyone who comes to our show isn't female and fourteen, either,' he adds, possibly as a retort to unfriendly critics who seek to prove that Bush's mixed male–female audience is a dangerous sign of incipient teen-idol credibility loss. 'Of course, when people want to belittle what we're doing, they make out that it is.'

Of course, in amongst all the positive interactions with fans, Bush's crew remains vigilant for those that aren't. As happened to the band in, of all places, Ames, Iowa.

'Well, you know, touch wood, God forbid, we don't have too many nutters,' Ross Duncan says. 'Usually it's fine. I mean, I've walked to delis for breakfast with Gav and he's had his beanie and his shades and Gwen's had hers on and nobody's known who the hell we are. It's really just when he takes his bloody hat off that problems start. And then there was the time in Ames,' he adds. 'We got him in the lobby about three in the morning . . .'

It transpires that an unbalanced chap decided he needed to meet the band. Ross recalls, 'He stole a rooming list from behind reception [in the band's hotel] and when Bone and Bill [Sitkowitz, tour security] came in, they saw this rather weird guy telling the receptionist that he worked for Interscope and needed Gavin's room number. Now, this is Iowa, and so the woman behind the desk goes bumbling round to find it and the geezer leaps over and steals a list. Fortunately, the band all register under pseudonyms so it didn't do him that much good.'

According to Bone, 'It was scary, because this guy rang my room and called me down to the bar just when they were ready to close. You should have heard the spiel that this guy gave me. Of course, part of my gig is knowing when something's up and I said, "Well, you know, I'll come down and meet you and we'll see if we can't help out." He said he was a record company rep, and it was really late and he'd just got in. So I threw some names at him that were common interests of us and this record company, and he didn't know any of them. So I called Ross, and I told the guy I was calling Gavin to have him come on down to meet us. Instead, I told Ross to grab Bill and call the cops, and he rounded everything up.

'The guy was quite a wacko. And as the night wore on, he got worse and worse, and by the time the cops arrived, believe me, his eyes were spinning around in circles.'

'When the cops turned up,' Ross continues, 'they did the whole thing: made him walk a straight line and stick his finger on his nose; try and eat an ice cream cone with his eyes shut, the whole deal. Anyway, they arrested him and had him kept in jail until we left the state. And we went down the next day to get the details on him, because we keep a database of the odd nutcase, so that if they ever appear again we have a profile to give the local authorities. And the funny thing was, we went down to the jail to get all his details, and me and Bill walk in and the band all bugger off next door to the thrift shop, and they all come out like ladies having had the finest shopping day out they've ever had.'

He laughs wryly. 'And I'm, like, two hours late for the next gig, and worrying about this stalker, and the band are all going, "Oh, look at my new shirt! Well, it's not quite new, but . . ."'

Bone concludes, 'At the risk of sounding like a melodramatic, neurotic fool, nine hundred and ninety-nine times out of a thousand, every meeting that we have with people in the street or a bar or restaurant is going to be a pleasant one. My job is to be ready at every single minute for that one time that it's *not* going to be. I scope everything around Gavin every single minute that we're out there. I don't take anything for granted. Because it only takes that one second where you take something for granted to send everybody home and nobody has an income. Not to mention a hurt friend or a dead friend. I take protecting Gavin very seriously. Far more seriously than he really likes me to, but I've been in this business twenty-one years and I know how quickly shit can go bad. It's just a fact of life.'

Of course, it isn't always dangerous out there. Sometimes it's just arm-chewingly boring. And sometimes, as Dave Parsons says, you've got to remember that even having a crew to do everything for you doesn't mean you have to become a pampered baby.

'Personally,' he says drily, 'I like doing things myself. I mean, I guess having somebody taking your suitcase to your room is not such a bad thing, but generally I'd rather do it myself. Otherwise you end up like, "Wow, I can't *believe* my suitcase didn't turn up."

But if you left it in your room and just relied on the fact that the hotel may pick it up and may take it to the hotel lobby for you and may put it on the bus then sooner or later it's gonna go wrong and it's not gonna end up there. And also it sort of gives you a bit of normalcy. I like doing things. I'm not very good at being totally lazy.' He reconsiders, and grins. 'Actually, I am quite good at not doing anything. But I'm not very good at lying down and watching telly and just vegging out. You can get really bored – *super* bored if you've got nothing to do.

'Being on tour, you realise that mostly what you do every day is exactly the same. You really get into this sort of routine and it's quite a dull routine. You know: you go to bed really late because you're hyper from the gig before. And then you get up, and you have to almost lower your expectations of each day, because if you have really high expectations for what you can do in a day, you'll get disappointed really quickly, because there's not really a lot that happens. You know, if you go to soundcheck and get there half an hour early, chances are someone's still fixing the monitor board. Then you tune up, and Nigel tries to fix his guitar pedal for half an hour and, you know, most of it really is just sitting around. In fact, you have to get *good* at sitting around. So you just do real simple stuff: listen to CDs, read and watch videos . . . basically, it's a lot like the stuff that everyone else does at college when they should be studying. Football games. PlayStation. Stuff like that. I guess if you're somewhere interesting, you go shopping. You get really good at shopping as well, funnily enough . . .

'I really don't know how else you should be using the time,' he muses. 'I mean, in some ways, you've probably got enough time to learn to speak five languages, or you could take a correspondence course and get a degree in law!' The twinkle in his eye suggests that the similarity to prison inmates turning to home study is not quite coincidental.

Mind you, you can always invite your friends over to watch you at your day job. Although Judith, Jasmine, Glynis and Sarah had been out to America to see Bush during the *Sixteen Stone* tour, it would be the band's sold out show at Madison Square Garden which gave Bush the opportunity to splash out on a real party, and invite family and friends from the UK to share in their excitement and triumph.

Sarah Chope says, 'Madison Square Garden; well, it's just one of those places you've heard of, isn't it? It was incredible to see, and absolutely everyone came over. I actually get quite nervous, and can't eat or anything, before shows like that, when there are lots of friends and family on the guest list. I don't know why, but I get really nervous for them even if Dave doesn't. He's always asking me, "Are you okay?" I remember being in the audience, watching the show from different places in the crowd, and listening to people shouting, "Bush!" And kids going mad, and shouting at everyone; girls shouting at Dave, too. And it's hard not to want to say, "Well, I know what colour of underwear he has on!" I remember standing in a queue for the toilets, and the young girl ahead of me had Dave P written in black marker across both of her hands.' Sarah laughs. 'I thought it was quite funny – I was tempted to say, "I quite like him too, actually", but of course you don't.'

Alex Tate, who would come over to see the band play in Buffalo, recalls, 'Honestly, I hadn't really paid attention to what Gavin was doing in America. I knew he was going to do his best and it was going well but, suddenly, he's ringing me up saying, "Look, you've got to come out here."' Having just made his first feature film, Alex 'was drowning in a sea of ideas and people; living in Soho, working all day, snoozing all night. I kept saying, "I can't come next month, because I've got two jobs on." I wasn't putting it off, I was just busy. And he's like, "You're coming. I've already bought you a ticket." So I've landed in New York, and this limo picks me up. I'm already getting out a hundred dollars and hoping that's enough to cover it, and then it pulls up outside a massive hotel. And I'm thinking, "Jesus, I don't know if I can afford all this. I can't afford the fuckin' limo, let alone the hotel. And what's more, can *Gavin* afford this?"

'I just thought he was saying thanks for being at every gig. You know, "I can't afford much but I can take you to America and we can have a laugh." So I check in, and there's the bus outside and we drive to Buffalo. And we drive past this huge stadium,' Alex says of the Marino Midland Arena. 'So I say to him, "Hey, soon that'll be *you* playing there." And he says, "Yeah, it's tonight." And I'm going [laughs], "Yeah, right, *right*." And Gavin looks at me and says, "No, that's where we're playing, and it's *tonight*." And I say, "Shit, no, it can't be, that place must hold, what, seven or eight thousand people!" In fact, it's actually a sixteen thousand capacity venue . . .

'So there I was in the dressing room and suddenly the place is full and I'm starting to understand. Then I hear sixteen thousand people shouting, "Gavin! Gavin!" And suddenly it hits me: *he did it!* And I'm jumping and shouting and he's trying to be self-deprecating but pretty soon he's doing it too. All the clubs and pubs and shitty times . . . and here it is: boy, you're going to get paid tonight. And he's like, "Right, Alex, you're coming on stage tonight. Come on, man, do some funky dancing.'

And some funky dancing onstage with his mate Gavin in front of sixteen thousand screaming American fans was indeed what Alex Tate did. 'So I go onstage and do this mad dance and I'm just exhausted in about fifteen seconds so I collapse in a heap and let the guys drag me off . . .'

Pete Black, Gavin's friend of two decades' standing and, as a photographer, a veteran of most of the *Sixteen Stone* tours of America, comments, 'Sometimes when you are having such a good time, you want to share it with all the people you love. And that's exactly how Gavin felt. He flew out Alex, and Mark, and Sacha, and his father, all because they'd never seen him play in America, and they didn't even know, really, what all the fuss was about. I remember speaking to Alex when he came back, and he said, "You know, what you described to us before I really couldn't believe. Not until I was there and I watched it, and even *then* it was still hard to believe." Because you don't think your friends are ever going to become superstars, do you? I'm sure not even Michael Jackson's friends did. But then again, did he even have many friends from when he was younger? Do many bands have them? You know, you see these documentaries on Madonna and Fleetwood Mac, and you don't see many people around them that they've known all their lives. What happened to Madonna's school friends? Didn't she like them, or didn't they like her?

'And it's only when you see it for yourself,' Pete reiterates, 'that you know. Because deep down, unless you're there, you're never going to believe it.'

Sacha Puttnam, also in attendance at that Buffalo show, remembers his own revelation. 'Something really struck me about the audience there. I saw a lot of disenfranchised young people, which I never really thought we were. Well, I definitely wasn't, but clearly Gavin felt that he was. And watching him, I saw the power in Gavin's psychology; the whole thing of his mum leaving and all that pain. Suddenly it struck me that I saw it being reflected in the kids who were there, and the more he pulled out from inside himself, the more people responded. What's cathartic for him was cathartic for them as well.'

Of course, it wasn't all catharsis. There were a few rock'n'roll parties to attend.

'Have you heard about the fourth of July party?' Ross asks, gearing up for a particularly choice anecdote. 'We played Harrowshea Stadium in Pennsylvania that day and [department store magnate and Interscope Records honcho] Ted Fields was having a huge party in the Hamptons. So the record company invited us, but everyone was like, "Aw, we're in Pennsylvania and we don't come offstage until half ten. Do we really need to go?' And I tell them that two of them did need to go, at least, as ambassadors, because they're the biggest band on their label. They weren't sure, but I need a decision, because I have to get a Lear jet booked to take us there. After all, I don't have a Lear jet I can just whip out and say, "Right, lads, we're off."

'So, eventually, Gav and Robin and then all of them decided to go. Right. So we stick the band on the stage, get the Lear jet. We had to fly from the Harrisburg airport, and I hear there's a curfew there, I think it's eleven o'clock. But it meant that the band had to come off stage, run into the limo, change in the limo. Of course, when we get there, it turns out that the curfew doesn't exist: I've been cracking the whip and everybody's sweating and we're all in suits and running around like idiots.

'Anyhow, we get on the plane, fly to Ruislip in upstate New York, where I've got another limo waiting for us on the tarmac. We get off the Lear jet, drive to Ted Fields' house up in the Hamptons. Massive marquees, absolutely everything, but in fact the party is nearly dead because by this point it's about one o'clock in the morning. And no disrespect to Ted Fields, but it's a bit dull. So Ted's obviously aware of this and goes, "Right, there's a nightclub in town." By this point we've been joined by Marilyn Manson and his crew. So there's Marilyn Manson in one stretch limo, and us in another and Ted Fields in his car, driving in front, to take us to this club. Now, Ted has come out with no ID. And in America, obviously that's wrong. You're a vagrant. But Ted Fields is no vagrant,' Ross laughs. 'He probably owns half the Hamptons. But as luck would have it, we all get pulled over. And this young cop comes up to Ted Fields and when he asks, "Where's your license, sir?" Fields says, "I've got no goddamn ID." So the cop tells him to get out of the car. Eventually Ted says, "Well, I think if you were to call one of your superiors you'd realise that I'm employing one hundred and thirty of you. And I'm good for this, and I'm not drunk, and I'm just taking these guys to a club." So the cop eventually radios in, finds out he's an ass, and off we pop.

'So we go to this club 'til about seven in the morning, and then go from the club straight to Ruislip Airport again as the sun's coming up. Jump on the Lear jet, fly from there straight to Saratoga Springs, get off the plane, another limo on the tarmac, straight to the hotel, and all the buses have driven overnight to get there. So we get out of the limo, and there's me, Gav, Robin, Nige, Dave, we're all stumbling round like zombies. Get all our bags off the bus, straight into the hotel, sleep until six or seven o'clock at night. Get up, go to the gig for dinner, play the gig at the Stack, and that was another day in the life of Bush.' Ross laughs.

Of course, even in a tour in which every day brings the same thing bar the odd Lear jet, some days are bigger than others. Such was the case when Bush headlined a gig at Dallas Raceway. For 500,000 people, making it, as John Marks says, the biggest ticketed event in rock history. The fact that Bush were meant to be on tour in Alberta in Western Canada at the time was not, as it transpires, enough of a deterrent for the promoters to give up and find someone else to head the bill.

'Yes, attendance was somewhere around half a million,' he notes. 'I don't know if we ever got an accurate count. To begin with, none of us were really sure about the event, that is to say if it was going to work out, so there were a lot of conditions sent to satisfy ourselves that it was. But you never know, until the day, whether all those conditions are going to be adhered to. Nonetheless they were, and it was a pretty momentous occasion.' He realised, he says, 'that not long ago I was at the Dragonfly watching them and now we're here in this huge stadium. That's a wonderful thing to experience with any band.

'They were intent on getting Bush,' he adds. 'We had every excuse to not do the show, but they were very very intent on getting the band.'

And so they did.

But it certainly made load-in a bit different. Dale Meekins recalls, 'We got our own 737 plane to get us down from Canada [the day before the show] with all our gear. Except our gear didn't fit into the bay of the plane. That was bad,' he says mildly. 'So we had to put a lot of the gear, like the cabinets, inside the plane, seat-belted into the seats. And the pilot was all freaked out about it, but our attitude was if it crashes, it doesn't really matter, does it? Who cares?'

In fact, Ross adds, even then all the gear didn't fit onto the plane. 'The people organising the event had promised me that the plane would be big enough. I've still got my fax, which lists every case, every dimension including wheels, and they said, yes, it will go in, and we got there and it didn't. So what we had to do was shove the remainder of it onto No Doubt's bus, and I had to bribe the bus driver to double overnight to Texas with all our shit on *his* bus. And he did. And he did it well. And we got there and we had all our gear and we did the gig and it was absolutely amazing.'

Of course, that's not the end of the headache, as Dale notes. 'Of course, then we had to put all the stuff *back* on the plane right after the show, and the rest into a big semi. And the plane was waiting on the runway for us with the engines running, so that we could get back into Canada. In order to get to the airfield we drove down the opposite side of the road in the tour bus with the truck behind us. And we flew off, and went to load in for the next show. That was a tiring day,' he concludes, ever the master of understatement.

Bone, challenging Dale's position in the understatement department, adds, 'To think that two years before we'd been in front of a thousand people, and we were now playing the biggest rock and roll event in the world. Yeah, that's pretty good.'

Gavin recalls arriving the day before the Dallas show. 'We ended up staying in this . . . motel really, the nearest one to the venue. It was packed with kids and people going to the show, too, which was a bit mad. So there we were hanging out at the pool at this roadside motel, and I was being interviewed, and it ended up being mayhem because there were so many people around. It was too hot to stay in our room, so we ended up standing in the car park. I had to lock the door to my room, because kids were banging on my door. And actually playing that show was ridiculous. I mean, five hundred thousand people! It seemed so weird that they'd all turned up,' he says, returning to his favourite semi-serious fantasy of an empty house. 'I mean, that's a lot of people to all decide they want to do exactly the same thing on the same day . . .'

On the subject of hotels, Ross offers an explanation. 'I had two options: I could either have us staying at the Four Seasons in Dallas or a LaQuinta Inn. But it makes more sense to be half a mile away from an event that half a million people are trying to go to, than it does to be in the Four Seasons in downtown Dallas. So I had to eat an enormous amount of excrement over that one,' he laughs, 'because when we drew up outside the LaQuinta, Nigel just went, "I'm not staying here. That's it."

'But it turned out to be so perfectly located,' Ross insists. 'I mean, it took a lot of research to find out that this was the right hotel, because it was on a back road that none of the people from the city were using, but I still had the police escort – six motorcycles! – to get us to the venue. In the event, we were so well-placed that there was no other bugger in sight on the road. It was fine, of course, once Nigel had got over the shock. And it was a great show.

'Mind you,' he adds, 'I hated it. In fact, I wore a Rage Against the Machine shirt the whole day saying "We have evaluated that your whole system sucks", because I was at war with the promoters. See, I never actually go to war with anyone literally. I never yell, I just do silly things like wear the odd T-shirt with a particularly appropriate slogan on it.'

Asked about milestones like the Dallas show and its attendant brag factor, Dave Parsons merely shrugs. 'The funny thing is that I wouldn't know who to boast about something like that to. If I had boasted about it, I don't know, maybe it wouldn't be as good. But it's brilliant, isn't it? Then again, no one believes statistics anyway, do they?'

It's hard to believe any hotel receptionists ever quite believed the check-in names the band was by now using, either. Nigel rattles off a selection of choice pseudonyms – River Thames, Reginald Perrin, Michael Caine, Harry Palmer, Thomas Pynchon – and when the listener laughs at the sheer ridiculousness, he replies, 'Well, that's exactly how you choose them. Trying to make everyone giggle in the hotel lobby on tour. That's your yardstick; if it makes people giggle, it'll do. And yet, no matter how ridiculous the names are,' he shakes his head, 'no one behind the desk *ever* gets the joke. Not even when I was called Mr Martin A Navratilova! So you ring up and ask for a Mr Martin A Navratilova, and all they do is say, "How do you spell that, ma'am?"

'It definitely wasn't a good choice in Japan. Judith tried to reach me as Martin A Navratilova in Tokyo and when she finally got put through, she said, "Don't you ever, ever choose another name like that again." '

Sometimes, of course, corny hotel pseudonyms can work in your favour. Robin, who has been particularly fond of calling himself Helmut Phelvet for no reason other than an oblique dirty joke and a chance to practise his fake German accent, recalls one such occasion. 'The idea is to have the silliest possible name, and it's always a constant battle to keep our standards up. Especially,' he adds, 'when you turn up drunk and have to remember it when you're trying to get the room keys.' On one occasion, however, he lucked out. After checking into a hotel in Düsseldorf as Barry White, when he returned to the hotel at two in the morning and opened the door to his room, the band's most voluble member was temporarily lost for words. ' "What the fuck?" ' he recalls exlaiming. 'I was in an upgraded deluxe suite with chocolates and champagne – but it was late, so all the ice had melted, and the champagne was just floating in a bucket. I guess they were fans of Barry, so they decided to do something nice for him. I bet they were really surprised when a skinny white guy turned up instead!'

25 SEPTEMBER TO 21 NOVEMBER, 1997

Melbourne, Sydney, Bangkok, Manila, Seoul, Osaka, Tokyo, Belfast, Dublin, Newcastle, Glasgow, Birmingham, Leeds, Cambridge, Southampton, London, Manchester, Newport, Luxembourg, Rotterdam, Oporto, Lisbon, Santiago, Buenos Aires, São Paulo, Rio de Janeiro, Curtiba, Mexico City, Honolulu, Maui

What's it like playing *really* foreign parts? According to the phlegmatic Dale, well, there's a simple answer. 'They've got different power. And mostly they don't speak English. So you tell one guy what to do, and he tells forty other guys. And, of course,' he grins, 'you can't ever find that one guy.'

Still, why not go, if it's there for the playing?

Mike Greek relates, 'The south-east Asian tour began in Australia, and we set up an event in Sydney for the first time called the Grudgefest, which was a free show to twenty-five thousand people, and the response was insanely good. They were going to do a show in Singapore, but it was at the time of the fires in south-east Asia, so the smog warnings meant that we weren't allowed to travel there. But everywhere they did play was mayhem, and the highlight was probably Manila, where there were eight thousand people and the audience were jumping over the balcony, fifteen to twenty feet, to try to get into the pit.'

Of course, the Manila audiences aren't the only people making unwise moves onto or from balconies at a Bush gig. Almost as soon as Bush were playing venues big enough for unplanned lead vocalist movement around said venue to be a threat to his own life and limb, Gavin Rossdale was doing exactly that. To the despair and frustration – not to mention sneaking admiration – of those who work for him and who consequently have to follow him around when he scales lighting rigs, throws himself into the audience, or climbs from one floor of a venue to the other the hard way.

'Well, you can only tell them,' Ross sighs. 'You can lead a horse to water, but you can't make it drink. I told Gavin not to jump off the stage in Chile. I told him not to jump off the stage in Brazil. And in Argentina. And he did it anyway. What can you do? I knew he would do it, so I had umpteen people waiting for him. But, you know, it's his deal and if he wants to do it, all you can do is say, "Look, Mexico City is not a wise place to dive off the stage." 'Cause you might go in for a laugh and come out in stitches. But he did it, and he survived, so maybe I'm the ass. But you know, you can only advise; at the end of the day he's insured and if he wants to do it, it's up to him. It does make my life and the security's life a lot more difficult. But you know . . . I'll tell you what he never would do; he would never endanger, wittingly, any of us. I mean, he has done it unwittingly, when we've had to go in and get him out. But he's always said, "Sorry about that. I know you told me not to . . . And are you all right?" As you wipe the blood off your forehead and say, "Yeah, Gav, I'm fine, how 'bout you mate?"'

'I don't know where he gets his energy from,' Ross marvels. 'I mean, I've seen him absolutely dead, dog tired, five minutes before going in front of a fifteen thousand people show in Miami. And then he'll pour a bucket of ice water over his head and go out and play one of the best shows I've ever seen him do. But as he says, as soon as it starts he's just an animal. You know, as soon as the show starts he's *him*.'

'He's always gone off like that,' Bone reports. 'Maybe because he's got such a deal with the fans, such a one on one thing that they just want him in there. They want to touch him and he wants to be touched. It's part of the night that the fans know is coming and they just can't wait. But oh, Jesus, he puts us through some shit sometimes. I tell you what, I have hung off a balcony, the *second* balcony, while Gavin sat on my shoulders and Bill has held him by the collar to keep him from falling off. Shit like that. And he's just . . . he's unreal. He has no idea. When Gavin wants to go, he just goes. Yeah, he's nuts. But boy, you can't beat it for response: the fans lose their minds and by the time he's done, he's got them worked into such a goddamned foam they don't know what they're doing.'

Dave Dorrell observes, 'I've seen Gavin doing things that are completely crazy. I've stood beneath him in some vain hope that somehow I wouldn't be killed by the impact of him falling on me and that I'd . . . *catch* him, I guess. I remember being at a festival in Canada when Gavin decided, while wearing a pair of four-inch high brothel creepers, that he was going to scale the lighting rig with a mic between his teeth. And it was just too fucking scary to watch. He was way on top of it where even the lighting crew don't go without support. And, yeah, I was very scared for his wellbeing. And I told him never to do that again, please. And I'm sure he *will* do it again. The threat of being ripped to pieces by fans has also made itself apparent once or twice and that's kind of scary, too, in a completely different way.'

Even the mere fact of touring south-east Asia brought its own scariness, as Ross recalls.

'For a start, we had this uncanny stroke of bad luck when we went to the Far East. Every day that we arrived in a country, the currency collapsed. Of course, we had all the fees paid in dollars so it didn't affect our income. But what it affected was that all the local promoters wanted to cut corners. We arrived in Thailand, and their currency sank. We arrived in Korea; their currency sank. Same in Manila; everything just went horribly wrong. As the band's representative, my duty was basically to say, "Let's just make this run like we expect it to run." But because of costs, the local promoters didn't want to supply adequate security. They wanted to bring the police in, because they're paying them off anyway. So in Manila we have nine thousand people in an arena, and I walk in with the band and all the lights are on. Like, *all* the lights. Every tungsten and halogen that you could possibly imagine in one gym is on. And so I go off to the promoter . . . and for some reason,' he grins, 'the promoter kept running away from me.

'Anyhow, there's nine thousand people in the arena, the band are in the dressing room, and I go out to see if everything's okay. You know, fifteen minute call, ten minute call, five minute call, you know the drill. So I go out fifteen minutes before and the lighting guy comes running up to me saying, "They won't put the house lights off, because they're scared there's going to be a riot." And I say, "Well, no house lights off, we're not playing, that's fine. We're not playing in the light, okay?" As I'm chatting to the crew at the front of the stage, some kid dives off a balcony. The military police wade in with their malacca canes and beat this kid into the middle of next week. Well, being Scottish and stupid, I decide to grab three of my crew and run in and stop it. Which is just humanitarian, really. So we get in the middle of it, and then I go to the promoter and say, "Right, I want all these military police people out of the building now or else the band don't go on."

' "Oh no, we can't do that, it's part of the licence," he says. Now you know, I've applied for licences before. I know what licences require in Britain, and I'm pretty sure they're not that far off, if a little bit more bendable, shall we say, in Manila. But I was like, "Okay, so you need to have some of them there. So the deal is you put all the military police outside. However many you need here for your licence, fine, but stick them outside in case there's a riot outside. I don't want any of them in the building."

'So I walk off back to the dressing room and I come out again, and there's another beating going on. So I was like, "No, this is really wrong now. OK, the gig's off." We'd been paid upfront anyway, because I didn't trust the guy. So I called Mike Greek and asked him to send me through a waiver that he was happy with, as the agent. And asked him if I pulled the gig due to certain circumstances, would he back me? And he said of course, and he faxed me through this paper. So we're looking at, like, ten minutes after the band are supposed to go onstage. By this point I finally get all the military police out of the gig but there's no security in the pit. So there's nobody anywhere and there's nine thousand people, so I'm wondering, Have I shot myself in the foot here?

'So I go to the promoter and I say, "Right. You need to sign this waiver." And without a word of a lie, nine thousand people are chanting and chanting for Bush, and I've got this guy at the side of the stage signing this waiver. On the side of the stage, in fact, and then I take it, fold it, pop it in my pocket, and say, "Right. How many crew did you have to load all this stuff in here?" Thirty-two, he tells me. So I ask where they are. They're all in the crew room. And I say, "Well, you'd better go get them, because we need them to work the pit. We'll give them all shirts so we can identify them. We'll do all that jazz, but we need people in the pit."

'Well, of course, Snow White and the thirty-two dwarves get up, don't they,' he laughs. 'Because this is Manila, so these people are basically knee-high. They can't even see over the barrier, let alone do any good. But the barrier is starting to move with the weight of the crowd. So I want to put the band on, but then the head of police arrives and says, "No no no. You don't put band on with lights off.

Riot. Be riot." So I say, "Well, I'm not putting them on with the lights on, so it's up to you. Whatever you want to do. You either put lights off, band go on, or you don't put lights off, band don't go on, then definitely got riot. Whatever you wanna do, mate, I'll be in the dressing room."

'So I went and played clever for a couple of minutes and they all argued outside in whatever language, and then they agreed. The house lights can go off. So I said, "Well, put them off. Let me see that they go off." So the lights went off, I put the band on . . . and chaos erupts. The place just goes mental. So myself and Bone are in the pit, and we're the only two that can see over the barricade. And I've got all these dwarves running around me; I'm tripping over them. And they're trying to hold the barricade up because it's beginning to collapse. So I'm deploying my legions of dwarves, just saying, like, "Push this barricade away from the stage so that it doesn't collapse and kill all of us."

'And then, out of the corner of my eye, I see this big bulk come flying over, like you know, *swimming* over the crowd. And stupidly, it's just my own reaction and I shouldn't have done it, but I react and turn to my left instinctively and go to try and catch this person, who turned out to be an American GI. He is massive. So I popped two vertebrae in my back, right there and then. Now Bone is about six feet away from me, the band are playing, the crowd are hysterical, and Bone will swear to this day he heard my back pop. It was hideous.

'In the end, I did save the guy 'cause I caught him by the shoulders and I stopped him banging his head on the floor. Then I let him go and the dwarves carried him out: "Hi ho hi ho, let's get the American out of here", basically. And I said, "Never mind, my back's fine." Because there's so much going on that it doesn't really register how bad it is. So you carry on, catching kids and all the rest of it, until a guy gets on stage. And I leap up, and before he gets to Gavin I've got him. But as I get down to house right to get this guy out of the barricades, I suddenly seize up. I can't move. I can't do anything. I was in tears. Two vertebrae had popped and the muscles went into spasm and it was the most miserable time I've ever had on the road, ever.'

In the end, Ross says, he had to be carried out of the gig in agony.

'So the next morning we had to fly to Seoul in Korea, where I lay on my hotel room floor, and I admit to crying like a baby. I've never been in so much pain. But it was a Sunday and we couldn't find a chiropractor. Nothing. And I'm lying there thinking, This is me, I'm knackered, I'm gonna be paralysed forever. And I've played rugby for years so I've had neck injuries and everything. Anyhow, Bone comes into my room and suddenly the room goes dark. It was the middle of the day, but it was like a solar eclipse. And Bone's like, "Hey lad. I got somebody who's gonna sort you out." And I'm lying face down, and I'm squirming to look round to see what he brought me to sort me out. Eventually I manage to see this guy who is the biggest Korean ever. He's six foot six and he's a Marine and he's one of our armed guards but he went to a Californian chiropractor school. And he doesn't speak any English, but says, "I have card! I have card!" And he's waving his bloody diplomas at me, but all I know is that he's so big he's blocking out all the sunshine. And I'm petrified. And I'm going, "Bone, is this really necessary?"

'So to cut a long story short, he rolled me around like a rag doll and like, two bullets, or cracks of whips, bang bang, and both my vertebrae went right back in. It still took me a week to walk, but they went back in. And for the record, the band could not have been better. I survived Japan, I was a mess, I was on painkillers, steroids, everything. And I have to thank the band that when it came to coming back from Osaka they all bumped together and put me in a first class seat. To me, that is payment enough for anything I've ever done for them. And when we got on the plane, I was immobilised, lying down on a stretcher. And Gavin took my painkillers and went to the stewardess and said, "He's on these painkillers every four hours, so can you make sure you give them to him? Oh, and every time he has one of them, give him some Cabernet. He likes Cabernet." And every four hours, a stewardess came round with a glass of Cabernet and my painkillers. I'll never forget that. It was just brilliant.'

In Bangkok, Gavin says, where the band played a small club, the ticket price was beyond the reach of most punters and the club was half full. 'So we just threw the doors open for half an hour, and let in everybody who had turned up to see the show.' And as for bootlegging and piracy, historically rife in south-east Asia, he says, 'Well, we're bootlegged and we're proud. Besides, a bootleg's not going to sound like a recorded studio record. But that's cool.

'In fact,' he adds, after worrying that he's creating a monster by revealing his largesse, 'one of my favourite things to do when I turn up at a venue to play, and I always do it, is that anyone who's there waiting outside at the time gets in free. Those kinds of things are fun. And it certainly shocks people. What's funny, when you see people's responses, is that it's just such a craply easy thing to do. And it always makes you laugh. I'm sure it's no big deal,' he adds dismissively. 'I'm sure everyone does it.'

But not everyone throws himself off the stage quite so regularly, as his crew colleagues have already elaborated. When the band reached Brazil, however, Gavin's luck with escaping injury ran out, leading to the only few dates in Bush's history when Nigel's co-guitarist was no longer Gavin Rossdale, but an unflappable and much more than competent Dale Meekins. The reason for his turn in the spotlight was less than ideal, however: at a show in Curitiba, Gavin's hand was ripped open by a fan attempting to pull his wallet off by its chain. How did he find himself in the situation in the first place? Well, do you need to ask?

All was going as per usual at the gig. 'And then Gavin had to jump off the stage into the crowd,' says Bone. 'In Curitiba. In Brazil. Off the stage he goes. So me and Bill were down there . . . and we got our asses whupped. He cut his hand right open . . . They tried to rip his goddamned finger off to get at his ring.'

'That was *real*,' Gavin says mildly. 'Someone pulling and prodding at a chain on me that had my wallet on it. I was out in the crowd, and there was Winston and Gwen watching, and I was fighting with all my life to hold on to my wallet. But they held on and my hand got sliced. It was quite dramatic,' he adds. 'Lots of blood.

'Brazil's just a mind-bomb,' he adds. 'It's got such a wicked reputation for being dangerous that everyone was on alert on arrival. We turned up in this mad 70s-style kitsch hotel with insane shagpile and strange wallpaper, and all-in-one furniture, like a long desk that turns into a chest of drawers and curves around a corner. And everywhere, there was a whiff of danger.'

Of Brazil, Ross says simply, 'They're all pathological liars. Really. Lovely country, and the promoters were good to us, but they lie to you through their teeth from the minute you get there to the minute you leave. Then again, you expect that. The only place you have to make sure that they don't lie is with the figures. You get them to send you the names of the hotels they're putting you in. And then you phone the hotels up yourself and make sure: "Are we actually in here or is the Argentinian president arriving and we all have to stay somewhere else?" That did happen to us, actually. When we arrived in São Paulo we were supposed to be in the best hotel in town. And we turn up and the crew has arrived before myself, as has my assistant Michael. But when he'd arrived at the airport, he'd been met by this poor girl Mariana. She was a lovely girl but she was having to lie because the company she was working for were making her lie. So when Michael arrived, she had to tell him about the hotels. "Oh no, I am so sorry, this information isn't right anymore, because you see the Argentinian president . . ." '

Ross grins. 'Now, this is where it gets like *Pinocchio* at times, you know. "The Argentinian president has flown into town and we didn't know and he's taken over the whole hotel. So now you're in this YMCA," basically. And it was pretty grim. I got food poisoning within five minutes and was sick all day. Nigel went into manic depression because the room was so dark. I mean, that's a joke, but it's not that far wrong. So I spent the day, in between being sick, on the phone to my UK travel agent. Eventually she got us rooms in this five-star hotel which was absolutely beautiful, and we moved out of the dump and I charged the promoter back the extra money because it was his fault, in my opinion. And then I found out that the Argentinian president wasn't anywhere near town. And it was like, "Oh, knock me down with a feather; they're *lying* to us." '

'So São Paulo was tough, but the shows were great. One of the best shows I've ever seen Bush do was the first night in São Paulo. That rocked; it's one of the legendary Bush gigs, without a shadow of a doubt. I mean the hairs were up on everybody's neck: the sound engineer's, the monitor engineer's, everybody, all the crew. And the crowd went insane and subsequently the second night sold out on the back of the first. Then we went to Rio and Rio's Rio, you know. The hotel smelled bad and . . . but it's Brazil! What do you expect? The Inter-Continental is one of the most famous hotels in Rio. And it's right on the beach. But it stinks. And everybody knows it stinks because the water there stinks. So you get, "This hotel stinks, Ross." "Yeah, it's the only one that we can stay in. Everywhere stinks here, mate. Let's take a walk down the road." "Oh yes, it all smells." So, you know, a couple of incense sticks and the odd Glade air freshener and everybody was happy again.'

According to Bone, the Brazilian security arrangements, while overbearing, were entirely justified.

'Oh, my God. In Rio, we had guards packing Uzis taking us to the nightclubs we wanted to go to and following us to the bathroom. And that's me and Ross, too, not just the band. If I would go to the bathroom, one of these guards would come with me, and stand outside the door, and wait for me to come back out and bring me to my seat. No, they weren't overreacting. People are kidnapped there daily, and they're stripped of their guts, liver and heart, because they have an incredible black market in organs down there,' he insists. 'They'd think nothing of whacking you in the head and gutting you on the sidewalk.'

It wasn't until they got to Chile, however, that the secret police turned up. And arrested Ross Duncan.

'Well, not me personally,' Ross clarifies with a grin, 'but it did happen to me as the representative of the band. We arrived from Mexico into Chile and the bill was David Bowie, Bush, and [Mexican rap stars] Molotov. And *they* had no work permits, but they lied at the border and said that they could produce them the next day at the show. Anyhow, they played their set and I walk into the gig with Gav and the band and suddenly I'm swooped upon in my tent by the Chilean secret police. And my interpreter, it turns out, is an illegal immigrant whose work permit has run out. So she runs away and I get taken away with David Bowie's tour manager to prove all our work permits.

'And I had permits for the 30-odd people with us, but they were all perfect because, you know, that's what I do for a living. I run around embassies. But for half an hour they couldn't understand me. And I couldn't understand them. And I was literally interrogated under the big bright white lights until I saw Maria Canalis from [South American promoters] Rock and Pop come by. And I was calling out, "Maria, Maria – help me!" And she came in and she chatted away in Gaucho Spanish to them all, and all the papers were approved and I was let go. But *that* was an interesting forty minutes,' he chuckles. 'The band were onstage, of course, so they had no idea! Meanwhile, backstage, here's poor Uncle Ross being beaten with a lead truncheon.' He exaggerates only slightly. 'And Gav was not very impressed. Not with me, but he was like, "What do you mean you've been arrested?" So I just said, "Well, I've just had the greatest forty-five minutes of my life. But never mind!" '

In the event, perhaps it's just as well that three and a half years of touring ended on a safe, and rather dull, note in Hawaii.

'It wasn't really that memorable,' Dave Parsons admits. 'It was beautiful, and a nice place, but Hawaii's not really – well, it wasn't my favourite gig ever.'

Nigel Pulsford is somewhat more blunt. 'It was horrible. The worst gig of the tour. We were finishing the whole *Razorblade Suitcase* tour in, like, a little tiny venue, three thousand people or even less. It was open air, and we played in a car park. It was the worst way to end three and a half years of touring. We should have gone to Chicago, or to New York and played the Roseland or something; played a big theatre, rammed full of people, for three hours. And do the Grateful Dead thing on them,' he laughs. 'But this wasn't really a great way to end the tour.'

Still, the band wouldn't forget the date of that last show in a hurry.

'Twentieth November 1997, was the last time we played,' Dave Parsons says instantly when asked when the Bush live circus wound up prior to a much-needed break and the recording of the band's third studio album, *The Science Of Things*. 'I know that date because I remember the whole of that year was spent concentrating on when we would finish. And thinking, "Great, what are you gonna do November twenty-first?" '

V

Living in a cage
Washing in a birdbath
Sinking in a fishbowl . . .
States we've been through

For the first time in a very long time, it was time to stop and Bush were ready to leave the road. That is, *really* leave the road, for longer than a few weeks and without a new album to make immediately, for the first time in years. Rediscover their friendships with girlfriends and wives. Hang out. Travel for fun. Be normal. That kind of thing.

That isn't to say that as soon as they began their holiday, Bush didn't put out another record anyway. Well, sort of. *Deconstructed* would hit the shelves in November, an eleven-track collection of remixes and electronica-mutated versions of songs like 'Mouth' [which featured on the *American Werewolf In Paris* soundtrack and became a format-crossing radio hit in the US] and 'Swallowed'. So, was it the band's third album? Well, yes and no.

In one of the few interviews Gavin gave around the release of *Deconstructed*, he told Canadian monthly magazine *Watch* that it was 'definitely not the third record', and that the remixers deserved all the credit for whatever was interest-worthy therein.

'At least they can't say it has anything to do with Seattle, thank God!' Gavin joked in the *Watch* interview. 'Seriously, we should have called it *No Big Deal*. If people like drum'n'bass and hip hop, they'll like it. Remixes are nothing new. I don't claim that we're breaking any kind of ground, and it's not a direction that we're trying to move in. If people don't like it, they can just not buy it. It's interesting, and it brings a smile to my face, that's all.

'It started out, very simply, as a couple of friends doing a couple of remixes. We were on tour so much, we couldn't do any extra tracks or B-sides. There was a track we did with Tricky ["In A Lonely Place", a Joy Division cover] that went over to America. Trauma heard a few of the mixes and they were like, "This is pretty good, you should explore this." We got a few people to do some mixes and, suddenly, it becomes a remix album . . . it's become a record, but it's really a collection of stuff.'

In the meantime, the band had some stuff of their own to be getting on with.

Dave Parsons and Sarah Chope wasted no time in living the high life abroad; although, in their case, that's 'high' as in feet above sea level, rather than luxury hotel lifestyles.

'As soon as we finished touring,' Dave recalls, 'we went to New Zealand and drove around there and stayed in a campground. Then we went to Australia and spent about three weeks in Sydney and went up to the Great Barrier Reef.' Successful bands have traditionally taken 'years out' of the UK to ease their tax burden but, Dave insists, 'we just did it anyway. We always go on holiday whenever we can. We really like exploring places'.

Sometimes even on short notice. In 1999, Dave made sure that Valentine's Day combined travel and romance via a surprise trip to Prague. Sarah says, 'I realised, "Oh, gosh, it's going to be Valentine's Day in a couple of weeks." So I told Dave, "Okay, it's your turn to sort it out." The day before, he asked me, "So, where's your passport gone to?" But he wouldn't tell me where we were going, and in fact wouldn't even let me see my boarding card, so I didn't know where we were going until we were on the plane!'

Recalling their post-tour adventures, she insists, 'New Zealand was wonderful. We got a camper van and just drove all over. And because New Zealand is so empty, we'd never run into people. We'd just park on a beautiful beach and sleep there. Robin joked to Dave, "Actually, you don't have to sleep in a van now, you know – you can afford a hotel!" But we liked it.

'We'd already decided to go to Sydney for Christmas, because my brother lives there. So we just added on a month in New Zealand first. You know, I don't think there are many people that either of us could travel with as well as we do with each other. We just enjoy each other's company,' she says simply. 'Not everyone would want to find somewhere that was the tallest peak in the area and walk up it. In fact, probably most other people would be like, "Why on earth do you want to do that?" '

Dave adds, 'Some people can't think of anything worse than that, and they'd rather go and stay in a villa with a cook and a maid. What I hate about that, about thinking, That sounds like a really nice hotel and it's really expensive, is that when you get there it's just full of rich people and they're really obnoxious and horrible – the worst people in the world. I'd much rather go and stay in the cheap place and meet people and have a laugh and be with someone that's interested in what I'm interested in. You know, it's much more interesting to go and talk to people in Rough Trade [record shop] than in [the posh shopping district of] Bond Street.'

The inseparable couple also found places worth exploring closer to home. 'We bought a little place in Cornwall in August [1998],' Sarah notes. 'It was just an area that we enjoy going to when we get out of London, which we do a lot. I don't know if Dave really wants me to talk about that,' she pauses. 'I suspect he thinks it's not very rock and roll. But I was looking in the paper one Sunday and saw a tiny classified advert for a place for sale in a village that we really liked. We decided to go out and see it. In the end, we didn't get that place, but we found another literally just up the road. It's really tiny, but it's only about five minutes from the sea, and it has a fantastic view. We had a big New Year's Eve party this past year, and about ten friends came down and a lot of red wine was drunk as we all went walking down to the beach at night. It's really nice to have something like that,' she emphasises, 'because our family and friends can go down there, too. It's a way of sharing your good fortune with people without being crass or handing people money.'

Sarah and Dave also headed over the Channel for France during Dave's year off. From January to March of 1998, Dave elaborates, 'We lived in Paris, rented an apartment. My brother lives there; he works in TV and I made some music for commercials with him. I really enjoyed that. I'd never really lived in another city before, and been there long enough to have a local bar and everything. It does feel weird not to have played live for so long, especially when you know you're going to go out and do it again. But it was nice, just having the time to go to Cornwall, or to go and see my mum.'

'In a way,' Sarah smiles as she reflects on Dave's year off and subsequent months in and around London recording *The Science Of Things*, 'I'm almost looking forward to him going back on tour. It was lovely to have him back for a year ... even if for the first few months we were bumping into each other all the time! Still, I'm glad we moved in together when we did. We might not go out with each other for two weeks at a time, because my female friends are really important to me and Dave's got his pub and boy things and football, but at least I know we'll run into each other at breakfast.'

According to Robin Goodridge, arguably the hardest-working man of the four hard-working men onstage in Bush, the year off 'was a year of being *still*. I definitely didn't miss touring until towards the end of the year, and until I started getting into the music we were making [with *The Science Of Things*]. I certainly didn't miss playing what we'd already been playing, because the excitement from touring always comes from a new record. Each time we make one, I can't wait to get out and do it again. Obviously you're going to be playing songs off each record, but the new stuff is what makes you want to go and do it.'

In the meantime, there was relaxation to be dealt with.

'In January [1998] I went to France for three months, near Cannes,' he says. 'Rented a big house out there in the forest ... and sat there and made music,' he exclaims, as though the irony of that statement in the context of relaxation amuses him. 'I did remixes for other artists, and messed about and explored ideas that I wanted to bring to this record. So I learned about computers and programming, because I'd done it once before with The Beautiful People but, five years on, technology changes. You know, understanding what's new and the leaps that have been made software-wise. But I was able to do it, and then stick a big black line through a lot of it and say that's totally irrelevant, don't go there. But some of it, I could bring to Bush.

'Glynis came out a few times, but basically I went out with a couple of the guys I was in The Bunch with. One of them was a really good engineer and the other one's a keyboard player. People came out, but I used it as sort of a monastic work thing. Just to explore the interior of my head, because when you don't have time to think, you don't really know what you've acquired. So then you can unpack all that you've absorbed over the years of touring. I got to think about what I wanted to bring to the new record. And realised I didn't want to make records on my own!

'The reason I went to the south of France,' he adds, 'is because Andy [one of Robin's Bunch bunch] has a dog and he lives in Belgium, so we couldn't bring the dog to England [because of quarantine regulations]. And being in England would have meant I might as well be at home. I'd never spent any time in France, before, and I really enjoyed it. It would be amazing to own a house there where you could go every summer for three weeks of the year. I probably will go there every year for the rest of my life now. If I had enough money, I'd probably buy a house there. Or Barbados,' he interjects. 'I could go there for the weekends on Concorde. Or in the winter. You know, tell everyone, "Well, from December through to mid-January, I'm in Barbados if you need me." It would be great. I went there in '92 or '93; I've got a friend who lives there now who's a helicopter pilot. It's great. It's not like a regular holiday. You can rent a house in a resort, but you can go out with him and go to beaches.'

Glynis recalls, 'There wasn't much for Ruby and I to do out there in France. She was only a year and a half old, so a place like that, with studio equipment and everything, was a bit of a nightmare with her pulling things out and stuff. Still, Robin came back every three weekends or so, I think. In fact that time came and went quite quickly, so we must have seen each other quite regularly.'

And, in May, Glynis and Robin began house hunting in their village near Horsham, and settled on a home a little, but not much, larger than their previous abode.

'I remember thinking about that change when we moved from the house that we were in to here,' she muses. 'I mean, it was a tiny little house but we were incredibly happy there. It was our first home and I do remember thinking when I left that I didn't need anything more than I had at that point, you know, and I didn't want things to change or things to spoil. But touch wood,' Glynis smiles, 'they haven't.

'I think I got used to Robin being around again,' she says. 'And I think I am going to find it harder the next time he goes away. That first time that their touring turned into a couple of years was quite exciting and all, but I think our lives have moved on. We sort of know where we are. I don't quite know how to explain it, but I think I'll feel worse about him going away this time. I know it's going to happen and I don't want to dwell on it, but I think it will be tough.

'I remember when Ruby was born, and Robin was away, feeling

quite alone,' she adds. 'And if I'd have a bad night, and Robin used to phone me in the morning because of the time difference, I'd be completely hormonal and talking rubbish!' She laughs. 'I remember thinking, You bastard! once or twice, too, but that's really only for such a short period of time. I'm kind of resentful of time he spends away in London now to do bits and pieces, because . . . well, I just like him being here,' she teases. 'Ruby will miss him when he goes, too, although children just get on with it, don't they?'

Nigel and Judith, too, did their share of travelling during their year out, decompressing from the almost inconceivable, if wonderful, changes the last few years had brought. Not least of which, of course, was their marriage, in July of 1996, after Nigel asked Judith for her hand twice, and even travelled up to Yorkshire to ask Judith's father's permission. In the end, she laughs, the third and final time, Judith turned the tables and proposed to Nigel. 'Well, it seemed like a good idea!'

The wedding was, of course, a perfect event on a perfect day, 'at Marylebone registry office [in London] with the whole family and everything', she nods. The previous two times, she insists, 'when Nigel proposed to me, I didn't really think he was serious! I mean, I think it was on my mind, but both times I was really freaked out. Especially because he was in a band, and I was working [as a BBC producer]. His life is so different to mine.

'Maybe I was afraid it wouldn't really work. I mean, how many people go off and turn into a supergroup? When they went to America the first time, and some of us girls went out, it was OK. It was really amazing. But on my birthday the first year, I think they played in Pittsburgh to a four hundred-capacity crowd. Really grotty, but absolutely packed. And there's me and Jasmine and Glynis up the front, dancing around and thinking, 'Wow, this is brilliant! But a year after, again on my birthday, they were playing the Palace in Auburn Hills [where, as Bone notes, the band set a one-day attendance record]. There were sixteen thousand people – can you imagine it? – producing absolute *waves* of screaming. Unbelievable. You can never believe it until you see and hear it for yourself.

'We still stay normal. But there are all these amazing people wanting to hang out with them now. You know, loads of people in bands and people saying things like, "Oh, yes, that's the man who owns Bloomingdales." Everything's really big time, and part of a world where people are spending money to be sociable and looking beautiful. And it's hard not to think, Oh, God, can I compete? Or am I just the hometown girl making cups of tea? I remember some journalists coming out to interview the band and one of them said to Jasmine, "Oh, are you the girl who walks the dog?" ' Judith raises an eyebrow. 'I mean, here she was with her own [modelling] career, and suddenly her boyfriend becomes a pop star and, to the nearest journalist, they just assume you're the girl who walks the dog.

'It takes a while to get used to any situation,' Judith explains, as she expresses surprise at having found herself in the position of 'rock wife', and 'retired' from full-time employment at 25. She now works in jewellery design – 'I enjoy it, but I won't make money out of it, because it takes about ten hours to make a ring, so maybe it's my way of saying I am something really!' – and freelance video editing, in order to have more flexible hours. 'It's strange, suddenly finding yourself a kept woman with a lot of money and a nice house. If you're used to working for your money and having any individuality, it's strange. And trying to buy Nigel a Christmas present – how can you do it? When there's a company that makes custom guitars for him that can be done to his exact specifications, how can you top that? I know it sounds really stupid, but it becomes hard to just treat him to something nice. You just want to feel like you can do something special, and it's hard.

'I know Nigel was amazed at everything that happened to Bush. He came back from the first tour and he was really freaked out. And when they come back, it always takes a few days to get used to it. You can go out on the road to see them, but I've just realised you can't fully appreciate it. Even if you see it yourself. Last year, I went out to a gig and got out of the car and almost immediately I could hear a girl shouting, "Judith, Judith, sign my T-shirt!" But the band have to cope with it all the time. And they get up, they get on the bus, they don't see anything, they play a gig and perhaps go to a party, and they get up and they get on the bus again. Every day's the same, really. And you've got nothing to talk about, besides saying, "How are you feeling, honey?"

'Nigel did start talking about it more after the second tour,' she elaborates, 'but mostly because I started quizzing him. "What's it like? What's it *actually* like?" It'd be his birthday and I'd be shouting down the phone, "Happy birthday!" And wondering, What's it like to do what you do? Even if you're in a situation where you're not playing exactly what you want to play, what's it like to be up there? And actually, asking him questions is kind of pointless, because you're talking about words. And it's about the music, it's not what they think about the music.'

Judith wasn't even sure, she says, that when it came time for a holiday, Nigel would be able to slow down. 'Even when I first met him, we had the idea of going on a holiday but, really, he didn't know anything about holidays. He had always worked. He was really scared at first about relaxing with me.' Reminded that Nigel has said how much he appreciates Judith's talent for being sociable, she concedes, 'Maybe he needs that, because he tends to work so much. But he's very charming himself, too.'

When it came time to head off on a year out, however, Nigel somehow managed to combine relaxation with ... well, more work. Some of the time, anyway. 'That year we travelled a lot,' Judith remembers. 'We lived in Paris for a while; someone lent us an apartment, right near Notre Dame Cathedral. It was wonderful realising that we'd been married for a while and we were actually able to spend time together at last. We're actually alone, and in a foreign country, and he's not working and hasn't got anything particular to do and hasn't brought his music over with him. Could we survive?' She laughs. 'And actually, we did!'

When the Pulsfords went to Tennessee to stay with Nigel's sister Jan, a musician and studio and label owner, however, music did pop back into the picture, as Nigel took the time to record his recently released debut solo album, *Heavenly Toast On The Paradise Road*. A diverse, mischievous and surprising collection of music – from effortlessly accomplished jazz soundscapes to impish Pixies in-jokes to John Cale-like hymnals to Beatlesque pop – it not only shows off Nigel's musical skills (on instruments other than the guitar, in the main), but also a rather impressive voice. In fact, according to his mother Madeline, who's clearly biased but no mean vocalist herself, it's quite an album.

'Oh, you'd love it,' Nigel's mother comments, just before its release. 'I'm playing my copy all the time. I know it well. I was quite surprised, you know, because it was so good. I'd never actually heard Nigel sing, besides with Gavin in the band. And I said to him, "You've got such a pleasant voice." It's not a great voice,' she clarifies. 'Not an Andy Williams or a Frank Sinatra. It's just a very good voice, and the tunes on it are lovely.'

'I spent years trying to work out what I wanted to play,' Nigel says when the subject of *Heavenly Toast On The Paradise Road* – named after the road he lived in in Stockwell – is broached. 'And the answer is that I never knew then, and I don't know now. I was playing what I did because I thought I should be playing it, it was expected of me. I play guitar in the confines of being in the band, but when I do my own stuff I hardly play guitar at all. I'm not really sure what I want to play. Is that a vague enough answer for you?' He grins. 'I didn't believe I could do it before then. Now I do. It's just annoying, having wasted that time. What a wanker I was. I should have done it when I was twenty, instead of waiting on someone else to do it. But maybe I didn't think I could do it, so that's why I didn't.'

Even this time, he says, 'I didn't start off wanting to do a solo album. I did it because my sister had just set up an Internet label [Collecting Dust], and the original idea was that I'd do an EP just to give it some publicity. And then when I was there [in Tennessee] I really got into doing it and thought, Oh, my voice isn't that bad. And it's just the stuff that came out, really. Some old songs, some new ones. Quite old-fashioned, really. But it was quite natural, with loads of different styles. That's the only problem; it's a split personality thing.' He shrugs. With plenty of company to help him split his personalities, in the event: *Heavenly Toast* features guest spots from Steve Turner, an esteemed Nashville drummer who has worked with the likes of Dolly Parton and Glen Campbell, as well as David Schnaufer on dulcimer and Jew's harp, and Ukrainian hammer dulcimer player Alexander Fedorouk.

The location for this work in progress was, Nigel says, 'in the middle of nowhere, and it was lovely. We sat around. We played around in the studio. Drove around in redneck cars. Looked at deer in the woods. That kind of thing.'

'Of course, next,' adds the workaholic Welshman with a smirk, 'I'm going to do another album in Chicago with my famous friends, I think.' By famous, he means the innovative artists famous in Nigel's independent rock pantheon, rather than MTV-famous types. 'I'd like to work with all the Jesus Lizard people, and Steve Albini, and the guys out of Silkworm. I saw them a few years ago and they were great.'

What's more, Nigel's year off gave him an opportunity to collaborate with someone that a slightly larger segment of the population would recognise as being famous. And of whom Nigel Pulsford is more than a little in awe. And not just because John Cale, like Nigel, is Welsh.

'Our US press officer Michael Pagnotta, who's become a good friend, also works with John Cale. And I said, "Well, if John ever needs a guitar player, I'm the man. I'm a huge fan. I'd love to do it. Any time." And of course I thought nothing more of it once I'd mentioned it until one day Michael rings me up and says, "We're doing this benefit thing in New York, and would you like to do it with John Cale?" ' Nigel recalls his sharp intake of breath and a big gulp. 'I said, "I'd love to do it!" And then a week later, the call comes: "Nigel? John Cale." Eeek!' Nigel laughs at himself as he tells the story.

'It was fantastic. We went to New York, and it cost me a *fortune* to do it!' he moans, rather less than half seriously. 'Well, it wasn't that expensive, but we did stay in a nice hotel. So I went along to SIR instrument rentals and rehearsed, and had to go away and carry my amp and guitar somewhere else just like normal. We rehearsed twice, and we did "Gun" and "Cable Hogue". And the story was that John is going to do "Pablo Picasso" with the band Live. So I'm like, "Humph, so I don't get to play on 'Pablo'!" The idea is that John and I and the other two guys playing with John would come on afterwards and do our two numbers. But when he and Live did a run-through of "Pablo Picasso", John goes, "Nigel, come over here." And there I was with my fuzzbox and acoustic guitar. And he says, "Let's try it again." And I launch into my horrible, Stoogey guitar, and I felt ten feet tall immediately. I had this old fuzzbox, made in 1961,' he elaborates, 'from *years* before I was born, called a Kettner, or Kimball, something like that. And it was an amazing sound. And Cale seemed pleased, because even when it wasn't turned on it sounded . . . *horrible*!'

And when Nigel and Judith weren't hobnobbing with former members of the Velvet Underground in New York, they were house hunting in London, and meeting estate agents who knew exactly where rock couples wanted to live. Next to other rock couples, naturally.

'I got taken around by an estate agent who, as soon as he found out what Nigel did, said, "Ohhh, so you're a band person. How about a nice property we have going next door to someone in Oasis?" ' Judith rolls her eyes. In the end, the Pulsfords settled on a des res in North London that needed a bit of work. Perhaps more, as is usually the case, than they expected, and that's before Nigel had a modest studio put into his basement so that he could work with other artists in his spare time. In fact, some of *The Science Of Things* would end up being tweaked in that very basement.

'We bought the house in October of 1997, and we moved in about a year later,' Judith notes by way of illustration of the sad truth that having the builders in always takes longer than you think. But a party during the Christmas holidays in 1998 illustrated just how much their living arrangements had changed. 'There were people still running around at four in the morning,' Judith laughs. 'And we couldn't work out where they'd gone! We used to live in a flat, and suddenly we live in a house in which you find yourself saying, "Oh my God, there are so many bedrooms in here. How did that happen?" We had over a hundred people!

'Can you believe having that much space?' she marvels. 'In London, everyone lives in flats, because it's too expensive. It was quite a change, after renting a place, and sharing rooms, and then suddenly buying a flat – I paid the interest on the mortgage, that was my contribution. And then suddenly we have this house. But it's a kind of security. You know that, whatever happens, we'll be okay.'

Nigel, too, alternates between being shyly house-proud of his first castle – as he flits from the piano to the sofa that the family dog insists on jumping on expressly against orders – and being faintly appalled at the seeming lavishness of what is, in the event, quite a modest rock star pad. He even points out, with scrupulous honesty, that his wine glasses cost a whopping £2.87 each.

'I don't feel guilty at all,' he insists. 'Well, maybe a bit embarrassed about the house. But if you had the opportunity to do it, and you didn't, you'd be a real fool. Plus,' he grins, 'it's sort of fun. I've got the studio downstairs, even if you can't always work at home. It's a bit of a responsibility, but as long as everything goes well, it'll be fine. And it's not about cash, or just about cash particularly. I love the space. You can clear your head. Living in London, it's a luxury not having a wall six feet away from you. And after touring and touring and touring, it's a nice change!'

Gavin acquired exactly that change himself, when he moved from the legendary basement flat in Montagu Square in early 1997. His new north London home, in contrast to the old one, also has walls more than six feet away from most places guests will end up sitting. And, in contrast to the old place, no one has to sleep in the kitchen. Or the hallway. Or the converted broom closet.

Nevertheless, like his bandmates, Gavin still upped sticks for a while when the band's year off presented itself. Partly because, as

Bush's songwriter, he had to come up with some songs for *The Science Of Things*.

'So,' he recounts, 'I just thought it would be really good to go and live in Ireland. Basically, I got the idea off a cross between Lennon's "Imagine" and a Picasso film about how he'd live in lovely houses and have endless streams of interesting people come to visit. And it was a cultural thing, not just a social thing; there would be all these energies going on.

'And so I had this arrangement where anyone could come and stay with me,' he says, adding that longtime London friends he hadn't seen in the past few years all made their way across the Irish Sea to his rented accommodation in the south-west of Ireland. 'Of course, I had to work eight-hour days in the studio, but they could stay. That was what Picasso used to do. So I found this white house in Ireland – though I didn't end up suddenly writing about rolling hills or how wonderful life is,' he jokes, an old punk through and through, half-afraid you might take him for another Van Morrison wannabe. 'But it's where I got in touch with my true self and experimented. I had all these art books with me, and songbooks, and then I went out there and I didn't get to many of them at all! I just found there was plenty to do. I just wanted to play guitar and play some bass and sing words over things. That's what people say about songwriting: it's fun to start with, but you have to immerse yourself. Just get up every day and do it. And I'd never lived in the countryside before, and it's intense sometimes. It just allowed me to open up a new spectrum in what I was thinking, which is why I hope this new record shows changes from within.'

Initially, not everything ran smoothly on a technical level. 'I got this studio put in, but it wasn't really working and it was a bad scene and there were a lot of technical hiccups. I had had the whole studio a year earlier, but I'd never used it. When I first got successful, one of the presents the label and the music publisher gave me was this equipment. So the first month in Ireland was very good, but there were all these people in the house, and I just couldn't get on with it.' He laughs. 'This whole perfect creative lifestyle and I couldn't get to it, with a lot of people milling around and no equipment working. A beautiful conservatory, and everything plugged in, everything ready to go. There's the microphone, there's the guitar, there's the drum machines already plugged in. Everything's in there, and you've just got to turn it on. So I used to have my little recording Walkman and, in the end, I wrote every song like that, with a drum machine and a guitar. It's kind of like the tail wagging the dog,' he adds with a wink. 'And, of course, I *am* the tail to my dog!'

Even without house guests, Gavin and Winston weren't completely alone. Longtime cohort Bone was convinced – though to be fair he didn't take much convincing – to accompany Gavin to Ireland.

'We had a tremendous time,' Bone enthuses. 'We walked two or three miles every day. We explored all the hills and nooks and crannies all around, and spent our nights drinking wine by the fireplace. We were up in a house in the mountains, and from our house, when you looked out, the next stop would have been Boston. That's how far west we were: jump in the ocean and swim until you hit Massachusetts.

'We had such good friends there in town, like the people who ran the grocery store. They were so gracious to us; invited us out to eat, invited us to their home. We used to go to McCarthy's pub in this little fishing village over the mountain. Brendan McCarthy's, a little hole-in-the-wall pub in a little village that was all fishermen. We had fun nights there, just listening to traditional Irish music, with a little coal fire in the place; all dark and cold and clammy and drinking Guinness.

'The thing is we both went there to write,' he adds. 'I write myself, and I was trying to finish a screenplay. And it was very difficult to get my juices flowing. Writing's tough. It's just like work,' he jokes. 'It was a wonderful time. Everybody loved it there. We had to kick the guests out. Nobody wanted to leave!'

It was good, Bone says, to see Gavin relaxed. 'Because we were completely left to our own devices, and nobody made demands on our time except him. He could get up when he wanted, eat when he wanted, work when he wanted, walk when he wanted. We were kind of a sovereign nation there. Gavin's a very intense workaholic kid, but he does know how to enjoy himself. And he knows how to get his free time and what to do with it. It was very important to him to have his daily walk, and he did. He'd go out walking and sometimes he'd be gone for four or five hours. I wouldn't know where the hell he went; he'd just go. Go and go, as far as he could possibly go, and then come back.

A year spent more or less off from work, give or take the odd album to write, would also give Gavin a chance to spend time with his significant other of a few years, Gwen Stefani. Paradoxically, it was probably only the fact that Gwen also fronts a successful pop band that made it possible for the two to see each other as much as they had thus far. Still, you can't always count on tour schedules to coincide. And it's nice, as Gwen says, to do normal stuff once in a while.

According to Gwen, she didn't know much about Bush at all when No Doubt began touring with the UK band in 1996, but she and Gavin became fast friends quite quickly. 'We were the opening band, and we were living on our bus. We didn't have hotel rooms or anything. We would just get to the venue and take showers in the locker room and then hang out the whole day. It wasn't like we were hanging out with Bush, of course, we were just hanging out with the crew and each other and having fun. Gavin was real sweet, but I was a bit worried, because once I met him it was like, "Oh no. He's *cute.*" Looking up at him, all I could think was, "Oh my God. *That's* what all the rage is about." And he was so sweet, and I was nervous about that. "Oh, no, what am I going to do? I'm gonna hide in my bus the whole time!" I just knew it could be complicated. I was in a really crazy part of my life, and me and Tony [Kanal, No Doubt's bassist] had been broken up for three and a half years, but . . .

'I was so young, compared to how I feel right now. Gavin's only, like, the second boyfriend in my life. I remember the first show we played with them; we were so excited, because we'd never done shows like that. Such a big place. I remember skating all day around the arena, and then the Bush bus pulled up and it was dinner time and everybody was eating and they said "hi" to us and that was that. And we watched them play and it was just, "Wow." The audience were really into them. And that was the first night. And from then on it was all a blur.

'I remember the tour kept on extending, and me and Gavin were like, "Yes!" Every time we heard the tour was carrying on, we were so happy, 'cause that meant we could hang out together. Of course, we totally got to know each other – that's what we spent the whole tour doing – but at the same time it was really sad. We were on different schedules, because, as I said, we were on the bus and they were in luxury hotels. And we would drive all night while they spent it sleeping. They wouldn't get there until after our soundcheck. And our relationship, we took it slow. I didn't travel with him or anything like that. It was a really hard time for me and Tony, but he was really good. He could have been angry. He deserved to be. But it was also very exciting. It was exciting on all different levels, as a person, because I was in this huge growing stage in my life, and as a performer. Our record was out and we were playing those big shows and I knew we were just getting better. Every night we had to prove ourselves to people in the back.

'I don't know what to say about Gavin.' She shrugs and smiles. 'I just took him how I found him. I mean, I see him in so many different ways now, because I've known him for three years. I just felt like this little tiny baby when I met him, and I just saw him as a really sweet person. I remember thinking, "God, he's so sweet to support bands." He's always signing autographs for everyone, takes the time out for everyone. He's super patient in that way. And he really loved going onstage. I was always there just before he went on, and he just loved to go out there. The whole band worked really hard. They were on tour for a long time. At that time I didn't realise it, 'cause I had never been on tour extensively. I was on tour for about two and a half years, but they went on tour for longer than that and they made a record in between. I still don't know how they did that. I mean, we're writing a record right now,' she says of No Doubt's third album, 'and we've already spent a year writing it. I just think Gavin's unbelievably driven. He's desperate about wanting to achieve and have this music come out. Seriously, I'm lazy compared to him. He's unbelievable, extremely driven and very committed.

'If something's not being done properly he won't stand for it, because he's a perfectionist. But he holds his friends so dear. His friends and family – there's not even a line between them. And he's so loyal to every girl he's been with. All his ex-girlfriends are still his friends. I think it's really weird,' she laughs. 'But there's something to say for it. He has this loyalty to anyone he's had a relationship with, boys or girls.

'Maybe it's a cultural thing,' Gwen suggests. 'London's a lot smaller, so people run into each other all the time. It's really weird. We'll be out in London and he'll know everybody, on every corner. I just go, "Wow, you are *too* popular." Here in LA it's different, more spread out. But I think that's a neat thing, the way everyone in London keeps up with everyone.

'I think he loves touring. You've got to be a certain kind of person to tour that kind of way, where your life becomes the road. It's not like, "Oh, I have three months now where I'm going to be on tour." It's like, "This is going to be my life now, for the next two years." It's a really weird space but it's also an amazing thing. You have basically no responsibilities; all you've got to do is make sure you put on a show every night. And that is so traumatic. You go out there and you don't even know what's going to happen. It could be the worst night of your life, or you could go into that one space that is like the most incredible feeling. And it's hard to describe, and it sounds so cliché'd and cheesy, but it's almost like an out-of-body experience. I know that Gavin's felt it. It's the greatest thing in the world to be up there performing. You wake up and all you have to do is exercise and maybe find something to eat in a foreign country or somewhere across America. It's the greatest life. And you have this little family of people that are with you that are all doing the same thing, and everybody's so into it and cares so much.

'And throughout it all, Gavin was my new friend that I could talk to. The only thing that was weird about it was this little whispering thing which would go around, because everybody wanted to know. It wasn't the crew, I'm talking about when you start doing interviews. People asking me about it. I'd be sitting with my band, and hey, *they* don't want to talk about it. It's boring. That part of it was weird,' she grins. 'So I just ignored it. It was my little thing. I didn't feel I had to explain myself. Mainly,' she theorises, 'what people want to know is what sort of person Gavin is. And he's the most loyal human being I've probably ever met, and so driven. Someone who has the energy to get what he wants done, done. But the funny thing is he has this little lazy side, too,' she adds. 'Like, he loves to eat ice cream and watch movies on TV, which is something we both have in common. Which is a really good thing, because he has, like, multiple personalities, and I'm still trying to get to know all of them. He has this driven side and then this side who wants to be lazy.

'He is extremes. And he's so sensitive. He can see a movie that can upset him for two days. And I've got to be careful about my jokes sometimes, because I have a real dark sense of humour sometimes, and so does he, but sometimes he says, "Oh, don't say that." He's very sensitive. He's like a guy, but he has a lot of girl qualities.' She laughs. 'And he always looks great. I'm not going to stand next to him unless I've done my make-up, that's for sure!'

At first, Gwen admits, 'I definitely didn't trust him at all. You know, I mean, I didn't trust *it*. I didn't think I'd still be with him in three years' time. And both of us are like, "Oh my God, how did we do that?" Especially since we don't see each other all the time. It's really hard. But I trust him; I know what kind of person he is. If he's anything, he's loyal, and I think that's a really good trait to have. I never wanted to go out with a guy in a band, and of course I was *in* a band with a bunch of guys. I know what you're like after being on tour for two years. Anything goes, and by a certain point you're just trying to amuse yourself. At the same time, though, most of the people you meet on tour are sixteen-, seventeen-year-old girls. And I don't think Gavin's the kind of guy who will hang out with just anyone. He doesn't like to be touched. He doesn't like to be poked. He's just like that about his space. He kind of has a guard up unless he lets you in.

'But I was never in that little waiting room. It was really that he forced me into it. I didn't want to get involved, because it was too complicated, but I couldn't help myself and here I am. He just pretty much sucked me in but he was always very welcome,' she adds with a smile. 'He's very romantic, and I'd never really been treated like that. Very sweet. He was always bringing me little presents. Sweaters. Just little things every time I saw him. Gosh, so supportive and so sweet. And I never thought about him as, like, being in this big band. I don't know why it never felt like, "Oh my God, no." Because I never really knew too much about his band before I met him. I wasn't like a huge fan before. I just never looked at him in that way. I don't ever think about it even now, except for maybe when I hear Bush on the radio.'

As for Gwen's legendarily close family, Gavin had already been introduced to them long before he was aware of it. 'Yeah.' Gwen laughs. 'The story was my dad saw him on TV when we were going out on tour with Bush. And my dad pointed at the TV to my mum, and he said, "Honey, there's your future son-in-law!" Before we started dating, he predicted it!

'Of course, Gavin must have been nervous meeting them,' she agrees of the fateful encounter at the Stefani home. 'We're like, the goody two shoes family, and he's the pot-smoking guy from another country. I think my dad always really liked him, but my mum was nervous. They must have read stuff about him when I was on tour, but they were fine once they met him.'

In fact, Gavin would meet Gwen's parents the night he had taped *Saturday Night Live*'s solo performance of 'Glycerine'. 'Yeah, that was the first night he came over. He came over and we taped it and then we all watched it. I felt a little sorry for him,' she adds, 'in an embarrassing kind of way.

'At the end of the tour, it was really sad. We didn't know what was going to happen or when we were going to see each other again. And it was really hard on me. I didn't know what was going in my life. I think he just said, "We'll just find each other." And I remember coming home from tour; I was still living with my parents and I was in the bathtub and I was just sitting in there, crying. And then my mum walked in with this huge bouquet of flowers from him. It was so sweet. And then every chance that we got, we went to see each other. Whenever we were off the road. If I was on tour and I had a couple of days I'd go to see him, and same thing for him. I think the first time we were together was when we were in France.' Gwen and Gavin would spend time in Cap D'Antibes with Mark Armstrong and other friends in the summer of 1998 and it was, Gwen says, a wonderful time.

'Even though I was, like, so out of it. I flew home, I spent a week with my parents at a beach house that we rented, and that was after being on tour for two years. And then I spent time with Gavin. I've never lived with a boy or anything, and here I am with this guy in a foreign country. I didn't even speak the lingo. It was really funny and it was romantic. But like I say, I was naive and now I'm not.'

Visiting London, she says, is often a blur, meeting all of Gavin's friends. 'I'm just like, "Hi," because they have all this history with him and I'm this American girl. But they're all so friendly and very welcoming in that way. And everybody seems to be like, "As long as Gavin's happy." Definitely *nobody* likes it when Gavin's not happy. That has always amazed me, that he has some kind of weird power over people like that.'

And his house? 'Oh, God, I think it's beautiful. Once again, I never met a guy who can cook, who can decorate a house, who can help me pick out clothes. You know, he has no limit on those sort of things. He's pretty much good at everything he does. I'm trying to think of something he's not good at, and it's hard. Though I think I might be a better swimmer than he is,' she laughs.

'We've been really lucky, in a way, that we have the same job. I think it's been a blessing for us. I can't imagine having a normal boyfriend with a nine to five job. My other boyfriend was in my band and we did the same thing, too. Our lives are so different to so many people. I think the long-distance thing is awful, but it gives you the space to be creative and put out records. I mean, Gavin's put a lot into this new record, but that's what it takes to make a good record great. All the work he puts into it is necessary and it's the same for me. Even though we complain about it every time we're on the phone – "Oh, I wish you and I lived in the same country" – in a way, it's kind of a blessing, because we both work really hard.

'And he's totally into me being me. It's probably what he likes about me. He definitely wants children, he wants a wife. That's another reason why I've been so attracted to him, because that's very important to him and to me, too. But he doesn't want me to just become a housewife. He's totally supportive. I mean, he's come and sat with me in the studio for hours. He's just really good like that.

'The more I come to London,' she continues, 'and get to know the culture and the people, I definitely feel I know him better and I'm less scared of him. Because sometimes he frightens me by his experience, by his history. I mean, our lives are so different. He comes from a crazy life. He struggled and had a really hard life. And I had it really easy. I had this lovely family. I have nothing to complain about: I mean, I got spanked when I was little one time or something. I think the more I get to know the people, the more I understand him and the closer I can be to him.'

As for Gavin's and Bush's long struggle to success, Gwen suggests, 'It couldn't have happened any other way. I think you need to go through those things to make it be real. What annoys me about the bad press the guys get is that if anyone's real, it's him. He's the singer and he writes the songs, he plays guitar. It's the music he loves and it's got influences like anyone else's. But all the lyrics, and just everything, is so real. And he's really sensitive, but he's also really strong. He's very thick skinned in that way. That's what I mean. One second he's so sensitive, like I don't know *anyone* that sensitive, and the next he's really strong. Don't ask me,' she laughs out loud. 'I still haven't figured him out!

'It's really sad that we're apart so much, but we have the rest of our lives to do that other stuff. We are both really understanding of the fact that this is not going to last forever, so we're just trying to make the most of the fifteen minutes we've been given. And we've been really lucky touring together, playing shows together, seeing families together. We've done a lot of things. And there's still more to go. I would love for our bands to tour together somewhere, like Japan.'

In the meantime, there's always the telephone. Ask Gwen if one of them plays the stereotypical bloke unwilling or unable to chat on the phone for very long, and she crows, 'Yeah, *I'm* that guy! I'm the one that's not good on the phone. He's so much better, and I'm the naughty one, sometimes, I think. But he's patient with me and understanding, because I've just been through that twenty-nine year thing, and it's a hard one.

'He always makes me feel special. He's really good at that. That's why I love him. He tries really hard to make me feel good about myself. That's important. And I thought I was romantic and obsessive about love until I met him. But listen, I don't even touch it.'

As for the press interest – what Michael Pagnotta wryly describes as the media's attempt to paint Gwen and Gavin as 'Queen and King of The Alternative Prom' – Gwen says, 'It's annoying sometimes when things aren't going great. But whatever happens, it's nobody's business. You are just trying to deal with it on a day-to-day level. It's your life. It's fun to talk about it, I guess, but at the same time, for both of us, the music's the most important thing to us and the relationship is totally separate.

'You don't know how weird it sounds to me when people use the term "celebrity couple",' she continues. 'Hey, I'm just this Orange County girl who has a boyfriend. I mean, of course people would say that, because my boyfriend's in a band, but when you're in the middle of it, you never think about it. It's not like you ever get used to people asking for autographs, or stop thinking, Wow, this is my life and people are interested in it. It's weird.

'We go out all the time,' she insists. 'Our lives are not that crazy. OK, we might have been a bit naive to go to Catalina together for a vacation. Going to a tiny little [resort] island with families with lots of sixteen year olds, yeah, that ended up being three days of thinking, *Please* don't take a picture of me in my bathing suit! It was the worst thing ever,' she exaggerates, laughing.

Of being in the public eye with Gwen, Gavin says, 'Usually it's all right. I remember me and Gwen and her family going out to Disneyland, and it was really good for a while. But as we were leaving – we'd been there all day and were trying to keep a low profile – a woman and her kids were there wanting to take pictures. So we did that for a while, but then we wanted to go, and we got, "Come on, you *owe* it to your fans." By the end, the mother was just screaming at us. And I didn't want to scream at this kid's mother, so I called the kid over and said, "You know, your mum's being a little bit naughty about this." '

Gwen continues, 'I think the hardest thing is when I go over to London because it's not like my life continues, it's like I'm on vacation all the time. It's really hard, because Gavin will be continuing to work, and I'll be left saying, "Hi, I'm here, I'm going to hang out now." Which can be really fun, actually, to have to force yourself to do that. But I kind of wish that we could try it being both of us working together. You know, like, "'Bye, I'm going to work". Right now, it's that one or the other of us always has to stop to be with the other one.'

As for Gavin's sojourn in Ireland, she says, 'I really loved being there when I visited. It was so beautiful. And it was amazing that he did all that; it was really dedicated to go off and work like that. The poor thing, he was going crazy trying to get everything working. I don't know how he does all that, just takes it further and further. And when he has to, he gets his work done really quick.

'I feel pretty loved,' she says simply. 'And yeah, we have our ups and downs. Sometimes you make a commitment and things aren't so good. And you have to go halfway around the world. But we decided that if we're not going to be together for Christmas, what's the point? One of us has to do it, and he's the man, so he did!' Gwen is referring to Christmas 1998, which would be the first Christmas Gavin Rossdale had spent apart from his own family. 'But I came over and got him,' she admits, 'and we had our Christmas dinners in England, and we flew over together. And we got here, both of us with jet lag, and woke up at four in the morning and had breakfast in bed and went back to sleep and it was so much fun. He came over to my family to have *my* Christmas,' she exults. 'And when we walked in, they were singing *Away In A Manger*. Everyone had a stocking with their name on it, and about four hundred presents per person . . .'

By then, of course, Bush's 'year off', which wasn't actually either an entire year, or entirely devoid of work, had been over for months. And *The Science Of Things*, as yet un-gift-wrapped and not quite ready for anyone's stocking, was still to be completed.

I've been waiting let me say
Been a strange 1,000 days

Not one, not two, but three editing rooms at Westway Studios were running at the same time as Bush completed *The Science Of Things*, co-produced along with *Sixteen Stone* producers Alan Winstanley and Clive Langer, engineer Tom Elmhurst and programmers Aiden Love and Johnny Rocstar, not to mention a string section, the assistance of old friend Sacha Puttnam, and a guest vocal from Gwen Stefani on 'Space Travel'. It might not have taken one thousand days, but Gavin Rossdale thinks it took too long to complete a set of twelve tracks which begins with the words '*I memorise the basics*' and ends with '*the best is yet to come*', with a number of career-bests and bold musical shifts in between. And, indeed, the best was yet to come, although in between the completion of *The Science Of Things* in March and its release in the autumn of 1999, the band would have a contractual difference of opinion with their label Trauma, and then resolve it, as the album's release date hung in the balance.

'I'm an endurance specialist,' Gavin smiles, when asked about the furious work rate and the long hours that he and his colleagues put in on this record. 'It was amazing. And we had a producer who got sober during the making of it,' he grins, 'and probably one programmer who's going to end up back in therapy. This has been a year of my life, and it has been a test of what we can do, and of what we are. The last record was our definitive recording as a band, and this is the record where you've got to take it that bit further.

'I'm happy with it,' he says. 'I was unhappy at Christmas [1998, when the record was originally scheduled to be finished] because I knew, when I listened to it, that there were tons of things still to do. And, of course, I still keep wondering why we can't do it in an afternoon! But I knew that record wasn't done, whereas now, I know it's the best we can do. Even if stuff wasn't right, and someone said, "Look, you've got to remix it and you've got to redo it," I'd say, "Well, someone else has got to redo it, then, because I've put my bit in as much as I can." '

In some ways, he says of the new album, 'it's softer. It's definitely more exposed'. Tracks like 'Forty Miles from the Sun' and 'Letting the Cables Sleep' reveal a more intimate sound to match their subject matter, although elsewhere 'English Fire', 'Prizefighter' and 'Mindchanger' rock harder than ever. The newfound softness in certain tracks might come from the fact that Gavin's vocals are more compellingly showcased than previously, as 'Forty Miles' shows.

Gavin smiles when it's mentioned. 'You know, I'm the only person who ever worked with Steve Albini who wanted the vocals lower [in the mix]! Everyone I know is always saying to make them louder, and then I get scared of it. I love the music being really loud, and the louder the voice gets, the smaller the music gets. Then again, you know what the words are if you write them, and when I think back to Pixies records – they were one of the first bands I paid attention to that had really different words – I've got about three sets of lyrics for every Pixies record. And that always frustrated me because I love words. So I'm trying to bring in a small balance, just to get used to them being a bit louder. It's like trying on a shirt my mum's given me or something, trying to make out it's a good fit,' he laughs.

Speaking to Gavin before the album's release, he confided, 'Do I worry about it? Sure, I am worried. I need to work out the final order of the songs, and I've kind of got moments when I'm happy with it. At the moment I find it hard to listen to anything Steve Albini has recorded, because I knew we'd forfeited that [by returning to Langer and Winstanley]. No one records guitars like he does. Trent [Reznor] is the clever one; maybe what we should have done was use Steve for a part of the recording, and done the rest ourselves. But, you know, it's relative: if my grandmother had balls, she'd be my grandfather. So I'll probably be happier with it in a little while, and also there's mastering, that really crucial process that stops things sounding wrong. We just need to go through the final process.'

Bringing Sacha Puttnam in to add string arrangements and keyboards to the record was, he says, a pleasurable experience from start to finish. 'Sacha's just really talented,' he says simply. 'And I love writing with him. I've always tried to find any excuse to get him to work with us. In fact, I tried on the last album; I sat with him in his house in the countryside and played "Straight No Chaser" to him on the guitar. I spent three days trying to get him to write a string part for it, saying, "No, make it more angry, more bitter, think of all the shitty things that have happened to you!"' Gavin laughs. 'And he'd say, "I just don't have it. Look around you . . . I'm not that angry!"'

This time, however, 'I knew what stuff I wanted from him. He's just so musical. His understanding and knowledge of music is not that of a pop musician. He's a really good piano player, and any good piano player understands the laws of harmony, things that people in rock bands don't know much about.' And having keyboards on a rock album is, he says, most definitely 'not wussing out. It's a case of finding the right notes that communicate that emotion. When Sacha plays on "English Fire" it's amazingly powerful; it just goes straight to your stomach. And when I was working with the string section, I would direct them by talking in terms of how it would affect your stomach. It's quite amazing, you know, because music is basically the distance between notes, the ringing of a note, and they all have physical effects on you. Nigel knows a lot about that stuff, but Sacha's really studied it. He's done the time sitting in classrooms for five years. If we ever took a keyboard player out live, it would be Sacha, which would be so fun, because that would just blow his mind.

'The only thing that scares me is that I don't want to seem as if we're treading ground. And when you've only still got the same four musicians and no embellishment, by definition you're treading the same ground. And when I got upset with the band during recording these songs was when I didn't want to make out that I'd never heard of the Aphex Twin. And I didn't want to be John Cougar Mellencamp – although no disrespect to John Cougar Mellencamp – and just stay really straight ahead. And the one sure way of pissing myself off was feeling there would be a lack of textural depth; I don't like it when bands have songs that sound the same. And I don't think we sound the same.

'Finishing a record is a weird time, full of self-doubt. I don't care about competing with any other bands,' Gavin explains. 'And I'm not embarrassed by having a younger audience, because I think any successful band has had that. Even The Clash,' he smiles. 'And even though it sometimes seems like there's a time limit on how long you can keep doing it. I mean, it never occurred to me how old Michael Stipe was, for example. Still, I always feel like I'm playing catch up. I remember saying to Clive, "Oh, God, I should have made so many records by now." And he told me, "You should look at what you *have* done." I always look at the weakest point, I suppose. Then again, Nick Cave made *The Boatman's Call*, which was his best ever, when he was forty . . .'

Not surprisingly for the frontman of a band whose career was made in the concert arena, Gavin spends much of the time he discusses *The Science Of Things* focusing on how it will translate to a live show.

'It's hard with just four of you, because basically there's only so much you can do. For instance, I really wanted, when we began touring again, not to have to play every song on the guitar. I thought that dynamically that would be really good. It's great to have your arms out and be expressive, and to be always stuck playing every single song and chained to a guitar, it's such a crutch. It'll be interesting to strip that away. Nigel is more than capable of playing a song on his own; he's a fantastic guitarist. The problem is that if you've had the power of two guitars coming out of those speakers and then you only have the power of one guitar, it's weird. Like when Polly [Harvey] did that first record with Flood when she had that band where she went out without playing guitar. I just missed her playing so much. I've got buckets of feel but I'm probably a pretty shitty guitar player. But I can't let anyone else play the song; in the parts where it's just voice and guitar, everyone has their own feel. I know what I'd be like,' he grins. 'I'd spend the whole time thinking, "No! That's *not* it!"

'And the truth of it is,' he adds with a wink, 'if I didn't play guitar, I'd have nothing else to throw!

'At one point, too,' he continues, 'I was also looking at getting someone who could work loops and this and that. But then it gets a bit like a big old fat sandwich to listen to, you can't really digest it. But then again when I just think of that song "English Fire", if

I heard it live, I would love to hear those strings on it. I mean, Nigel can play strings. And I think it's probably better to keep it to the band; there's something better with just the four of us being there.'

However the configuration would work out, there was an audience waiting, as European agent Mike Greek observes. 'I can't speak for America but, for the territories we deal with, people are desperate to get Bush touring again. The demand to see the band is building all the time, and it comes down to the fact that word-of-mouth keeps spreading. People, fans, are constantly ringing us up – how they get our number, I never know – and trying to find out when they're going to play again and what the details are.'

In the meantime, the four band members in question weren't the only ones aware that, according to the band who made their last record in under a month, taking the best part of a year to do the next one was not only not very punk rock, it wasn't very Bush.

Alex Tate laughs as he relates a telling second-hand anecdote. 'Apparently, Gavin was at a party sitting next to Mani, an ex-member of the Stone Roses [who famously took years to complete their second album]. And Gavin was complaining, "God, I've been working on this record for seven months." And then he caught sight of Mani, who retorted, "Try fucking five years, mate!"

'He played me a song the other day and he said, "I've been having problems with this track, but I think I've finally got it right." He just knew that he hadn't pushed himself yet. He knows the Bush formula, he's just got a little bit bored and wants to expand. People like David Bowie have shown him that you do need to carry on beyond that big bang. Experimenting with musical shapes is hard, especially where their songs have always been "you've got to make it big, and then ease back, and then build and build and build!" But Gavin says, "I can't do that forever." And, of course, he's in a band with three other people, and they all need to do their part.

'But it's good,' Alex grinned as he offered an early review of *The Science Of Things*. 'And "Forty Miles from the Sun" – cor, what a sublime piece of songwriting that is! Gav's really showing off his bouncy little lyric action there.' More seriously, he adds, 'Of course, they're all a little anxious about this album. Because, hey, they've never made a third album, for a start, and after having a year off when they hadn't had a month off in years, well . . .'

Asked to comment on the recording process, manager David Dorrell offers a typically tart reply.

'Of course, the best judge of when something is done is the artist. Always. Should Picasso, who in the course of a number of hours, almost, did *Guernica* and thereby captured in it the full horror of modern times, have spent longer? Should Rembrandt, who went back to a canvas time and again and where the layers reveal the development of another great classic, have taken less? Are you going to argue with Rembrandt about what's finished and what isn't? That it could have been better? Whether it was as good as it needed to be? I don't think so,' he retorts.

'I think it was just a case that this was an album where they were going to take more time and more care over than, certainly, the last album. Which was by no means slapdash, but which was just a different approach and technique. In attempting to grow as a band, and in an attempt to increase the palette of colours that they paint with, it was inevitable that things would be gone back to time and time again. Certainly every time it was seen that there was room for improvement,' he concludes.

Of the programmed elements on the record, most obviously on the massive 'The Chemicals Between Us', Dorrell observes witheringly that so-called 'dance' elements are hardly new to rock music. 'Trent Reznor does fine. Rob Zombie does fine. Rage Against The Machine have always been very smart in their use of stuff. It's only Luddites who believe that you can't pull it off successfully. I think we already bridged that divide with [the *Deconstructed* remix of] "Mouth". And I think when Gavin did the demos for this album in Ireland, he was already programming stuff himself, and it had already taken a definite shape in his head, so he knew there was going to be a future for the two elements on this album.'

According to Gavin, 'I wanted to keep the album modern, and by modern, I mean Aphex Twin. It's not pioneering, because obviously we had Kraftwerk in the 70s doing that stuff, but it's modern in that it's pushing the boundaries. But if we'd done too much of it, you know, I was aware that you could become the tail wagging the dog, running after an idea. I didn't want to be ever conceived as trying to acclimatise myself into the *Zeitgeist*, into what's happening now. If you try to do that, by the time it comes out, it'll be something different anyway.'

Clive Langer who, with longtime colleague Alan Winstanley, also produced *Sixteen Stone*, wasn't expecting to find the two of them back in the studio with Bush. He says. 'One minute I'm doing this score for a film and then I'm in the studio with Bush. And I sort of drank my way through it. I had to give up drinking by the end of it, because my body wasn't coping.'

Back in a state as close to hale and hearty as a studio-bound producer ever is, Clive says of these recording sessions that 'for me, working with Bush isn't like producing bands, especially these days. I mean, Gavin makes a lot of the decisions because that's the way he is. On this album I think of myself more as a caretaker than a producer, just making sure everything's all right. He has that effect on people; I look after him, go running round after him. And I put my little bit in and I like to think I can help, but often I just have to step back. I don't want anybody to get the wrong impression; my main concern is always to get it made and get it done.'

There's a crucial difference this time, he says, compared to the twelve-week session which produced *Sixteen Stone*. 'They had played those songs live a lot, whereas with this one, they've never played it live, so there was a lot of rehearsing. My job is to make sure it sounds just as tight. Gavin's intense, everybody's intense. And you could tell him if you thought he was fiddling too much, but that doesn't mean that he's going to stop. He's got his own strong mind.'

When asked how the band knew what needed fixing, Langer laughs.

'I think once you've made an album or two, you can figure all that out. It's really common sense. It's more musical things: let's re-do that, or that sound doesn't work. And everybody keeps themselves busy; Nigel always has a lot to say and Robin has a lot to say and Dave has a bit less to say. He comes in and talks about the bass. But they're all pretty involved. But it's difficult with Gavin at the moment because I think he is really looking forward to making an album on his own, and I had to remind him that it's the Bush album here,' he smiles. 'That's part of my job. But quite often I just leave him alone, because his ideas are quite good. He doesn't need interfering. I've learnt that with artists before like Kevin Rowland; it was sounding good, so leave it. I'm not the Trevor Horn of grunge.' Clive laughs.

'They're fun to be with, and bright,' he says of the band. 'You know, they might be a bit competitive and bitchy – it's a lot like the dynamics of a public school, in fact – but then you go and have a drink and then everything's great. Maybe that's pretty healthy. Well, maybe not healthy, but normal. Though, personally, I went to an all-boys school and I avoided those guys who were trying to outwit each other,' he laughs.

Sacha Puttnam, this album's visiting professor of keyboards and strings, enthuses, 'I really looked forward to working on the record. Suddenly, I was getting away from school at three thirty, running off to the studio to join them. It was wonderful: "Wow, you've got me out of my mundane life."

'The weird thing for me, though,' he muses, 'is that while Midnight was totally based on a friendship, I see that Bush is very much a working partnership. And being a visitor, when I was in the studio, I'd try to be as inclusive as possible, just so no one thought there was any kind of ego involved. I think Nigel is a really, really talented man,' he adds, 'and really clever with musicians, and it must be strange when suddenly there are twenty other people helping to make your album. Maybe it's the difference of age, because when I think back to Midnight, even if I'd come up with the worst bass line in the world, the attitude would have been, "Sach, it's your bass line, you do it," and they'd have lived with it. Whereas now, I think if Dave came up with something that wasn't working, it would be the old elbow and someone else would fix it. The important thing in a band is never to make anyone feel they're not wanted, regardless of what happens, so that someone feels they're just an extra person who plays an instrument when the band goes on tour.

'Obviously it's Gavin's thing, and none of them are shy about saying that it's his band, and that he calls the shots. Gav even calls the shots with Dave [Dorrell] a lot; I've watched him working his way round him. So perhaps he values me when I come in, because I don't really care. I mean, of course I care because I want it to be absolutely wonderful. But if I think a part sounds like another song, then I just say, "Actually, that sounds like that bit over there." And they look at me like, "What are you saying?" But it's good to get it out, because then you can say, "Right, well if we do that to it, mess it around, then it's going to work better."

'I think Gav treads a clever little line between being close to the band, and using that power he has. I have a great worry about power. I hate to use power. Gavin seems to do it in a clever way. But the next stage for Gavin, which will be lovely, will be a situation where Dave can grow, and where Nigel can grow, and Robin, and then you can really have a band that lasts for ever and ever. But this album is the crunch, isn't it? I think they've got enough good singles to pull it through. And if they go out to the people, then they'll get it. They really will.'

Of Gavin's assertion that he is an outsider, Sacha says, 'I think it's in his head. But I think it's quite lonely to be the top dog. If you're going to run something, you're the one who has to be aloof, because you have to be setting the example to everyone. My dad never gets friendly with the crew, because you know that one day you might have to fire someone. It definitely is a psychological thing. So that might be the explanation for the outsider business. But I think if he didn't have that, if he was more arrogant, he wouldn't be so charming. And sometimes I've seen him when he was stamping his foot, but I love people who have power and are generous with it.'

Nigel Pulsford, contemplating the months spent working on *The Science Of Things*, smiles at his own impatience. 'At the time, it seemed as if it went on for so long! Dicking about on the same bloody songs. All the songs with programming on them have changed the most, probably because it was new for us and no one quite knew how it should sound, or had a clear idea of what it should be. We just knew that whatever we had wasn't it.' It's far different, he says, from a situation in which 'you work within the constraints of a limited budget, and you just give yourselves two weeks because you can't afford to go and buy another whatever, because you haven't got any money, so you have to do the best you can'.

Clearly, he admits, Bush have moved beyond those constraints. 'And there's a learning curve, certainly, but also there's a not-sure-what-it-should-be curve,' Nigel argues. 'So there was exploration, which we all said we'd give ourselves time to do on this album. Then again, I'm sure we wasted some of it.'

Still, he says, he's 'very excited about what people will think of it'. He grins. 'I never really like records when I've finished making them, because I've heard them too much and there's no fun involved in hearing them. There's fun involved in hearing them in a year's time, though. I'm glad that it's over, more than anything. Because we'd had time off, no one was playing that well when we started. It got better; everyone got playing really well, but it took some time.'

That time, however, gave the band the opportunity to decide which tracks would make the cut. Of the seventeen tracks the band worked on, Nigel says, 'it got very obvious what should be on and what shouldn't. It's a bit longer than fifty minutes, but only just. If it's too long, it's never as good. And these days, most records are just too long!

'And the actual songs are all really good,' he insists. 'I don't think there's a bad song on it. And songs are always better when they're live. Six months from now, I'll be listening to it and go, great. And "Dead Meat" sounds really good; "Space Travel" sounds really good. And in six months, it won't sound safe at all.'

X

'The actual writing is easy. Anyone can tell you the hardest part about writing is being there. Some songs take five to ten minutes, but it's taken me ten years to get to the point where I can write them.'

When Gavin Rossdale came off the road from the *Razorblade Suitcase* tour, he had no new songs stored up. Thereby providing himself, if accidentally, a clean slate when he went to Ireland in early 1998 to begin writing the band's third proper album. 'When I was in Ireland, I made a point of just sitting down and writing and writing, and used as much of it as I could, and just tried to get it done. I care about all of them, you know,' he says of his lyrics. 'I want them all to go to a good home!'

Of the record's title, he says, 'I like that mixture of specific – "science" – and not specific – "things" – because it's really personal somehow, and intimate. This record is partly about the idea that you invite things into your life; you know, that we are all "*servants of our formulaic ways*",' he elaborates, quoting 'Greedy Fly' from *Razorblade Suitcase* in the process.

'It's also about the way that time after time we seem to surround ourselves with certain situations. And I was thinking about Darwin, how everyone I know is obsessed with the Internet and highways and byways, so I was thinking how things are explained; the science of things. In the last few weeks of being in Ireland, I was a bit obsessed by our formulas and what we all invite, and who we meet and what we're attracted to. What we're attracted to about people and about things. And you just see the thread that runs through the record.

'The reasons why you connect with one person and not another are seemingly unexplainable. Even if, yes, ultimately most things are explainable. But who people decide to be in love with and who they want to be connected with, that's where it starts to get tricky. Although maybe it's not,' he adds with a smile, aware that the man of contradictions is second-guessing himself yet again. 'Some people would say there's a formula to it, because generally you'll find people will go out with the same type of person, and generally spend the same length of time together. Before this,' he notes, 'I've had two serious relationships that lasted five years dead on. Really weird. But it is brilliant, isn't it, behavioural science and anthropology. That's what I'd like to have studied. Evolution. How people are.'

Human relationships are, he admits, complex; perhaps even too complex to be expressed in words. 'I mean, it's pretty bizarre, apart from the fact that I adore her, that I have a girlfriend who lives in America. It's not a logical step. It's twisted. And whenever I speak to my friends and I'm just dying for Gwen to be here, I think of that. And when I come back off tour – and I don't want to sound like I'm feeling sorry for myself, though perhaps I am a bit – everyone else goes home to their partners, and they have wonderful homes set up together. And whenever I come back, I get Winston, and even then, he's angry at me for being away. The whole idea of coming home means comfort, and the comfort of the one you love, and so it's a shame not to have that. But whenever I speak to anyone who has it, they'll say, "Well, it's never perfect, and it's not fun every day." And I'm like, "Yeah, but I don't care! I'd love to try it!" So I'm still stuck with this illogical thing, even if it might possibly change in future. But you go by the person, not the location,' he smiles.

'A record has to be relevant, personally relevant,' Gavin theorises. 'But I think with this record, I've given up that belief that songs should always be directly about yourself, every minute of the day. Especially because, even without trying to be contradictory, you may have a certain attitude towards something which is directly the opposite of how you feel the next day, let alone the following week. The totality is what's important. There is some personal stocktaking on here, in the sense that maybe I wasn't really saying what I was thinking in the past, or I didn't say it very clearly, or very well. Or I was correcting myself, proofreading. But if something is a personal stocktaking and you're happy with the results, you think, "Fucking hell, these will live forever." ' He laughs. 'Or as long as CDs last, until they wear out. But of course I'll be dead by then. Triumphant!

'I'm not trying to be wiser or calmer,' he emphasises. 'No, I hope those things never change. I haven't calmed down, but there are times when I feel calm. Basically, I'm completely contradictory. As soon as I think about something, I think about something else at the same time. I don't change my mind, it's just that everything is . . . fluid.

'If you don't question yourself, you are left with arrogance. Though sometimes it's good to be arrogant; maybe arrogance is like direction. But I like taking in other people's points of view as well. It can be helpful,' he laughs, raising an eyebrow in the direction of his own headstrong tendencies. 'Not always, but it can be.'

'Warm Machine', which begins with the line *'memorise the basics'*, is, Gavin says, 'some degree of trying to understand how you're meant to be. Putting yourself in a context. So often, you feel right off the mark, so you attempt to conform but you know that you're not pulling it off. Your suit is ill-fitting, and your shirt is actually just a bit too tight around your neck, but you're trying to look like you're meant to look.

'And that's why the next bit goes, *"tread slowly for I know there's a thousand miles to go without blinking"*. That thing of trying to keep stoic, as if you're all right, when maybe you're not. It's a "save me" song. The "I'm really trying to deal with it all" song, which is where the line *"I'll take the help, I'll take a slice"* comes from.' He looks at the lyric sheet. 'A slice of help. That's a weird image.'

Of the ambiguity between the words "warm machine" and "war machine', Gavin says: 'Yeah, I love that confusion, and the song has some of both, because that's an integral part of it. So as long as it doesn't get that treatment Springsteen had with "Born In The USA", which was an anti-war song and it got used to enlist people,' he adds. 'I don't want it to be taken as that.

The oppressively lithe 'Jesus Online', with its Internet-era *'wires around the world'* and the seductive and subtly malevolent presence of a mysterious *'computer carbon girl'* is, Gavin says, 'this album's version of "Swallowed", because this is how we're going to ask for help in the next century. And this is how much you get pushed around by how much you can love somebody.'

He looks down at the lyrics. ' "*Computer carbon girl* . . . you know, I got a computer, so I had to write about one. When I was wondering what it must feel like to be great.' Not, he says, that he knows anyone who does.

'It's just like a love song with a little bit of an angle, because we all sometimes feel that if you love someone too much, you feel a bit vulnerable. And when you feel vulnerable, you just get paranoid. You think that people think they're perfect, and they probably don't at all. But it feels really powerful to be able to sing, "*to be perfect just like you*". Because you know no one can really feel perfect. But when you hear some people speak, you'd think they fucking were.'

As for the unsettling, Edvard Munch-like images of a '*perfect black dress/perfect grave*', Gavin admits, 'Yeah, I just had to turn left at that point. Because people can drive you to the grave, kill you; people always talk about that. Sometimes,' he reflects, 'I'm so conscious of how much work it is to write the words to an album. It's nice to be through it, looking back at it and not having to sit there with a blank bit of paper going, "*Wherever she sends me*" . . . and nothing else!'

'The Chemicals Between Us', whose lyrics gradually mutated as the song underwent various musical incarnations taking it beyond 'traditional rock' into a fusion of beats and guitars, came about 'because I was at the boredom threshold. How many times can you do the same thing? I was trying to push myself, and I think it had a lot to do with starting the record on my own in Ireland. And that I thought it would be one-dimensional to have another record like *Razorblade Suitcase*. Then again, *Deconstructed* is total remixes, so they're all different.'

As for the lyric changes, 'it was a bit of pushing myself. To me, when I changed all the lyrics at the end, it just really needed it. It just lacked a dynamic. I thought they were too simple, simplified, as they were, and needed a bit of seasoning. It's about the differences and distances between people. The thing I hate about falling out, breaking up, or arguing with someone that you love and someone you've been through loads of things with, is that you want to say, "Hold on, we're the same people as that time not long ago when everything was so wonderful, and now look what we've done to ourselves. How did we get here? Look what we've become . . ." '

Writing about relationships does, he admits, run the risk of hurting other people.

'Yeah, I felt guilty about that every time I'd ever been in a relationship, because I always think that my songs are a bit like diaries. And even though I might not sustain a certain feeling, all the most outlandish and weird imagery that I've used has just been a way of describing how I felt at the time. You know, I've never thought, "Wow, what's it like to have a punch in the mouth?" Because I know,' he laughs.

'When I look at my lyrics, I realise sometimes they're pretty disparate and disjoined and malfunctioning . . . Because that's how I felt. And my attention span is sometimes so chronically bad that I just get bored of myself. Whereas for Gwen, she's so sweet – oh, God, that sounds condescending! – when she writes a song. It's one idea, it starts, and then goes through the whole song. But that's just virtually impossible for me; it's not something I could fathom. Sometimes I think I've done it, but then I look at what I've just written, and I go, "Nope, look; you bled that bit in; you contradicted here; you changed that." '

'English Fire', perhaps the album's sonic standout as its raging guitars clash with a deeply unsettling keyboard swell courtesy of Sacha Puttnam, is also a *tour de force* of venom. 'Oh my God,' Gavin says as he re-reads the lyrics. 'That's so bitter, that one. It's just a good-riddance song; that empowered moment of detachment. And craziness. And thinking, "Thank God you just said that to me, because you make me sick."

'I think that even though I've tried to not be that way, there are really repressed elements to the English character. And of course, being male, the whole idea is that you know who you're meant to be, and you're not meant to be too frank about how you feel. I was always getting in trouble for being oversensitive, for coming across like a freak, for identifying with certain things and people. I think it's an English thing to be a bit uptight. Anyway, again it works on two levels. "*We'll hang ourselves by the English fire*"; which means, we'll ruin ourselves by the fact of our repression. And, at the same time, that there's no comfort in hanging ourselves. We'll die by who we are.'

When asked if the chorus '*All my love*', which repeats four times, is an apology for the rest of the song, or a way of softening its venom, he says, 'No. It's just bitter, bitter and aggressive. You can say "all my love" and really mean – nothing. You know, it's love as talk. It's between lovers, but in an aggressive, icy, stamping way.'

Asked if older life experiences resurface when he writes songs, years after the event, Gavin laughs. 'Oh, absolutely. I have loads of little rooms of disease to draw on. And it's the vengeance thing again here,' replies the man who repeatedly refers to his allegedly vengeful 'triple Scorpio' nature. 'It's not active vengeance, where you go out and cause someone harm. It's just knowledge against them, or truth against them, or empowerment in your future dealings, which in itself is a form of revenge. The biggest revenge is to be all right with somebody. If someone fucks you over in some way, the biggest revenge you can have is to obviously ignore them. And to be in a position where they wish they still had some connection with you. That's the ultimate one.

'I've got plenty of shit stored up; loads of shit on tap,' he smiles, when asked if creating an album in the happier circumstances surrounding this record, compared to those of *Razorblade Suitcase*, made writing more difficult. 'One phone call I got today was my aunt Maggie, who wanted to speak to me. That's the first time she's ever rung. Wanted to speak to me, to say hello. And what happened to her, that's the biggest tragedy in my life, and I've never written a song about it, and I've always wanted to. I can't; I don't know how to do it. I don't know how you'd put that in a song.' He shakes his head.

Asked to reply to the view that leading a life with some creature comforts is antithetical to creativity, he laughs dismissively. 'That's the kind of argument from people that don't write, because you can't possibly think that everyone who ever writes anything of value is living in the gutter. It's like Rainer Maria Rilke's *Letters to a Young Poet* said; you should be able to sit in a prison or a palace. It's your imagination that matters, so the trappings, good or bad, are merely the trappings. The intrinsic thing is your message, your song.'

'Space Travel', which features a guest vocal from Gwen Stefani, is the result 'of living in Ireland, and feeling very removed. This was just when Tony Blair was in his first months in office [as the first Labour Prime Minister in the UK in two decades]. It was all that matey-mateyness, all that hype about a new England. And yet there I was, a fucking freak, stuck in a hunting lodge in Ireland, thinking, "Shit, I'm missing it all again!" But it all seemed a bit false, a bit grins and short trousers.' Of the Labour victory, he says rhetorically, 'Is it progress? I don't know. It's a progression in time, but I don't know whether having that Blair government in England and how it affects us is progress. Whether it's now a better place to be.

'So some of this – *"They're polishing the government"* – is just mistrust, and knowing you don't have a good handle on what's going on. Most people don't understand what's going on in politics, and most people couldn't really give you a clear opinion about whether we should abolish the power that we've had for three hundred years or a thousand years, or what to think about the Euro. It's a slightly more advanced version of "them and us", I suppose.

'I've always hated really simple, angry music that concentrates on "them and us", though. You know, the old "they'll never get us, they'll never beat us down". It's such an insecure image; insecure in the sense of not knowing who they're talking about. Obviously when The Clash did it and punk was a revolution it made sense. Now, I don't know. It's hard for people to be political and have any good tunes. I suppose Chumbawamba would be the ones with the best tunes, if you had to pick.

'So there was a little bleeding of politics in there, but maybe it's really about that person inside everyone who wishes they could just take a little spaceship to the place they think they should be and then they'd feel whole. And as for the line *"I employ spies to stroll the gravel"*, well,' Gavin grins, 'there was a lovely drive there [in Ireland]. And it's also playing slightly into the caricature side of fame, like David Essex in *That'll be the Day*. You employ a lot of people; every single band that's successful has a whole bunch of adults working for them whose livelihood is wrapped up while they're working for them and with them. The fear about being paranoid and being in an ivory tower while you're in a successful band is that it's totally possible. It's a really easy trap to get into. Sometimes you just get paranoid, and wake up and decide that everyone is bleeding you dry and it's all wrong and, you know, it's just not right how it is.

'Employing spies . . . it's funny because, the way it's worded, it could go either way. They could be spies where they're telling me what's going on, and keeping cool, or it's like, I've fucked up, I'm getting someone who's just gathering bad information about me for someone.'

Is it hard to trust people? 'I dunno. I might be a mug. But no, I think you can just see in someone's eyes and in their motives. You have to trust your instincts. We all have to make such assumptions every single day.'

Of their collaboration on 'Space Travel', Gwen Stefani says, 'Working with him on that song was kind of embarrassing but kind of fun, to go in there and sing and having him saying, "Can you sing it a little more English? You sound too American." Of course what he meant was, not have such an accent.

'I was excited,' she adds. 'I felt honoured to be on somebody's record, especially my boyfriend's. I mean, it's beautiful. I think if anyone would put you in their song, that's a really big honour. It's history. And it's nice to think that I might be in some of those other songs, lyrically, even if I'm the one that's beating people over the head with a hammer,' she laughs, referring to a line in 'The Chemicals Between Us'.

'With a lot of Gavin's songs, I wonder what they mean, because my music's really straightforward, and his is made up of all these little metaphors. But when he does break them down and explain them, they are so beautiful, so poetic. I know a lot of times people can't figure them out, but I know the author,' she grins triumphantly, 'so he explains them, and I'm learning from that as well.'

'Fantastic; she was a great singer,' Gavin says of the collaboration. 'Gwen was just [snaps fingers] like, great.'

In fact, he's just as pleased to talk about Gwen's new songs, written for the follow up to No Doubt's multi million-selling *Tragic Kingdom*. 'Some of the songs are so pretty, and one of my favourite ones was just about her, because she has changed so much. People change in relationships; they learn from each other and change through each other. And it's not because of me, I've just been around to witness it, just seeing her blossom and change. She's now twenty-nine and she was twenty-six when we met, and she was such a tight, closed little flower. She seemed so much smaller then, scared. And she just really blossomed as she went through that whole crazy zero to superstar thing. And handled it so well and never got pissy or weird or full of it. I think that's one of the reasons we get on so well, because it never seems to affect us too much as people. She's very much the same, and very normal and very easy. I've met supermodels who are so self-important and so full of themselves you just want to laugh. And then you see someone who's really talented and really special, just being normal and doing normal things. And I like that. It's like a calm in the eye of the storm.'

Returning to her work on 'Space Travel', he says, 'It just made me really happy to have her sing on it, and I suppose it also makes me giggle – just me being a prat, I suppose – when I think of her songs, the really pop, really sweet ones. And then I get her to sing my stuff, and I can't help it, I just thought it was really perverse to have her singing "*my future lies*". It just appealed to me to push the envelope. I just thought it was strange, if you have an emotional connection to someone, that you would be singing those words together. Because lies, in this case, could mean either thing. I'm really happy with that line. Sometimes the most fun things are the ones that only time will tell the truth of them. And the real meaning of that line will only reveal itself in five or ten years' time. And we can't do anything about it now,' he adds. 'And I mean, even the line "*I employ spies*", the ambiguity of that. Who knows, I'll probably still employ them by then. I'll be doing my *Boatman's Call* and I'll have a core of two or three people who help me go touring around bars in Oklahoma.'

'Forty Miles From The Sun' 'is like the apocalypse. What I like about this song is that it's so cinematic; I just think of Kubrick, or Kurosawa's *Seven Samurai*. Just space and fields and sadness and white noise and windstorms and sand everywhere, where you can't see anything, and weirdness, and a funny spaceship in the corner. It's really *wide*, this song, like the falling apart of everything. It's really bleak, like someone's journey into their own dissolution.'

He runs a finger over the lyrics. ' "*Our coats beneath the layers*" … "*We should sleep late*" … I love all that figurative stuff. It's like looking at those paintings upstairs,' he says of his much-loved paintings of displaced and dissolving human forms by Francis Bacon. 'And you can close your eyes and just have that feeling of … of seeminglessness, you know, even if that's not a word.'

'Disease Of The Dancing Cats' refers, in title and lyrics, to Minimata disease, named for the Japanese fishing village where mercury poisoning from industrial effluent caused widespread convulsions and deaths amongst the people and the animals who fed on contaminated fish. The mention of orangutans, Gavin smiles, is simply because 'They're my favourite animal.' He laughs. 'It's my festival song. Maybe my World Wildlife Federation festival song, even.'

'Dead Meat', he says, is a song about Dorothy Stratten, the

Playmate whose murder at the hands of her violent ex-boyfriend was the subject of the Bob Fosse film *Star 80*. 'That was the focus, the start, her story,' Gavin says. 'Maybe I had an idea of the sort of revenge which isn't direct, but which is indirect, the sweetest sort. So I was happy about that. And I liked the idea of her coming back to haunt this place, this person: *"I'll be your poison/I'll be your pain/I'll be your struggle to be sane."* Fuck, imagine if you could control the madness in someone's head. Wow. I'm not violent, though I have violence in me. Personally, I'd love to be Clint Eastwood and just punch a few people out now and again, but really the ultimate power is when you infiltrate someone's mind and control their sanity.'

'Letting the Cables Sleep' is 'about a friend of mine, who's so brilliant and so cool. He's one of my best friends, certainly one of my best friends in America. He's the only friend I made when I was living in LA. And I just found out that he's HIV positive. You see, he didn't tell me for months, and I was hearing this rumour, so I just called him up and asked. Because for all of us, there's a stigma attached to it all, and ignorance, and I was very defensive about the idea that it might be true, because of how people are treated. So whenever people would mention it, I would say, "Don't be silly – where did you hear that?" So when I rang him up, I said, "You know, I've heard something and I need to talk to you about this." It was weird, because I'd just spent time with him, two or three nights a week for a month, because he was in Los Angeles at the same time. For a month we were totally hanging out. So he goes, "Yeah, it's true."

'If you look through the song, you wouldn't necessarily know it was about someone finding out they were HIV positive, but once you know that, I'd imagine it would make much clearer sense. But if it wasn't that, it's someone isolated – *"you in the dark"* – and I was just trying to understand how he was dealing with that. You've got to reel from all that, reel ten thousand miles. I cannot imagine the courage you'd have to have and the places you would be forced to go in your head. The mind boggles at it. So, I just wanted to hear him tell me about it.

'And obviously living in Ireland, that's all the *"breaking the waves"* stuff, and *"watching the lights go down, letting the cables sleep"*, well, everyone needs rest, needs a place where they can just be themselves. It was a real gift that I thought of that image. Where I was living up on that hill, before I had arrived the power had been out for two weeks because of these mad storms, so they actually had people in the village come and dig a trench up the hill to put all the power cables in. Letting the cables sleep ... that's my favourite image on the whole record, and the lyric I like the most.

'When I'd written the song, I sent my friend a letter asking if I could use it. I wrote, "I'm really sorry about this, and obviously I haven't told anyone, but you've got to tell me if I can talk about it." And he said to go ahead, that it's just prejudice that says no one must talk about it, and it's really important to let people know.

'He's nearly died a few times, and he's my age. Whenever you know someone who's in such a grave situation, it just teaches you to reappraise your angles, see where you're coming from. And he says he's learnt so much about what's important; the way you treat people and the way you are treated.

'I got a letter from him the other day,' he continues. 'He writes,

"Very few people are blessed enough to come back from the dead. My doctor said it's a miracle I survived. Ironically, as I write this letter there have been two new news reports on CNN about AIDS. And what with Planet Of The Apes *being my favourite film I find it really funny. I'm finishing this letter having spoken to you on the phone. Congratulations. Man, you work so hard and are so driven, I really admire your work ethic. I'm inspired by your perseverance. I'm really happy to hear you say you'll talk about the AIDS issue. Listen, Gav, the main reason people get it is ignorance, and people not talking about it. My doctors told me that I was probably exposed to the virus when I was eighteen or nineteen years old, and I'm thirty now. That was a time when people didn't think there was very much of a risk for heterosexuals, and now AIDS is the biggest killer of young men aged twenty-five to thirty-five, and it's only second after drink-driving amongst teen mortality statistics. Kids think they're invincible; at least I did. Anyway I'll do some research and get some good statistics for you. It really means the world to me that you can actually save lives by talking, as I told you on the phone."'*

Gavin puts the letter down. 'So he wants me to talk about it. He's amazing; he's nearly died twice, and they call him the Comeback Kid. It's good,' he says simply. 'It's good to talk about it.

'This was all about distrust, this "*prisoner or passenger*" bit,' he says of 'Prizefighter', which closes the album. 'Just like the line about "*employing spies*" in "Space Travel". I like the fact that over an album, certain themes recur, because they do, and when I sit and go through the lyrics, I see that there is a shape to them.

'It's a weird collection of words, this one. It's trying to look at where I was fitting in, and looking at the people around me, thinking what their relationship was to me. That's as in everyone I've been out with.' Asked if his lyrics are ever messages to those people, he replies, 'I always wanted my girlfriends to read my lyrics. Just because, if they didn't read those words, it would be strange, because it's a huge part of my life.'

As for the meaning of the word 'prizefighter', he says, 'We're all prizefighters. I mean, the mere fact that we're here, even if there are certain people we've lost, is because we're survivors. And everyone is just trying to be a survivor of some kind, because we've seen people go.

'I'm very conscious of the fact that I got to make a career out of music. And I know what it took to get there, and how it was and how it went. And nowadays anyone who has a really good job is some kind of fucking prizefighter. Anyone who has a really good life – and that's nothing to do with money – but just has a rewarding life, is a prizefighter. Because it takes a lot to be able to define things about your life that really satisfy you and make you feel like there's some sense or some purpose to your life. And when you're trying stuff and continually get knocked down, it may be wholly untrue, but you cannot help but feel invalid in some way. You feel beaten. And it's a terrifying, slippery slope. Which we all have gone through, and some people still live it, you know. Go to any estate in Tottenham or Moss Side. Or the gang stuff in America. That's the first thing I noticed when I got to California, staying in Venice by Electric Avenue; there were gangs there, and people were shooting. I don't know if they were killing each other that night, but I heard gunshots all the time.'

Told of his younger sister Soraya's assertion that he often remains closed, and would rather suffer through his own difficulties when offering to help others with theirs, he pauses to consider.

'Yeah. I think it's very true what Soraya says. I mean, I live with those things, you know, and even making this record, there are dark fears and dark feelings about that, and all those dark feelings about my own fears for love and children. Not that I want children right now,' he adds. 'But I think those things come up. And sometimes people like to pick over them. F Scott Peck talks about how women like to talk about their problems. They don't need any solutions, they just want to talk about them, and as soon as they start talking about them, it helps. And men just like to solve things. If you have a problem you just try to solve it.

'I don't often talk to people about myself. Mainly because I can't really articulate those fears and feelings myself, and when I can, I just second-guess myself, and I know what the answer is but it's just hard to solve. So yeah, she's right; I'm just not one of those people that just comes in and goes, ME!' He laughs.

'I think also it's tempered by the fact that I have a twisted feeling I'm really privileged and really lucky because I have all these trappings, so it's kind of dumb saying, "Shit, yeah, life is really bad." Well, it may feel bad, but I've got this roof over my head, and if I want to go to Shelter and just sit and talk to someone else about their problems, it might make me reconsider how valid my problems are. But if they're valid, they're valid within my own space and therefore I don't really feel the need to discuss them when they're not ripe for solutions. It's not like taking an eraser, and you've just rubbed out the problem there by talking about it.

'My lyrics might seem cryptic,' he adds, 'But I think they're as clear as anything to me. There's stuff I obviously have to hold back and not say because it concerns other people, but also sometimes because it concerns stuff about myself that I don't want to reveal.

'And for me to talk exclusively about the problems of my personal life,' Gavin shakes his head, 'it's like, well, they're so obvious, the problems of my personal life, and if I didn't want them I shouldn't have them. It doesn't alter the fact that your choices bring problems, but I just think that I try and spare people in my own life stuff like that.' He allows himself a mischievous smile. 'And maybe I'm just saving it up for a moan on a rainy day.

'I put a lot of it into my music. And I remember what Lorraine once said to me, how it was all right for me, because whatever pain I had and whatever problems I had, I had this great outlet. Think about it: the physicality of screaming about my complaints, or singing about joys. Every day when I'm on tour I get to do this cathartic thing where you can go through all your problems. And the weirdest thing is that when I get so wrapped up in my personal life, and things really drive me crazy and I'm right at the edge emotionally, that's when I feel like I'm on fire when I perform. Thank God I have that outlet. And if I didn't, all these emotions that well up inside would have to find a way to come out. Or else you just burst, or malfunction, and you become the Edward

Scissorhands of emotions. You're lost. That's obviously why music is such a therapy, such a power, when you think of the comfort it gives people, since the beginning of time. I mean, its healing powers are just amazing; even when it's really sad, there's something so empowering about facing the demons. And about facing how broken up you are about something.

'Which is why I always love lyrics. And I believe in the power of lyrics. Obviously not everyone listens; someone like Sacha really very rarely listens to lyrics, doesn't care, and it's all about feel for him. So I think that while that's true what Soraya says, I've complained and told people about things about myself that, you know, normally people don't do. Millions of people have our records; that's a lot of people to be open to. So I guess maybe it's also a desire to still keep something to myself. I mean, if you give everything out, what do you have left? I don't really understand people who just tell you *everything* when you socialise with them. I'm scared of self-obsession and, because of what I do, people ask me all the time during interviews about myself. It's such an unnatural state to be in, to really indulge and discuss yourself, and how you think, and why you did this or that. I mean, no one ever did that with Van Gogh,' he adds.

'Maybe what I've done is not express too many things to people, to have a level of being cut off and, to a degree, to have a strange emotional life – to have weird connections with some people, and weirder connections with others – because I'm just a slave to writing songs and being in a band. There are things I probably would confront about myself, and probably that I may even change in future, but I just give myself to the work, I suppose. Because it just takes everything.

'But there has to be a balance, of course. You have to live, too. I don't want to be a lonely old git aged forty-five, going, "Oh, my God, I've given all my life to music, and now I've scared everyone off!" '

And then Gavin Rossdale laughs.

'You know, it's still a job, but it's a much better job. It's repetitive, but it's not the same as grinding a great big hole in a piece of steel all day . . . and it pays a little better.' – Nigel Pulsford

What's success like, then? Bush get asked the question all the time, whether it's about being famous in America and dozens of other countries, or whether it's about their steadfast insistence on caring about the support shown for them in their own country.

'Have we made it in England?' Nigel smiles, repeating the question he is asked so often, even now when the band are a platinum-plus success in the UK. 'Yes, of course, as much as we ever thought, and more. I remember the Pixies doing two nights at Brixton Academy and I thought, Jesus, they're huge! I remember seeing them here in '88, '89, and then going to America and no one had heard of them whereas, here, they were almost like the Bee Gees in terms of popularity. Imagine if we could be as good and as big as that, we thought, just imagine.

'How flattering that people like us,' he smiles. 'You can't not be pleased. I hate people who are rude to their fans. Jesus, it takes so little to be kind, and if you're rude to them, then you destroy them. You don't have to be difficult, even though you feel difficult. They put all those dollars in your pocket. You shouldn't be mean, even at times when you're so knackered you feel mean. If I feel mean, I don't go to the after-show meet and greet; everyone has their off nights, when the rest of the band say, fine, don't worry, we'll go without you.

'Our fans are great. They bring us the most amazing presents. I remember doing a show in the winter, in Maine. And, in the deepest snow ever, we went out to the car park at the back of the venue, and there was a mum and two kids waiting for us. And we had to flounder through four feet of snowdrifts to get to them and they'd got these lovely presents for us. Really sweet, seeing the mum hanging out with the kids. I have to say the parents of these kids are amazing, because they put up with so much to participate in their kids' favourite music . . . and then they realise that you're just a few years younger than them, or even, sometimes, the same age! All I could do was grin and say, "Look, I'm as bemused as you are, so don't worry."

'What happened to us was good fortune, rather than luck. You can make your good fortune; luck is being in that one right place at the right time but, to be fortunate, you have to follow that through. And maybe it's all about sticking at it. If you go to Normal or Moline or Grand Rapids, they'll love it, they'll never forget you, but most bands don't bother. And the headlines say, "Suede Take America", and all they did was play the Irving Plaza in New York. And yeah, it's a slog. Clubs are cold. There are no showers. Get in a van. You know, bands like the Toadies drive themselves everywhere; The Jesus Lizard do that, too. That's the only way they can afford to do it, because tour buses cost three hundred dollars a day.

'And yes, popular music may be narrow, but you don't have to stay popular. I was reading an REM interview and they say the same thing and of course it's easy for them to say it now, because that's what bands who aren't successful say, and bands who've been successful for ten years and sold thirty million albums. People who should sell those amounts of records are Alex Chilton, or Pavement, or The Jesus Lizard. People who *deserve* to be famous. There's this whole misapprehension in the credible indie world about popularity, and ultimately it's a silly little cliquey thing. It's nice to be number one in the real charts, in the big charts but, at the same time, sure, I suppose it would be nice to be credible, too. But then, do you want to be credible with people who don't like what you like?'

Steve Albini who, to his probable disgust, is a touchstone to many of the cliquey indie credibility crowd Nigel mentions as well as a hero to Bush, clearly has no qualms about their success.

'It was a total surprise to everybody that they were popular, and that in itself validates the concept that people buy the records they want to buy. Other bands were getting a lot more notice in the press and a lot more pushed on the radio, and in contrast Bush just keep building the sales in an old-fashioned way. They got played on the radio because people liked them,' he adds. 'The music industry does, of course, have a phenomenal ability to make hits. They've got the big guns and they walk. And so a band like Hole, who make unlistenable records, are able to get played on radio and TV and headline tours, because there are things about that band that can be sold *despite* the music, so they'll sell those things and the music rides along on the coattails.'

Bush, however, did it as a genuine people's band. 'If anybody had thought Bush were going to be popular,' Albini points out, 'Gavin would have been on the front cover of *Cosmopolitan, Playgirl*, and had feature interviews in all of the gay icon press and so on. They could have made an awful lot more of a big deal about Gavin being an attractive young man, and they didn't. But if anybody had thought that Bush had a chance, that stuff would have been done. I honestly don't know what they were offered, but my suspicion always was that they weren't asked to do anything to promote the record because nobody thought they had a chance. That's how they were able to concentrate on touring.'

And that, of course, is from whence the Bush success sprang.

Ask Gavin Rossdale if he's ever allowed himself to feel triumphant about tens of millions of record sales, and he says no.

'I think it's because I don't feel triumphant. I just enjoy this karmic space, I suppose,' he laughs. 'Plus I just feel really lucky. Of course I feel good about stuff, but you always get judged just on the records, on the music that you make, so all of the other things, all of the accolades you can get, be it an award or people saying good things, they are always tempered by things that don't go the right way. We've got so many more records to make. And I'm not done yet. I wanna be triumphant when – when my head starts to say triumphant. Which will be when I'm dead. Dead. Triumphant. See ya. Because it's ongoing.

'And plus,' he grins mischievously, 'I hate smug bastards.'

As far as fame goes, and the sycophancy that trails around after it, he says, 'It would be embarrassing to have people around you like that. Life is too short, way too short. The idea of having people like that around me just makes me want to puke. And I see that with people I meet, with big superstars. They have people around them that just find them hilarious. "God, you're really funny . . . And every record you sell makes you funnier!"

'I've seen so much being in a band. Being successful, the lever of hysteria and craziness; the good things and bad things, truths and truisms and sycophancy. The tension is amazing whether you are rushing onstage in front of two thousand five hundred people, or five hundred thousand people in Dallas. And I love walking around to see the activity beforehand, see everyone at work. I think when you're surrounded by all these things, you can be triumphant in instances. You can feel triumphant about a tune or putting a show on. But if you're the person or the band, you have to go on. You feel good about it, of course, but something about being triumphant signals the end. It means you're being retrospective about it. Where with me it's like, "Yeah, that was good. But what do I do next week?" It's just ongoing. I want more, whatever it is.'

Success, he adds, may lie in finding your own voice. 'I love lines like [Dinosaur Jr.'s] "*I feel the pain of everyone*",' he says. 'It's that thing of people singing in bands who are isolationists, who drown out the world . . . with a microphone.' Gavin smiles at the paradox. 'I love that. Of course, that's how we all feel in bands. That's how all bands who reach levels of volume and playing power are: born to complain, and to magnify your complaints a thousandfold.

'But, of course, as I think I've proved in every song I've ever written, everything contradicts and everything's tempered with something, and everything has its price. And of course there's tons of stuff to complain about. And it's a dangerous game, what we do, because it's so public. We get the chance to be totally washed out. To do a shit record. To fail. And then wait, and then every now and again get the update on how we're *not* doing . . .

'But no, it's not inherently dumb being in a rock band. I don't think you have to work especially hard for it not to be dumb. Of course, the top level of it is, can you make the records that count, that speak louder than anyone. It's just a weird medium. It's so twisted and torn up. I mean, the worst thing about being a musician is that the minute it all starts to go well for you and you get financial backing and stuff like that, is exactly when most people lose it and it's all taken away from them. It's the most destructive thing. Music is such a wide, varied thing. I feel really underground. I mean, rock bands have no media profile, certainly in this country, though it's changed a bit with Oasis. And I've always liked being part of that more subversive thing, that counterculture. And I still feel part of my own life. I don't feel trapped. I feel more confident. I feel like I belong. I get the chance to make records.'

Success frequently means money, of course: 'It's just a way of keeping score', as the band's press officer Michael Pagnotta puts it. It can mean helping your friends, too.

David Yow of The Jesus Lizard recalls, 'In May 1996 we played a show in Austin, Texas, where I allegedly threw a beer can into the audience and this girl claimed it hit her in the head and caused her permanent mental and physical damage. And so the whole process was going on with the lawyers and everything, and after about a year and a half into it, my lawyers suggested I declare bankruptcy. And I had just bought a house and things were going so great and I wasn't getting depressed at all. So the idea of facing bankruptcy tore me up. I was completely down. And I was talking to Gavin on the phone and I told him about it. And he immediately said, "I can help, I can help! I can loan you – no, I can *give* you – ten thousand dollars." '

He shakes his head. 'That's tremendous. I mean, sure he can afford it, but what's more important is the fact that he offered to do it. With no hesitation at all. In that conversation he explained he never thought that he'd be in the position that he's in – you know, he used to not have any money – and he said, "You know, I can do these sorts of things now." '

'There are times I've fucked up financially and I've wanted to call him,' Alex Tate says of his longtime friend. 'You can't believe how much I've wanted to go, "Hi Gav! It's me, Alex! Could you just send me a big cheque? Thanks – 'bye!" I haven't, but I know what it must be like for other people; maybe they weren't as lucky at sorting it out. And maybe I'm saving it up, like a Get Out Of Jail Free card,' he laughs. 'You only use it once, so maybe I'm waiting for a situation that's so fucked up . . .'

Is he surprised at Gavin's generosity in helping others?

'Well, you would, wouldn't you?' Alex asks simply. 'I don't think he wanted to make a zillion quid, he wanted to make a living. And once you've made a zillion quid, it's not that comfortable. He's a real soft touch.'

Pete Black insists, 'The only difference between Gavin now and Gavin years ago is that he has a bigger bank balance. He's doing what he enjoys doing, and he's become famous for it. And I'm proud of him for that, because it didn't just happen overnight. And, to be honest, he's not famous and rich to me, he's just Gavin. And if I praise him, it's not because I'm trying to be a sycophant, but because I have good cause to praise him. Lots of things in my life have happened where he's been the only friend who has been there, and he has stood by me.'

Success when you've waited so long, Dave Parsons says, is a particularly sweet kind of success. 'Everyone's had their ups and downs, so you get a bit more humble, I suppose. It was funny, because the first time I came back from tour, everyone was buying me a drink down the pub because they didn't want to be seen having me buy them one. It's really strange, because you're thinking, No, wait, you haven't got any money. And I've just earned some money, and I've got a pocket full of *per diems* I haven't spent, you know, apart from anything else . . .

'Yes, it's a job,' he continues. 'Well, not a job, but it's something I go and do. I get on a plane and I go and do these absolutely bizarre things. You know, if we didn't have proper newspapers and radio and things, no one would even know I did it,' Dave smiles. 'They would just say, "Yeah right," and they'd think I'd been in prison for the last few years!

'What's the bond that we have between us?' Dave considers. 'I think it's music, and I think it's some sense of achievement and pride in knowing that we're good at what we do, really good, as a band.' And that, he says, is success. 'You know those stories that you hear of bands who are quite successful, but they don't even like each other? They can't stand to be in the studio together. How do bands function like that? Why are they doing it if it's not fun anymore and they don't like each other? It's really strange, that idea, and we have never got anywhere near that. Success is simply making good albums and playing well and making it sound good. And I think even though everyone's got a completely different thing – Nigel reads Thomas Pynchon and watches *Star Trek*, and Robin lives in the country, and whenever you go to the airport, Gavin will meet someone he knows – but the thing that's more important than any differences is the music. It has to be.'

And maybe measuring your success at doing what you do is, indeed, simple. And maybe it's about realising that, eventually, if your aim is true, even the most spiteful criticism from a handful of nay-sayers does not matter a whit. Anton Brookes, a London press officer who has represented and befriended bands from Nirvana to the Beastie Boys and Smashing Pumpkins to Hole, looked after

Bush on their first UK release, when not only did a record company switch scupper the chances of *Sixteen Stone*, but the notoriously pack-minded British press did their best to crucify Bush, their music, their frontman, and indeed anyone who liked them.

As a touchstone of alternative credibility of the sort Bush were proclaimed by those papers and magazines to lack, Brookes' comments are unstinting, pointed and revealing.

'We went to see them at a rehearsal early on and thought, Yeah, this is really good, really powerful, and we wanted to get involved.

'We saw quite quickly that people in the [UK] press resented them. One, because they reckoned they sounded like Nirvana, and two, because they'd done well in America, without the British press' say-so. You're not allowed to do that; we've not granted you this permission. But speaking to Gavin and getting to know him, it was clear that the influences Nirvana had were the same influences Gavin was working from: you know, Big Black, Pixies, Sonic Youth, Jane's Addiction, Hüsker Dü, and the Replacements. And if Bush were that calculated, then people like Albini would never have worked with them. He's a free spirit; he's never going to do anything that he doesn't like and he's never going to do anything for the money.

'And of course every British band wants to be big in England. It doesn't matter how big you are in any part of the world, everyone wants to be big in your own back garden, and the British media just weren't having it whatsoever. I really thought Gavin was sincere, and honest, and of course he liked Nirvana, and I'm sure he's the first to admit they were a big influence on him. But talk to almost any band, and the band they're going to cite as an influence is Nirvana. I think in the UK there's not been another band that made people want to go out and pick up a guitar like Nirvana did. And, you know, if you were to look at Gavin's record collection, and to look at mine, you'd probably find about eighty per cent of the same records. Though his is probably a bit tidier than mine.

'Certain bands, whatever they do, they're never going to be accepted by the press; for whatever reason, they're never going to be fashionable. Gavin and the band have been honest about their role and what they're trying to do, and they'd do interviews with people who smiled at them and then went away and wrote "grave-robbers" and "the corpse of Cobain". You never think they can sink any lower, but they always do. As they did with Kurt when he died; they had a field day. In fact, the media turned on him as soon as they could, because he was in that position of success. One day they decide they're going to go for you and they do. They do with every band that we've dealt with, at some stage or another. And then you're out; it's as simple as that. You could play the best show ever and you know you're going to get a kicking. And that was the same with Bush; they played good shows and you'd stand there, thinking, That was a really good show: the crowd was there, the kids were going mental. And you'd read the review, and it would be like someone just ripping your heart out.

'I bet if I'd rung you four years ago,' Anton says pointedly, 'to tell you about Bush, you wouldn't have wanted to know either. People who slag them off, probably half *their* record collection is the same as Gavin's too. You could talk to him about practically any new record, something really obscure, and not only had he bought it, but he could tell you what the tracks were and had already read the liner notes.' He laughs. 'And really . . . can he help how many records he's sold?

'Every record is ultimately judged by its sales,' he concludes, 'and by that yardstick they're a great band. But you strip all that away, and they're *still* a great band. The kids who go to gigs in their Mudhoney shirts and Nirvana shirts and Bush shirts – their view is, if it rocks, it rocks. Does it rock? Is it any good? That's one great thing about youth – not everyone reads the *NME*.

'Most bands,' he adds, 'they'd sell their soul to have a tenth of the record sales Gavin has. But Gavin's never sold his soul. He's revealed it, but he's never sold it.'

Z

You'll never know how much you shine . . .

'How unusual is the Bush story?' Dave Dorrell stirs an espresso with two abrupt twists of a spoon and adopts a look halfway between outright mockery and reflection.

'I think there are merits in *all* stories,' Dorrell parries, perhaps because as a former music journalist he's told so many of those stories himself. Or perhaps because he's unwilling to show his hand, or perhaps because it isn't such an appallingly stupid question after all. 'I think it's as fine a story as many others. It's no more unusual than the strangest stories out there. But I think I believe in fate a lot, probably to keep my libertarianism in check. As much as you think you can do what you want to do, you sometimes get the feeling that it's almost pre-ordained, and the strange aspects of the Bush story are married to kind of mundane facts. And if I look at it from my own perspective, which is all I can really do, I find it very strange. I find it *amusing*. And hugely eventful. I think we've covered a great deal of ground in the last few years. Is it any more strange than the Oasis story? Probably not. But it might be more strange than the Blur story. *I* don't know.' He shrugs.

'I don't think you can judge it or value it against anyone's experiences but your own. And to that end, I think it's been quite crazy and quite wild and quite fun, and I don't think I could have predicted – I don't think anyone could have predicted –

that when I first bumped into Gavin again in Los Angeles, that the story would have gone as it did. We all have hopes, of course, and I suppose you visualise stuff, and perhaps if you can visualise something then it *can* happen. And I suppose when I first thought about getting involved with a band, I thought, like any manager, whether I could visualise this band onstage at Madison Square Garden, or at Wembley.

'And I suppose I was stupid enough to think that I could. And years later when Bush did get to stand on that stage at Madison Square Garden, I suppose I felt a little sudden chill. Because of expectations fulfilled, and thereby surpassed, you know,' he grins. 'All of your craziest dreams when you were standing in a two bob-an-hour rehearsal studio in the Harrow Road. So yeah, you know, I suppose it's a mix of equal parts everyday life, the mundanity of business, the yoke of hard work and determination and ambition – married to the insanity of headlining the biggest ticketed event ever in the history of man. Or *whatever*,' he shrugs again.

'Living it up on the Disney jet, flying between Toronto and LA. Being chased down 42nd Street in New York City by hordes of fans. It's everything. Comedy, tragedy, and the rock and roll soundtrack.'

He smiles. And finishes his espresso in one gulp.

Tread slowly for I know
There's a thousand miles to go
Without blinking

The sun sets behind Primrose Hill; the dark gathers into the kitchen and spreads across the table. Winston sighs doggily and shuffles, snuffles, pads out into the hallway in search of something only dogs can see. Gavin stares through the window and across the bricks and rooftops of NW1.

'In theory, how much more do you need to know about someone, outside of their songs? I mean, the songs should give you enough,' he says. And if there's a residual gentle chiding of me and my set task, now that it's almost done, it's friendly, thoughtful, rather than pointed. 'For me, with every single record I've loved, I've never really needed to know that much about the person. Or ever really cared. Or ever really cared to meet them. I mean, if you do that, generally it's going to be a disappointment.

'You know, I always had this inbuilt feeling that to a degree our success would always have a ceiling on it, a cap. And it's just continually blown me away how far it can reach, because I'd always assumed the world of mass success was the domain of some kind of lowest common denominator, puerile, vacuous, simple.' He shakes his head, the twelve-year-old punk in him welling up for a second. 'I just thought whatever we had would be restricted. And it makes me happy that you can ...' He searches for the word.

'That it's true that you can blow the building up from the inside. And go over the fence. And jump up and down, and shout, "It's all right! I'm still *me*! Yeah, I know it looks weird that I'm over here, but it's still the same!" You've got to let it be known. Still the same. Yeah . . .' He drifts off. 'You've gotta let it be known . . .

'You know, at certain points I've been thinking, Did you have a good enough story to write? Could this story really be interesting enough? When I think of greatness, it's ridiculous to compare what we've done to anything significant. Greatness isn't one thing you've done, it's a body of work. It's a career. There's a lot of people who come from the school of thought that until you're sixty, I mean, what the fuck have you got to say?'

That's the first thing you said to me, eight months ago, I tell Gavin.

'Was it?' He looks back at me and laughs.

How strange is what's happened to you, do you think? I ask.

'It's insane. Insane. But in order to stay sane, you have to pretend it's the way it was meant to be. I feel like I was born to do this. It's what I've waited all my life for, and it's the first time I've felt right. When we first got successful, it wasn't a case of, "Hah! Told you so!" It was like, you may not have believed that this is always what I was meant to do – that's you in the infantile sense of them and us, you as in anyone who didn't believe – but I just felt as though being allowed to make music and have a career in music was like being allowed *home*.

'Like being allowed into a place where,' he continues, 'although there will always be people better than you, and people worse than you, it's all relative and all to people's taste. But the fact of being able to say *this* is how I can live my life means so much to me, because it's where I thought I always should have been. I could never, when I was younger, articulate where it was I was meant to be. But having got there, and having this band, felt – normal. I didn't know how far we could take it, or how far it could go, and I still don't know.

'Because it's not over yet,' Gavin Rossdale says. 'It's not over today. This is just an opening.'

The best is yet to come

DISCOGRAPHY

The albums so far (singles and key radio tracks marked in bold).

Sixteen Stone

> Raindogs howl for the century/A million dollars a steak
> As you search for your demigod/and you fake with a saint
> There's no sex in your violence . . .   'Everything Zen'

Released December 1994 on Trauma Records
Produced and mixed by Clive Langer and Alan Winstanley
Recorded at Westside Studios, London

Everything Zen/Swim/Bomb/**Little Things/Comedown**/Body/
Machinehead/Testosterone/Monkey/**Glycerine**/Alien/X-Girlfriend

Razorblade Suitcase

> In the middle of the world on a fishhook/
> You're the wave/you're the wave/you're the wave . . .
>   'Swallowed'

Released November 1996 on Trauma Records
Recorded by Steve Albini
Recorded at Sarm Hook End, Berkshire and Abbey Road, London
All songs by Gavin Rossdale, Mad Dog Winston Music Ltd

Personal Holloway/**Greedy Fly/Swallowed**/Insect Kin/**Cold
Contagious**/A Tendency To Start Fires/Mouth/Straight No Chaser/
History/Synapse/Communicator/Bonedriven/Distant Voices

Deconstructed

> We're just a wish away/27th letter
> Much maligned/beat me clever
> Say you will/nevermind . . .   'Bonedriven'

Released November 1997 on Trauma Records
Remixes by Greg Brimson and Pete Coyte, Hein Hoven, Goldie and
Rob Playford, Philip Steir, Barry Ashworth, Lee Spencer and Jason
O'Bryan, Fabio Paras, Mekon, Jack Dangers, Lunatic Calm, Derek
DeLarge
'In A Lonely Place' produced and mixed by Tricky at Platinum
Island Studios, New York and Bush 8-Track, London

All songs by Gavin Rossdale, Mad Dog Winston Music Ltd, except 'In A Lonely Place' (Ian Curtis/Peter Hook/Stephen Morris/Bernard Sumner)

Everything Zen (The Lhasa Fever Mix)/**Mouth (The Stingray Mix)**/Swallowed (Toasted Both Sides Please Mix)/Synapse (My Ghost In The Bush Of Life Mix)/History (Dub Pistols Mix)/ Personal Holloway (Soundclash Republic Mix)/Bonedriven (Beat Me Clever Mix)/Insect Kin (Drum And Bass Mix)/Comedown (Lunatic Calm Mix)/Everything Zen (Derek Delarge Mix)/In A Lonely Place (Tricky Mix)

The Science of Things

> I memorise the basics/making strange faces
> Tread slowly for I know/There's a thousand miles to go
> Without blinking . . .   'Warm Machine'

Released November 1999 on Trauma Records
Produced by Bush with Clive Langer, Alan Winstanley, Gavin Rossdale
Recorded at Westside Studios and Mayfair Studios, London and Sarm Hook End, Berkshire
All songs by Gavin Rossdale, Mad Dog Winston Music Ltd.

Warm Machine/Jesus Online/**The Chemicals Between Us***/English Fire/Space Travel/40 Miles From The Sun/Disease Of The Dancing Cats/Mindchanger/Altered States/Dead Meat/Letting The Cables Sleep*/Prizefighter
(*Produced by Gavin Rossdale only)

Recommended reading

Bush: Sixteen Stone Tour
Pete Black (photos) and Peter Martin (text)
Omnibus Press, 1997
US ISBN 0.8256.1602.8, UK ISBN 0.7119.6341.X

Official Bush website

www.bushnet.com

INDEX